CENTERS FOR TEACHING AND LEARNING

CENTERS FOR TEACHING AND LEARNING

The New Landscape in Higher Education

MARY C. WRIGHT

JOHNS HOPKINS UNIVERSITY PRESS | *Baltimore*

Johns Hopkins University Press
2715 North Charles Street
Baltimore, Maryland 21218
www.press.jhu.edu

Library of Congress Cataloging-in-Publication Data

Names: Wright, Mary C., 1971– author.
Title: Centers for teaching and learning : the new landscape in higher education /
    Mary C. Wright.
Description: Baltimore : Johns Hopkins University Press, 2023. |
    Includes bibliographical references and index.
Identifiers: LCCN 2022049905 | ISBN 9781421447001 (hardcover) |
    ISBN 9781421447018 (ebook)
Subjects: LCSH: College teachers—Professional relationships—United States. |
    College teachers—In-service training—United States. |
College teaching—United States. | Education, Higher—Aims and objectives—
    United States.
Classification: LCC LB1778.2 .W75 2023 | DDC 378.1/20973—dc23/eng/20221220
LC record available at https://lccn.loc.gov/2022049905

A catalog record for this book is available from the British Library.

Special discounts are available for bulk purchases of this book. For more information, please contact Special Sales at specialsales@jh.edu.

CONTENTS

The definition of *educational development* used in this book is "helping colleges and universities function effectively as teaching and learning communities,"* and I would like to thank the many communities that informed this work. First, I owe much love and gratitude to my husband, Russ (Merrimack College), and my son, Lawrence (Oberlin College). They have lived with these ideas for years now and often helped with looking up a center, double-checking numbers, and talking through preliminary ideas. Your books are next! Thank you to my family (Mom, Dad, Laura, and Dan), who supported me through this process.

I offer a huge thank-you to Deandra Little (Elon University) and Joel Purkiss (Baylor College of Medicine) for reading initial full drafts and offering valuable feedback. Thanks also to the anonymous reviewers who offered generous and constructive comments. I am grateful to Inger Bergom (Harvard University) and Eric Kaldor (Brown University) for talking through methodological questions, as well as Charles Carroll (Brown), Carolyn Wood (Harvard), and Mary Jo Callan (Brown) for offering valuable reading suggestions about different types of centers and integrative emphases. Thanks also to Laura Cruz (Penn State) for sharing a range of smart insights and preprints on topics ranging from integrative emphases to SoTL and CTL spaces. Thank you to Josh Kim (Dartmouth College) for the original encouragement to contact his editor, and to Greg Britton (Johns Hopkins University Press), who believed that "it was time" for a book on CTLs.

*Peter Felten, Alan Kalish, Allison Pingree, and Kathryn Plank, "Toward a Scholarship of Teaching and Learning in Educational Development," *To Improve the Academy* 25 (2007), http://dx.doi.org/10.3998/tia.17063888.0025.010.

Thank you to the CTL directors who agreed to be profiled in the spot-lights and quotes in the book. CTLs can be vulnerable spaces, and I appreciate the trust you put in me to spotlight your work.

It was a joy to work with two students / recent alums on this work. Em-majane Rhodenhiser is credited in chapter 3 for her coding of CTL workshop topics, and Justin Voelker gets a shout-out in chapter 5 for his careful detailing of CTL participation counts, satisfaction metrics, and learning outcomes in CTL reports.

I am also grateful to the communities that over time have welcomed, supported, recognized, and challenged me—somewhat like a personal Hub-Incubator-Temple-Sieve support network. These include Center for Research on Learning and Teaching colleagues at the University of Mich-igan, Sheridan Center for Teaching and Learning colleagues and senior leadership at Brown University, POD Network friends, members of the Rhode Island Teaching and Learning group, Ivy+ CTL directors, and, most recently, *International Journal of Academic Development* (*IJAD*) co-editors. We are all working at the center.

CENTERS FOR TEACHING AND LEARNING

How Many Centers for Teaching and Learning Are There?

THIS BOOK PROJECT began with a simple question: How many Centers for Teaching and Learning (CTLs) are there? In 2017–18, when I was serving as the president of the POD Network, the US professional association for educational development, the executive board would read about or hear this question frequently. At the time, we did not have a precise answer, so it felt as if we were asking the intellectual equivalent of "Guess how many jelly beans there are in the jar."

This lack of knowledge, however, has consequences for CTLs. The Integrated Postsecondary Education Data System (IPEDS) tracks every college or university that receives federal student financial aid, serving as a near-complete map of US higher education and its evolution over time. This resource is a rich repository for research and practice. The lack of a parallel resource for CTLs is a clear gap. As one scholar of CTLs argued, "The field of teaching development has been hindered because the population of TLDUs [teaching and learning development units] has been unknown and because research has had to rely on samples of convenience."[1]

Although I began this book prior to the start of the COVID-19 crisis, the role of CTLs during the pandemic underscores the importance of having a better understanding of their work. Prior to the pandemic, scholars suspected that there was a significant pivot in the work of CTLs, but they also concluded tentatively: "The responsibilities and impact of CTLs are growing and . . . learning innovation is at the heart of this shift. Further research needs to be done before any definitive conclusions on CTL changes across higher education can be made."[2] As I document in this book, both the number and scope of center mandates continue to grow, and organizational change is at the heart of CTL work.

History and Biography

A classic text in my home discipline, sociology, is *The Sociological Imagination* by C. Wright Mills, which establishes the idea of connecting one's individual circumstances (biography) with larger structural forces and institutional context (history).[3] Therefore, I begin this book about larger changes in the landscape of US educational development by situating my own story within it. The term *educational development*, rather than *faculty development*, is used to reflect a relatively recent pivot in the work—the move to more broadly engage with constituencies beyond faculty as well as an increased emphasis on the organizational work done by CTLs. Although there are several excellent definitions of *educational development*, I find this one to be most useful: "helping colleges and universities function effectively as teaching and learning communities."[4]

I entered the field of education development through a nontraditional path. In the middle of my PhD program in sociology at the University of Michigan, I took a graduate class on faculty development, as it was termed then, from Dr. Constance (Connie) Cook, the director of the Center for Research on Learning and Teaching (CRLT). Suffice it to say that the course was revelatory and life changing. Eventually, I took a full-time position at CRLT, the first teaching center in the country. After four years, I changed emphasis to assessment and evaluation and developed a small group at CRLT that continues to focus on this integrative area. In 2016, I became director of the Sheridan Center for Teaching and Learning at Brown University in Providence, Rhode Island. The Sheridan Center was formed in 1987 as the Center for the Advancement of College Teaching, with a focus on the preparation of graduate students as teachers. In the years that followed, its mission grew to include faculty and postdoctoral scholars. When I joined in 2016, I was asked to integrate student learning areas into the Sheridan Center, which then came to also include writing, English language support, and academic tutoring. Around that same time, Sheridan became an assessment-infused center when we added one (later two) staff member to focus on evaluation, assessment, and curricular development. In 2020, I was appointed associate provost for teaching and learning, the Sheridan Center added another integrative area, digital teaching and learning, and it revised its mission once again. Currently, I have the good fortune to collaborate with about 40 full-time staff, 11 provost's faculty teaching fellows, and hundreds of student leaders to carry out our mission.

In my story, there are threads of the narrative that is woven throughout this book: broader aims, increasing integrative trends, expanding constituencies, and Hub, or centering, orientations to the work. The years I spent serving as president of the POD Network also influenced the themes I raise in this book, particularly in the sense of doubt about our positioning: How many of us are there? How many are doing what we are doing? What orientations join our work, which can seem so institution specific? How are we organized? Why are some depictions of CTLs so negative and how might these be countered?

Key Questions

Because this book originated from questions, the chapters are also organized around inquiries.

What are our aims? The research presented in this book analyzes CTL audiences and goals to better understand how they are represented in center statements of purpose, or missions, values, visions, and goals. Chapter 1 focuses on three questions about aims. First, who (or what) are the intended constituencies of CTLs, and how do these vary from the findings of prior research on center missions? Second, what are the key ambitions of CTL work, and how do these aims differ by institutional features and CTL characteristics, such as age and personnel size? Finally, how have CTL goals changed over time?

Answers to these questions are important for several reasons. First, in thinking about purpose broadly, it can be a useful benchmark, whether for starting a new center or for regular strategic planning. Additionally, for a field that is heavily engaged in working with instructors around backward design and learning outcomes, it follows that our CTLs should do the same.

In chapter 1, I examine the explicitly articulated aims of over 1,000 CTLs through their mission, vision, goal, and values statements. I identify key constituencies named in these statements and track how these differ from a previous smaller study of center missions. I also examine 9 common CTL aims (7 from the prior study and 2 emergent) to understand how CTL priorities have shifted over the past decade. I argue that these aims suggest a distinctive change vision for CTLs, balancing individual relationships and organizational change aspirations. This chapter also establishes the rise of learning-focused aspirations.

How do we get there? Chapter 2 switches focus to strategy, or how centers theorize—also through statements of purpose—that they can reach their stated aims. I continue to reference CTL statements of purpose to examine *theories of change*, or strategies for how change will occur. The presence of explicit theories of change is critical for enabling the process of organizational transformation.[5] The orientations can also help centers prioritize their activities, which is especially critical in an era of scarce resources.

In chapter 2, I use a sociological lens to group these strategies, adopting a framework originally developed by sociologists Mitchell Stevens, Elizabeth Armstrong, and Richard Arum that served as a "critical integration" on the scholarship around the sociology of higher education.[6] The Hub-Incubator-Temple-Sieve (HITS) framework offers four metaphorical lenses for categorizing key CTL change strategies. I situate each orientation within sociological or organizational change literature, noting strengths and cautions to each strategy. Finally, I examine trends in the articulation of CTL strategies using a previous study of verbs employed in CTL mission statements.

What tactics do we employ? Common program and service types found in CTLs are examined in chapter 3. These involve initiatives that are shifting the unit of analysis of CTL work to promote change more effectively across scale, from the individual instructor to the course and institution. In chapter 3, I also investigate questions such as What are the most frequently offered program types today? and How have CTL programs evolved over time?

How are we organized? Chapter 4 turns to organizational structure with a focus on numbers of personnel, leadership characteristics, and governance structures. I also examine the increased integrative trends of these units. The chapter explores how CTLs are moving beyond a teaching and learning mission to collaborate or integrate with units traditionally found elsewhere on campus: instructional technology and online learning, assessment, writing, service learning and community engagement, and career and leadership development.

Additionally, chapter 4 explores common questions about CTL organization and governance that frequently appear among educational development discussions, such as What is the average size of a center? Regarding faculty advisory committees, how do you set one up? What percentage of CTLs include IT support? I link responses to these practical questions to the integrative trends noted in the first half of the chapter, arguing that the organization of CTL governance structures—mixing formal structures like boards and informal engagement approaches like fellows programs—is a response to other organizational trends.

How do we make our work visible? Chapter 5 focuses on evaluation of CTL work. POD Network surveys and educational development articles suggest that a constant challenge for directors and CTL staff is finding time for evaluation. Additionally, educational development work is periodically critiqued by external organizations and found to lack rigor. In chapter 5, a database of over 100 CTL annual reports is used to examine the evaluation frameworks that CTLs do employ. I end the chapter by noting how the HITS framework can also be used as a CTL-specific evaluation method to align with the nature and values of educational development work. This chapter also offers recommendations for CTL annual reports.

The conclusion, which is oriented to both CTL staff and senior leaders, summarizes the key themes in the book and documents how center aims, theories of change, and tactics align. It also presents practical suggestions for CTL strategic planning.

Other Portraits of Educational Development

Over the past 20 years, educational development in North America has greatly benefited from three key surveys of the field. *Creating the Future of Faculty Development*, published in 2006, was an important overview of educational developers' perceptions of future trends and signature programs. Mary Deane Sorcinelli, Ann Austin, Pamela Eddy, and Andrea Beach surveyed 999 members of the POD Network in 2001, analyzing 494 surveys (50% response rate). The researchers argued that the field was being defined by a new conception of organizational collaboration, which they defined as the "age of the network."[7]

In 2016, an updated study, titled *Faculty Development in the Age of Evidence*, was published by many of the same authors: Andrea Beach, Mary Deane Sorcinelli, Ann Austin, and Jaclyn Rivard. In 2012, the authors distributed 1,382 surveys, and 385 were returned (28% response rate). The surveys were complemented by over 100 interviews about centers' signature programs. While the trends of the early 2000s called for increased intra-institutional collaborations, the latter half of the decade witnessed changing faculty roles, an increased focus on student success, and more urgent calls for instructors to use evidence-based practices. According to the authors, these new challenges defined a distinct moment of educational development work, the "age of evidence." The researchers describe this period as being characterized by "a focus on assessing the impact of instruction on student learning, of academic programs on student success, and of faculty development within institutional mission priorities."[8]

Temporally sandwiched in between these two volumes is *Coming in from the Margins*, edited by Connie Schroeder, Phyllis Blumberg, and Nancy Van Note Chism. This survey-based study was open to all members of the POD Network who identified as CTL directors (N = 477) in

2006. There was a response rate of 32%, or 149 directors, and the survey data were complemented by interviews with 8 CTL directors, 8 CTL directors' supervisors, and 2 supervisors' supervisors. The authors' focus on CTL mission statements, which were uploaded to the surveys, is also an important component of this study. Rather than a broad overview, *Coming in from the Margins* focused specifically on CTLs and their roles in institutional initiatives, noting the enabling and limiting factors of this organizational development work. Contrary to some prior depictions of educational development work as being limited to individual impacts, Schroeder, Blumberg, and Chism concluded that the majority of directors were very involved in institution-level efforts, such as assessment and student success initiatives. Overall, *Coming in from the Margins* highlighted the important role of CTLs in organizational development.[9]

All three of these books have been tremendously influential on the conceptions of and practices in educational development. However, all are based on self-reported data from CTL practitioners. To quote a title of a famous study in biology education, it could be a problem if "what we say is not what we do."[10] Further, the response rate in these studies (ranging from 28% to 50%), while typical for survey research, raises concerns about the reliability of findings. It is also a potential limitation that all survey respondents had to be members of an educational development professional association to be contacted. Although the POD Network had over 1,400 members at the time of this writing,[11] it is certainly possible that not all CTLs are represented by a POD Network member, particularly at less-resourced institutions.

Here, I use a web-based approach as my central methodology. This web methodology is explained in detail below (and in appendix 1, I describe my statistical methodology), but it has both strengths and flaws. On the positive side, it offers the potential for a widespread and systematic look at CTL practice in the United States that is not filtered by professional association membership nor propensity to respond to surveys. Additionally, it offers the opportunity to align aspirations about the work (such as mission and goal statements) with organizational artifacts of the work (such as program offerings and annual reports). Third, perhaps better than surveys, it helps illuminate how CTLs directly communicate their aims, strategies, and tactics to their key stakeholders, which may include both on-campus and external communities. Finally, with rapid developments in web scraping and AI technology, it may offer the framework for a more frequent update regarding directions in the field as compared to the 10-year periodicity with which most studies tend to align.

There are clear drawbacks, however, and the most obvious one is that to be included in this study, a CTL would need to have a web presence. I anticipate this to be less of a concern in 2020, when I collected my data, than for earlier studies because of the current pervasiveness and reach of the internet. However, I did locate 13 CTLs (out of over 1,200) that either did not have a website at all or did not have a functioning site. For those that did have a site, I observed that, occasionally, key pieces of data, such as program lists, were behind institutional firewalls; therefore, this approach may also impact sub-findings, such as analyses of program types. Second, as the director of a busy CTL, I know that websites do not always keep pace with the activity of work, and sometimes web documents may lag actual activities. Again, this may present holes in data, perhaps disproportionately for smaller centers that have fewer staff to update web resources. In short, I maintain that no single methodology for large-scale analyses of CTL work, whether surveys and interviews or analysis of web text, is perfect. My hope is that each can offer a helpful lens, ideally contributing corroborating evidence about this important sector of higher education.

To add richness to the statistics presented, I interviewed 13 CTL leaders about their centers' programs and strategies, and corresponded with others by email.[12] These narratives are woven throughout several chapters. The centers were selected because of their diversity in institutional types and as illustrations of CTLs with strong strategic emphases in one of the four orientations featured in this book (Hub, Incubator, Temple, or Sieve), integrative tendencies, or evaluation practice.

A second caveat is that this book focuses only on Centers for Teaching and Learning in the United States. As a "researcher of one" and working as a CTL director during a global pandemic, I wish I had been able to take on a broader scope, but I know my limits. Educational development, or "academic development" or "staff development" as the field is often termed in other parts of the world, is structured and practiced differently in other countries.[13] I hope other researchers are inspired to apply similar broad approaches to educational development in their own contexts.

How Many Centers for Teaching and Learning Are There?

What exactly is a Teaching and Learning Center? A Teaching and Learning Center (TLC) is central and dedicated space where ongoing excellence and support in teaching and learning is the primary focus, staffed by professionals with expertise in pedagogy, teaching innovation, and student learning.

—WEBSITE OF HOUSTON H. HARTE CENTER FOR TEACHING AND LEARNING, FOUNDED IN 2019, WASHINGTON AND LEE UNIVERSITY, VIRGINIA[14]

As noted, the originating premise for this book was to better understand the number of CTLs in the United States. Based on anecdotes and a systematic analysis of job ads,[15] it appeared that many institutions of higher education were starting or growing CTLs, but there was little evidence on which to base that claim. If we did not know how many units were engaged in this work, how could we understand the trajectory of the educational development field? Over time, I felt an increasing urgency to understand the reach and impact of the central organizational unit in which I have worked for over 20 years. Indeed, as I began my investigation, I discovered a valuable foundation of systematic studies tackling this same inquiry that reach back almost 50 years.

In 1975, John Centra, then a project director at the Educational Testing Service, sent a letter to the president of every US college and university asking if they had what they "would consider an organized program or set of practices for faculty development and improving instruction."[16] Of the group surveyed, 1,044 institutions responded that they had such practices or programs, which was the majority (59%) of those who responded to the letter (N = 1,783).

About 10 years later, Glenn Erickson, a director of the Instructional Development Program at the University of Rhode Island, lamented that "we had never had a decent mailing list of 'development' practitioners, yet we claimed to be committed to putting such folks in touch with each other," motivating a similar study.[17] Mailing a letter to chief academic officers at all four-year colleges and universities, Erickson asked for names and addresses of directors or coordinators of "what are typically called faculty development, instructional development, or teaching improvement programs or activities."[18] Among the responses, 750 chief academic officers provided the names of over 1,000 personnel who engaged in such work. Erickson concluded from his research "that the 'faculty development movement' is neither dead nor in decline."[19]

Fast-forward another 10 years and Sally Kuhlenschmidt, then director of Western Kentucky's Faculty Center for Excellence in Teaching, engaged in a similar endeavor, albeit now with the aid of the internet. In 2010, using a variety of records, such as POD Network member lists and Google searches for terms like *professional development*, *Center for Teaching and Learning*, and *staff development*, Kuhlenschmidt identified 1,267 teaching and learning development units (TLDUs). Notably, her criteria indicated that the presence of a website was not a sufficient condition for being included in her list; the unit had to serve postsecondary instructors, have responsibility for teaching development, and be engaged in delivery of "'pure' pedagogy, not only teaching involved in using technology."[20] Further, if the unit had a distinct program for graduate teaching assistants, it was listed as a separate program, which reduces Kuhlenschmidt's CTL estimate to 1,182.

Kuhlenschmidt concluded, "For the first time in many years, it is possible to say what is typical or not in terms of institutions supporting the presence of TLDUs. . . . Sustaining the data set will require the cooperation of the research community through sharing newly gleaned information and corrections."[21] Although Kuhlenschmidt's important work rigorously documented the extent of CTLs, she did not use the list for further research, calling on others to do so. While there have been highly influential studies of individual educational developers that reflect on their centers' priorities,[22] the organizational strand of work that identified the CTL as a key unit of analysis did not continue.

Now, almost on the 10-year cue of similar studies about educational development, I pick up Kuhlenschmidt's call. In the final part of this chapter, I circle back to the question that triggered this book: How many CTLs are there? This section identifies the number of US CTLs as determined during a web search conducted from 2018 to 2020 and analyzes these numbers by institutional characteristics and historical data.

In December 2018, I began this project with a web search that was conducted in two phases. First, the Center for Teaching Excellence at the University of Kansas has maintained a list of centers that includes about 400 US CTLs. To complement this list, I conducted a web search of every US state using the keywords *faculty development* or *center for teaching*. I also conducted a web search using *medical school* and *faculty affairs* or *faculty development*. In December 2018, I was able to identify 1,184 centers or programs.[23]

With these data, the POD Network created a new interactive Centers and Programs Directory, which was publicized in *Inside Higher Ed* in May 2019[24] and on the POD Network discussion list in June 2019.[25] Currently, CTLs can be added to the list from any location in the world. As of August 2022, 1,291 were listed from multiple countries, but because the site is open access, it now includes some units that do not include any teaching focus. While I find that it no longer offers a precise count of US CTLs, I was able to use the tool to find 13 additional centers that do not have a website. Although these 13 CTLs are not included in the analyses in chapters 2 through 5 and the conclusion, they are included in this chapter.

In 2019–20, using a 2018 IPEDS list of postsecondary institutions, I double-checked all college and university sites where there was not already an entry for a center. I accessed these institutions' websites to look more carefully for the presence of a unit, reviewing common institutional locations like the office of the provost or human resources and using the internal search engine.

Using this extensive list of CTLs, for the second stage of my research I refined and confirmed that the entries aligned with prior scholarship criteria for constituents of an educational development unit. In this stage of the research, I wrestled with how to create an operational definition for a Center for Teaching and Learning. To do this, I primarily utilized Kuhlenschmidt's criteria: the unit had to serve postsecondary instructors and have responsibility for teaching development. Also in alignment with Kuhlenschmidt's benchmarks, the CTL site needed to be more than a list of resources; rather, it needed to signal active interpersonal work (e.g., consultations, workshops, institutes, symposia, programs, or other campus activity). However, I also deviated from Kuhlenschmidt's approach in two ways. First, I did not separately code programs for graduate teaching assistants because my unit of analysis is the organization. Additionally, Kuhlenschmidt distinguished centers that focus on "actively delivered 'pure' pedagogy" from those that addressed "only teaching involved in using technology," and she excluded the latter.[26] That distinction was difficult to operationalize, and I felt uncomfortable in making the judgment that units that focus only on teaching with technology were not fundamental to "helping colleges and universities function effectively as teaching and learning communities," that is, engagement in educational development work.[27] Therefore, I included technology-focused centers in my study as long as they met the other criteria detailed here. Although many of the units in this study were identified by titles other than "Center for Teaching and Learning," in this study, *a Center for Teaching and Learning is a unit that serves a postsecondary audience, focuses at least part of its mission on teaching, and is actively engaged in interpersonal work—such as consultations, programs, or services—that goes beyond a digital list of resources.*

This second stage of research took over a year and allowed me to refine my list to 1,209 unique CTLs. Recall that Centra identified 1,044 programs or practices in 1975, and Kuhlenschmidt found 1,182 teaching and learning development units in 2010. In short, the number of Centers for Teaching and Learning has grown, and grown steadily.

Because some institutions have more than one center, what proportion of higher education institutions are affiliated with a CTL? Using the Carnegie Foundation list of institutions of higher education, over a quarter (26%) of all institutions have at least one CTL. Again, the proportion of colleges and universities associated with a CTL represents an increase, up from 21%, as seen in Kuhlenschmidt's study.[28]

Although CTLs are the key focus of this book, one growing trend appears to be the rise of the educational development consortia. In my research, I identified 11 large networks or groups of colleges and universities that share educational development programs and resources such as small grants.[29] While receiving little attention until now, these network educational development initiatives offer an emerging model of work, the "meta-center." These units included regional groups of peer institutions, such as the Great Lakes Colleges Association, as well as large state system consortia, like the Institute for Teaching and Learning, a hub for the state university campuses in California. (In some cases, the network included institutions that already have a CTL, joining them together in a partnership.) If including these systems or multi-institutional hubs, an even higher proportion of postsecondary institutions (27%) are affiliated with a CTL.

While news of a CTL that is closing due to politics or financial constraints always reverberates loudly, the field of educational development in the United States continues to grow. Additionally, the reach of CTLs is considerable. The majority of students in the US (60%) are studying in colleges and universities affiliated with a Center for Teaching and Learning.[30]

Institutional Characteristics

The distribution of CTLs among US colleges and universities was determined using several institutional characteristics, including Carnegie classification, control (public / private not-for-profit / private for-profit), region, mission, selectivity, and size. Because Kuhlenschmidt's study used many of these same variables, this allows for a comparison of trends over the past decade.

Carnegie Type

In 2020, CTLs were most frequently located in doctoral universities (table I.1), which is consistent with Kuhlenschmidt's findings. However,

TABLE I.1. Presence of Center for Teaching and Learning, by institutional Carnegie type, 2020

Carnegie type	Percent of institutions covered by a CTL	Number of institutions with CTL	Percent of CTL dataset	Number of CTLs
Doctoral	78%	324	28%	342
Master's	45%	309	26%	313
Associate's	15%	231	19%	235
Baccalaureate	25%	183	15%	183
Medical/health	16%	51	9%	106
Other special focus	4%	21	2%	29
Missing	—	—	<1%	1
Total	**26%**	**1,119**	**100%**	**1,209**

NOTES: Disciplinary-based CTLs were assigned a special focus category even if they were not a separate IPEDS institution. Dashes indicate that data were not applicable.

in comparison to an earlier study, both doctoral universities and master's colleges or universities saw increases in the proportions of institutions that housed a CTL (72% to 78% and 40% to 45%, respectively). The presence of CTLs also rose sharply for baccalaureate colleges (14% to 25%). In contrast, there were small declines for associate's colleges, from 17% to 15%; however, if institutional networks were factored in, there was a relatively constant presence from 17% to 16%. Special focus and tribal colleges are combined in Kuhlenschmidt's study and, therefore, it is difficult to make comparisons over time.[31]

The early historical roots of CTLs are found in larger research universities,[32] and this legacy remains to this day. Using the finer-grained 2018 Carnegie classifications, the institutional type that is most likely to have a CTL is a doctoral university with very high levels of research activity (94%). Among master's institutions, the size of the institution matters for representation. Those with larger programs (55%) are more likely to be affiliated with a center, compared to medium (40%) and small (28%) programs. For baccalaureate colleges, those with an arts and science focus (42%) are over two times more likely to have a CTL compared to diverse fields (20%). Within the special focus categories, medical schools (62%) are most likely to embed a center, followed by engineering schools (14%), but faith-related ("faith flag") institutions (2%) are least likely to have a CTL. (The "faith flag" is defined as a faith-related special focus institution in the Carnegie datafile, rather than an institution with a faith-based mission.) Among two-year institutions, the institutional type with the most CTL coverage is high-transfer/high-traditional colleges (33%). Two-year arts and design colleges and technical professions–focused colleges are least likely, with no representation of CTLs.

Control

Public colleges and universities were most likely to be connected to a Center for Teaching and Learning, followed by private (not-for-profit) institutions (table I.2). Private for-profits were least likely to be affiliated; only a small fraction (7%) had a CTL. When focusing only on public and private non-profit colleges and universities, the proportion of US higher education institutions with CTLs rises to 31%.

In comparison with Kuhlenschmidt's study a decade earlier, the proportion of public postsecondary institutions with a center remained about the same (from 37% to 38%). In turn, CTL representation at private non-profit colleges and universities increased substantially (16% to 25%) and rose at private for-profit colleges (1% to 7%).[33]

Diverse Missions and Focus

The presence of Centers for Teaching and Learning at US institutions of higher education with diverse missions is shown in table I.3. In 2020, over one-third of Historically Black Colleges and Universities (HBCUs), Hispanic-Serving Institutions (HSIs), and women's colleges had a CTL.

TABLE I.2. Presence of Center for Teaching and Learning, by institutional control, 2020

Control	Percent of institutions covered by a CTL	Number of institutions with CTL	Percent of CTL dataset	Number of CTLs
Public	38%	626	61%	742
Private (not–for–profit)	25%	427	38%	457
Private (for–profit)	7%	65	1%	8
Missing	<1%	1	<1%	2

TABLE I.3. Presence of Center for Teaching and Learning, by diverse mission, 2020

Mission	Percent of institutions covered by a CTL	Number of institutions with CTL	Percent of CTL dataset	Number of CTLs
MSI	34%	220	19%	234
HBCUs	46%	46	4%	46
HSIs	35%	120	11%	133
Tribal colleges	0%	0	0%	0
Women's	38%	12	1%	12
Faith-based*	1%	2	<1%	2

*As indicated by the "faith flag" in the Carnegie Foundation 2018 datafile but does not reflect that other institutions in the dataset are affiliated with faith-based missions.

However, there was very little presence in faith-based institutions and there were no centers at tribal colleges.

When compared to Kuhlenschmidt's study, an encouraging trend over the past decade is an increase in the number of CTLs at institutions serving diverse student populations. For example, over the past 10 years, the number of centers at minority-serving institutions (MSIs) more than doubled (109 to 234) and coverage sharply increased (14% to 34%). The proportion of centers at HBCUs also doubled (23% to 46%). Likewise, HSIs were a fast-growing segment of US higher education, and their CTL numbers kept pace. From 2010 to 2020, HSI CTL numbers grew from 66 to 133, with coverage rising from 17% to 35%. Although the overall count of postsecondary women's institutions declined over the past decade, the number of CTLs increased. For women's colleges, there was an increase from 7 to 12 CTLs with coverage also rising (from 13% to 38%). However, as in Kuhlenschmidt's study, no CTLs were found at tribal colleges, which suggests a needed area of attention for the field (or a limitation of web-based methodologies).

Region

Consistent with the population increases evident in many states in the southeastern United States, the largest number of CTL-affiliated institutions were in the Southeast region, which includes these US states: Alabama, Arkansas, Florida, Georgia, Kentucky, Louisiana, Mississippi,

TABLE I.4. Presence of Center for Teaching and Learning, by region, 2020

Region	Percent of institutions covered by a CTL	Number of institutions with CTL	Percent of CTL dataset	Number of CTLs
New England	43%	105	10%	117
US Service	37%	7	1%	7
Mid-East	29%	201	18%	215
Far West	27%	165	15%	185
Great Lakes	27%	162	15%	178
Southeast	24%	252	22%	270
Southwest	24%	102	9%	106
Rocky Mountains	24%	38	3%	40
Plains	20%	84	7%	88
Outlying areas	3%	3	<1%	3

North Carolina, South Carolina, Tennessee, Virginia, and West Virginia (table I.4). This follows patterns seen a decade earlier, with the Southeast United States having the greatest presence, followed by the Mid-Atlantic/Mid-East and then states in the Far West.[34] However, institutions in the New England region (Connecticut, Maine, Massachusetts, New Hampshire, Rhode Island, and Vermont) were most likely to be affiliated with an educational development unit.

Compared to 2010, CTL coverage grew sharply in New England, increasing from 28% to 43%. Coverage also expanded over the decade in nearly every other region, with the Rocky Mountain (17% to 24%) and the Mid-Atlantic/Mid-East (22% to 29%) areas showing the sharpest increases. This was followed by the Great Lakes (21% to 27%), Southeast (20% to 24%), outlying areas (0% to 3%), Southwest (21% to 24%), Plains (18% to 20%), and Far West (26% to 27%). Only US service schools showed a very small decline (38% to 37%), but because of the small numbers in this group, it translates only to a net decrease of one CTL.[35]

Selectivity

As a measure of selectivity, the 2018 Carnegie classification dataset categorized US postsecondary institutions into three groups: inclusive (ACT scores in 25th percentile, below 18), selective (ACT scores 18–21), and more selective (ACT scores greater than 21).[36] The selectivity of an institution is associated with CTL presence. About three-quarters of more selective colleges and universities house a CTL compared to half of selective institutions and a small proportion of inclusive institutions (table I.5). This dimension of institutional characteristics was not examined by Kuhlenschmidt, so historical comparisons are not possible. Because CTL work is related to student success,[37] this trend is certainly one to monitor in the future.

Size

To understand the relationship between presence of a Center for Teaching and Learning and institutional size, fall 2017 student enrollment data were divided into full-time equivalent (FTE) quartiles: very small (5–391 student FTEs, n = 1,081), small (392–1,558, n = 1,082), medium (1,559–4,961, n = 1,082), and large (4,962–103,975, n = 1,081). Generally, the larger the institution, the more likely it was to house a CTL (table I.6).

Using 2009 IPEDS data, Kuhlenschmidt found a moderate correlation between the number of FTE degree-seeking students and the presence of a teaching and learning development unit (r = 0.51, p < .001, N = 4,389). Using similar data for fall 2017 FTEs, there continues to be a statistically significant association for CTLs, although diminished in intensity (r = 0.43, p < .001, N = 4,326).

Conclusion

Centers for Teaching and Learning are a growing organizational unit in higher education. The first US CTL was founded in 1962 at the Uni-

TABLE I.5. Presence of Center for Teaching and Learning, by selectivity, 2020

Selectivity	Percent of institutions covered by a CTL	Number of institutions with CTL	Percent of CTL dataset	Number of CTLs
Inclusive	17%	527	49%	586
Selective	50%	274	20%	244
More selective	74%	281	24%	294
Missing	13%	37	7%	85

TABLE I.6. Presence of Center for Teaching and Learning, by student enrollment quartile, 2020

	Percent of institutions covered by a CTL*	Number of institutions with CTL*	Percent of CTL dataset**	Number of CTLs**
Q1 (very small)	2%	17	23%	278
Q2 (small)	10%	103	23%	278
Q3 (medium)	32%	342	23%	278
Q4 (large)	61%	656	23%	278
Missing FTE data	<1%	1	8%	97

*Computed using fall 2017 full-time equivalent enrollment (full-time plus one-third part-time) FTEs to align with other data on the 2018 Carnegie Classification datafile. Quartiles are: Q1 (5–391), Q2 (392–1,558), Q3 (1,559–4,961), Q4 (4,962–103,975).

**Computed using 2020 student FTEs, with the following quartiles: Q1 (29–2,218), Q2 (2,219–4,618), Q3 (4,619–10,136), Q4 (10,137–87,002). There are more missing values for CTLs because special focus CTLs not associated with a unique IPEDS institution are excluded (e.g., a CTL focused on only one disciplinary unit).

versity of Michigan, and less than a decade later, Centra identified 1,044 programs or practices. In 1986, Erickson found over 1,000 personnel working in faculty development, instructional development, or teaching improvement. However, the first organizational study did not arise until 2011, when Sally Kuhlenschmidt identified 1,182 teaching and learning development units, which covered 21% of US institutions of higher education. A decade later, I find an increase in both numbers and coverage. In 2020, I identified 1,209 Centers for Teaching and Learning. Over a quarter (26%) of all institutions had at least one center, impacting the majority of postsecondary students in the United States. Over the decade, CTL coverage grew in nearly every US region. Although the key focus of this book is Centers for Teaching and Learning, the emergence of the educational network amplifies the reach of CTLs. When considering consortia, CTL coverage represents a slightly higher proportion (27%) of postsecondary institutions.

In spite of increased presence, institutional characteristics shape this landscape. While the vast majority of doctoral institutions housed a Center for Teaching and Learning, a minority of institutions in every other Carnegie type were associated with one. Compared to private institutions, public colleges and universities were more likely to have a CTL. A much greater proportion of more selective institutions were affiliated with a CTL compared to inclusive and selective ones. Institution size based on student FTE was positively correlated with the presence of a center. Encouragingly, there were sharp increases in the number of centers at most institutional types that serve diverse students. However, the lack of a CTL is most striking at tribal colleges, where both prior research and this current study were not able to find a single example. There was also less of a presence at faith-based institutions.

The remaining chapters in the book make the claim that Centers for Teaching and Learning play distinctive change roles on our campuses, particularly around student and faculty learning-related aims. The ideas presented may be useful to current educational developers and serve as inspiration to other campuses to develop and resource even more of these influential units. Rather than focusing only on the CTLs that typically get profiled—namely, well-established centers at doctoral institutions and baccalaureates, usually PWIs (Predominantly White Institutions)—subsequent chapters highlight a range of center examples, including those in medical schools and other disciplinary contexts, associate's and master's colleges, and diverse institutional missions. My hope is that this book will spotlight a range of exemplary practices but also commonalities in aims, strategies, tactics, and organization when working "at the center."

CHAPTER 1

What Are We Trying to Do?

Key Aims of CTLs

It must be borne in mind that the tragedy in life doesn't lie in not reaching your goal. The tragedy lies in having no goal to reach. It isn't a calamity to die with dreams unfulfilled, but it is a calamity not to dream. It is not a disaster to be unable to capture your ideal, but it is a disaster to have no ideal to capture. It is not a disgrace not to reach the stars, but it is a disgrace to have no stars to reach for. Not failure, but low aim is sin.

—BENJAMIN MAYS QUOTE IN THE 2020 VISION STATEMENT OF CUNY HOSTOS COMMUNITY COLLEGE'S PROFESSOR MAGDA VASILLOV CENTER FOR TEACHING AND LEARNING, FOUNDED IN 2003

T HE DEVELOPMENT OF a mission statement is often one of the first steps for strategic planning in institutions of higher education. The mission statement defines "what the organization wants to be and whom it serves"[1] or, as described by four educational developers, "what you do all day, every day, as simply part of doing what you do."[2] Indeed, the CTL mission statement quote that opens this chapter notes the importance of setting ambitious aims. Through the lens of their officially stated missions and goals, how do CTLs define their own goals and sense of purpose?

Answers to this question are important for several reasons. First, in thinking about purpose broadly, missions and goals can be useful benchmarking information, whether for starting a new center or for regular strategic planning. Additionally, for a field that is heavily engaged in working with instructors around backward design and learning outcomes, our CTLs should do the same. The 2018 American Council on Education (ACE)-POD Center for Teaching and Learning Matrix, which set operational standards for CTLs, noted that "accomplished/exemplary" CTLs should have a mission, vision, and goals. Others describe the creation of a clearly defined mission and goals as the very first step that a new or re-envisioning center should take.[3]

In the context of higher education broadly, missions, visions, and goals can help guide decision-making, focus resources on what is most important, and serve as a powerful motivational and communication tool to those inside and outside of the institution.[4] The 2010 study of CTLs, *Coming in from the Margins*, found that center missions serve four purposes:

- Missions help sustain centers in times of fiscal constraint because they align institutional and center objectives.
- Statements of purpose clarify roles and expectations for CTL staff and key collaborators.
- CTLs with missions that explicitly embed ideas of innovation and change are more adept at navigating transformation.
- Missions can legitimize a center's role in leading larger-scale change initiatives around teaching and learning. Specifically, center directors who indicate that their missions enable their involvement in larger-scale work report spending a significantly higher proportion of their work time on institutional initiatives compared to those who do not.

Schroeder's research clearly suggests that the content and substance of missions are not mere verbiage.[5]

In this chapter, I investigate the explicitly articulated sense of purpose found in CTL statements of mission, vision, goal, and values, which are documents I collectively refer to as *statements of purpose*. I also look at other artifacts of purpose. For example, I examine the names of centers and what we can learn from those organizational titles. Although CTL names do not offer a great deal of nuance about purpose, they nonetheless can offer significant information about key priorities. For example, Ozarks Technical Community College's *Center for Academic Innovation* in Missouri likely has a different focus than the *Center for Active Engagement and Scholarship* at Governors State University in Illinois, which may again be different from Tennessee's Southern Adventist University's *Center for Teaching Excellence and Biblical Foundations of Faith and Learning*. See the word cloud of the most frequently used terms in CTL names displayed in figure 1.1.

This study relies on statements of purpose and CTL names from 2020. In fact-checking the book in 2022, I noticed that there have been some updates, some small (e.g., the CTL became a named center or the mission statement used different language but had a similar emphasis) and some large (e.g., universities merged or the name and mission of the CTL changed after a reorganization). Name changes discovered by August 2022 are noted in the text, and other updates are described in the notes. It is also important to call out the stasis in this dataset as well: of the names and missions cited in this chapter, most did not change. US CTLs are fluid organizations and can be vulnerable to senior leadership transitions. Despite the capacity of CTLs to be both change agents and

Figure 1.1. *Most frequent words in CTL names. Note: Displays 150 most frequently used names; proper names excluded.*

objects of change, I believe that the trends described continue to be descriptive of them in aggregate.

Method

Among the 1,209 CTLs identified in the last chapter, 1,196 (99%) had a functioning website. While most (57%) had a statement formally titled "mission," an additional group (34%) posted a mission-like statement with these components: key constituencies, programs, or aims. One in five (20%) formally identified goals, and smaller proportions included a vision (15%) or described their values or guidelines (8%). Missions, goals, visions, and values are technically different genres; for example, a vision statement is typically aspirational/inspirational, while a mission should be pragmatic and achievable.[6] However, all of these statements are similar in describing intended aims and, in most cases, how a center plans to achieve them. Additionally, in reading through these 1,605 texts, there was some blurring of the genres. For example, goal statements frequently offered a fuller articulation of center aims and intended purposes compared to mission statements, and values statements often described similar ideas. In short, it seems reasonable to combine these statements to best understand CTL stated aims. Therefore, rather than analyze each type of document separately, I triangulated the 1,605 texts into a broader genre that I call *statements of purpose*. Nearly all CTLs (92%) had a statement of purpose, including one or more of the following: mission, mission-like, goal, vision, or values. After consolidation, there were 1,105 statements of purpose. These texts are at the foundation of the analyses in this chapter as well as the next.

In this chapter, I compare my 2020 analysis with Connie Schroeder's study, *Coming in from the Margins*. Schroeder's book is based on a 2006 survey sent to CTL directors. The survey included a voluntary upload option for mission statements, and she received and analyzed 100.

Using very similar methodologies, I compared the statements of purpose from my study with the missions Schroeder analyzed. Although the methods were not identical, this approach offers a glimpse into changes in the field over approximately 15 years (2006 to 2020). I focus on two specific areas of CTL aims:

1. *Who*: Schroeder described this element as the "constituency component" or "constituents of the teaching and learning center."[7] For this analysis, I compare my analysis of 1,105 CTL purpose statements with Schroeder's of 100 missions. Here, *constituency* is defined as the key parties that are invited to directly collaborate with or utilize the center.
2. *Why*: This element examines themes in the aims or articulated purposes of the CTL. Here, I also use Schroeder's analysis of 100 mission statements for comparison.

In chapter 2, I address the third typical element of missions: "what," or "actions and efforts to fulfill purpose(s)."[8] All variables that are used for statistical analyses are described in appendix 1.

Who: Key Constituencies

Schroeder's analysis observed an increasing integration of constituencies into center mission statements. *Coming in from the Margins* found that most missions "do not identify faculty as their exclusive constituency," which "reflects migration from the earlier, but narrow, circumscription of the role teaching and learning centers play and constituents served."[9] Has this trend continued?[10]

In 2020, CTLs describe a mean of 1.50 constituencies per center, with a range of zero to eight. (The maximum number of constituencies that could be identified is nine; see table 1.1.) By Carnegie type, CTLs at associate's colleges identify the highest mean number of constituencies, an average of 1.59. This was followed by small differences in other Carnegie types: doctoral (1.57), medical/health (1.47), baccalaureate (1.45), master's (1.42), and other special focus (1.37).[11] There were no statistically significant distinctions by control, CTL age, nor time of coding (i.e., websites visited at the beginning of 2020 versus the latter half of the year). While there is no significant difference by MSI status, women's colleges (mean = 2.10) tended to report a broader base than coeducational institutions (mean = 1.49).[12] This may be due to the greater inclusion of (female) students in the institutional missions of women's colleges historically.

TABLE 1.1. Constituencies identified in CTL mission statements, by percentage of units at Carnegie type, 2020

Constituency	All (N = 1105)	Doctoral (n = 324)	Master's (n = 290)	Associate's (n = 206)	Baccalaureate (n = 167)	Medical/ health (n = 90)	Other special focus (n = 27)
At least one named constituency	90	87	91	93	90	96	85
Multiple constituencies	43	44	38	52	41	35	37
Faculty	78	70	83	77	81	86	70
Staff/ Administrators	20	15	16	35	20	11	15
Community/ All employees	12	15	13	16	5	6	4
Students	11	10	9	7	17	15	15
Educators/ Instructors	10	13	5	10	7	11	22
Academic units	8	11	8	2	7	5	4
Part-time/ Adjunct faculty	6	4	7	10	3	5	0
TAs, graduate students, or postdocs	5	14	2	1	2	1	0
External constituencies	3	3	2	2	2	6	7

NOTES: Statements of purpose could include more than one constituency. Percentages are presented for unique Carnegie type. (See appendix 1 for methodology.) One institution is missing Carnegie classification information.

Institutional size had some impact: instructional FTE ($r = 0.13$, $p < .001$) and student FTE ($r = .09$, $p < .01$) have weak positive correlations with the reported number of constituencies.

How do these trends compare with previous research? Constituencies identified in 2020 CTL mission statements are presented in table 1.1. In Schroeder's study, most (80%) of the 100 mission statements named at least one constituency served by the center.[13] In 2020, a slightly higher proportion (90%) of the mission statements reference at least one direct audience for the center's work (table 1.1).

Another point of consistency is the centrality of faculty in CTL missions. In Schroeder's study, faculty took center stage, named most frequently (78%) as a sole constituency or with another group.[14] Despite significant changes in CTLs over 15 years, faculty are still by far the most frequently named audience, identified at exactly the same proportion (table 1.1). Faculty appear in over two-thirds of missions across all institutional types but most frequently in medical/health contexts.[15] Additionally, about 1 in 10 missions reference the more general "educators" or "instructors," which is cited most frequently by CTLs in other special focus contexts.[16] In spite of increasing calls to center part-time or adjunct faculty in educational development,[17] they are infrequently referenced explicitly (6%), although in 2006 missions, adjunct faculty appeared to not be mentioned at all. (It could be the case that "educators" or "instructors" are less-specified references to part-time and adjunct faculty.) By Carnegie type, CTLs at associate's colleges are most likely to explicitly identify adjuncts.[18]

The focus on faculty is also reflected in many center names that spotlight this constituency. For example, as seen in figure 1.1, *Faculty* by far dominates the reference to any specific constituency in CTL names. Despite the use of other terms to describe the field,[19] it is interesting that *Faculty Development* appears strikingly more often (152) in a center name compared to these alternatives: *Professional Development* (44), *Educational Development* (6), *Instructional Development* (2), and *Academic Development* (1).

In 2006, academic staff—generically or with certain titles like "counselors"—were named in 19% of missions, and this was the second

---

The **Faculty Center for Teaching and Learning** (FCTL) at the Community College of Philadelphia, Pennsylvania, was founded in the early 1980s. Stephanie Scordia, currently Title III Professional Learning Coordinator, noted what the center name underscores: "We are faculty teaching faculty." This is highlighted in the very first and last lines of their mission: "As a faculty driven effort, the Faculty Center for Teaching & Learning is uniquely positioned to be at the forefront of faculty development, programming, and research at Community College of Philadelphia. . . . We are committed to serving all faculty, full and part time, across disciplines or programs."

most frequently named group.[20] This is a consistent pattern more than a decade later. In 2020, the second most frequently named audience is also staff or administrators, and at about the same proportion (20%). Another point of continuity is that staff/administrators are always named in tandem with another group (most frequently faculty), which is interesting given the rise in leadership-related functions of CTLs (more on this in chapter 4).

Associate's colleges reference staff/administrators with more frequency compared to other institutional types.[21] This may be due to a higher proportion of adjuncts at community colleges and the teaching-focused mission of these institutions, heightening administrative responsibilities for mentoring.[22] It is also the case, however, that some CTLs at these often less-resourced institutions bridge pedagogical functions with human resource mandates. For example, in California, the San Diego Mesa College's Campus Employee Learning unit coordinates "a variety of professional learning opportunities for all faculty, staff, and administrators to experience and enjoy in their roles as lifelong learners and educators."[23] Similarly, the Teaching and Learning Center at John A. Logan College in Illinois "works with departments to promote all training to faculty and staff."[24]

In 2020, after faculty, staff, and administrators, there are significant drops in the frequency by which other constituencies are identified in center mission statements. Schroeder found that institution-wide constituencies, identified by terms such as "all educators" or the "community of peers," were identified in 16% of the statements. Schroeder described these as "weak references to the entire institution,"[25] and in 2020, we observe these broad identifications with somewhat less frequency: 12% name the "community" or "all employees," most frequently at associate's and doctoral institutions.[26] Specific academic units such as "departments" were also infrequently mentioned in both 2006 and 2020 missions, but with higher frequency more recently (at 4% and 8%, respectively). CTLs at doctoral universities were most likely to identify academic units as a constituency.[27]

Despite the many similarities in mission-named constituencies, there is one key distinctive trend: the rise in student-focused constituencies.

In Schroeder's study, 2 missions (2%) named students and 11 (11%) identified teaching assistants. In 2020, over 1 in 10 missions (11%) reference students as a core constituency of the center's work, and an additional small group (5%) names teaching assistants, graduate students, or postdoctoral scholars (table 1.1). Students are most frequently identified at baccalaureate institutions, and this trend may signal growing "students-as-partners" initiatives,[28] which are described in more detail in chapter 3.[29] Postdocs are named very infrequently (only 11 centers mentioned them specifically) and were therefore coded with graduate TAs. References to graduate students, teaching assistants, or postdocs varied by institutional type in predictable ways, with most references at doctoral-affiliated CTLs.[30]

Another shift is the mention of constituencies outside of the academy. External constituencies were not listed at all in Schroeder's study, but there are a few references (3%) in 2020. Examples include the Center for Teaching Excellence at Milwaukee Area Technical College in Wisconsin, which seeks to "build the workforce our industry partners need and improve the community we share"[31] and the California Baptist University's Teaching and Learning Center, which "equips Kingdom professionals to live out the Great Commission in service to the university, the community, the church and the world."[32] The Center for Excellence in Law School Teaching at New York's Albany Law School states that its goal is to "provide a pedagogically sound and innovative program of instruction to meet the changing needs of law students and legal educators, as well as the clients lawyers ultimately serve."[33] Although small in number, this may signal a nascent trend for CTLs to be more focused on stakeholders external to the academy. There are no significant differences, however, in identification of external constituencies by institutional type.

Approximately 15 years after Schroeder's data collection, there are some important changes—and a striking lack of change as well. Far and away, faculty continue to be most frequently identified as key collaborators. Part-time or adjunct faculty are infrequently mentioned, but because this category of instructor was not mentioned at all in Schroeder's analysis, their numbers may be an increase. Staff are also referenced with striking consistency.

These data suggest that there has been a shift in the breadth of constituencies served. As noted, a higher proportion of CTLs identify at least one direct audience in 2020. Additionally, while Schroeder identified a mean of 1.18 constituencies,[34] I find a small increase in 2020 to 1.50 audiences per center. Examples of this broader base range across institutional types include the Center for Excellence in Teaching and Learning at the University of Connecticut, whose mission-like statement at the time indicated that it collaborated "with individual faculty, teaching assistants, students, departments and the academic administration,"[35] and the Teaching and Learning Center at the University of Tennessee's Health Science Center, which invites "faculty of all ranks, staff and students at all levels" as well as "departments, offices, programs, and colleges."[36]

Across centers, while the proportion of CTLs that reference work with faculty, staff, or administrators stayed about constant, there is simultaneously an expansion into aims of serving students, organizational development to serve academic units, and, in some cases, a broadening to external groups like patients, clients, and the community. Because of this broadening of stakeholders, the next section examines changes in purpose over time. Is it the case, as Schroeder hypothesized in 2010, that the "integration of constituencies into center mission statements may signal the changing mission of centers"?[37] Have the stated aims or purposes of centers also changed over time?

Why: Key Purposes

Statements of purpose offer valuable insight into Center for Teaching and Learning goals and aspirations. As with analysis of constituencies, I again attempted to replicate Schroeder's analysis with some small variations. *Coming in from the Margins* identified 17 aims in CTL mission statements. In trying to use the same codes on the 2020 dataset, however, I found myself struggling to distinguish purposes that seemed like a desired end state (e.g., develop a culture of teaching) and those that appeared to be a vehicle to reach that end (e.g., offer programs, provide resources). Therefore, I maintained 7 of Schroeder's "purpose components" that signal an intended outcome, and I added new codes for emergent aims that arose frequently in my 2020 dataset.[38] (Discussion of how CTLs achieve their aims is described in chapters 2 and 3.) While there have been small changes in espoused constituencies of centers over time, there are much more significant shifts in articulated aims.

For this chapter, I again analyze statements of purpose from 1,105 centers. Table 1.2 displays all aims that appear in at least 10% of 2020 purpose statements and compares them, when applicable, to Schroeder's study. While a deductive approach captures most of the key aims that continue to guide CTLs in 2020, there are two additional emergent themes that are not noted in prior scholarship but occur with frequency (in approximately 20% of CTL statements of purpose). These are (1) fostering scholarly and creative work and (2) promoting diversity, equity, and inclusion (DEI).

The vast majority of CTLs (94%) articulate at least one of the aims shown in table 1.2, and three-quarters (75%) describe multiple goals. Other aims that occur with less frequency and are therefore not elaborated here include course modality (8%), service (6%), curriculum (6%),

TABLE 1.2. Most frequent CTL aims, 2020 and 2010

Aim	2020 (% of statements of purpose)	2010 Schroeder (% of missions)
Student learning*	65	14
Instructor outcome**	50	~22
Change or innovation	37	22
Culture, climate, and environment	22	12
Scholarly and creative work	20	—
Diversity, equity, and inclusion	19	—
Support of institutional mission, strategic plan, or goals	18	28
Teaching effectiveness and excellence***	18	~24
Community building	11	13

NOTES: The 2010 aims are derived from Schroeder, "Aligning and Revising." Dashes indicate that data were not collected on this topic.

*In Schroeder, this aim is named "Learning."

**In Schroeder, this aim is named "Faculty-focused" (22% of missions) or "Serving multiple educators" (14%). The proportion is approximate because the overlap is unknown.

***In Schroeder, this aim is named "Teaching and learning" (24% of missions), "Teaching; classroom instruction" (fewer than 12%), and "Pedagogy" (fewer than 10%). The proportion is approximate because the overlap is unknown.

advising and mentoring (4%), community engagement (3%), and learning space design–related (1%) outcomes.

Student Learning

In their overview of the history of the field of educational development, Sorcinelli, Austin, Eddy, and Beach defined the 1990s as the "Age of the Learner," which marked a paradigm shift that moved the focus away from faculty and the dynamics of teaching to students and the outcomes of learning.[39] However, if that description is characteristic of the late 20th and early 21st century, then CTL missions are a lagging indicator. In Schroeder's study, 14% of CTLs noted "learning" as a key purpose, and it was only the seventh most frequently identified aim.[40] Somewhat more popular was "teaching and learning," which was stressed by 24% of centers. Turning to surveys of educational developers, a very small proportion (7%) noted that a key goal in 2016 was to "partner in the learning enterprise," although a much larger group (57%) indicated that it was important to advance new initiatives in learning and teaching.[41]

In 2020, the majority of centers (65%) include student learning as a key aim (table 1.2), marking one of the most significant shifts in articulated CTL ambitions. Learning is also the single most frequently listed purpose of CTLs at all institutional types except for medical or other health profession contexts (table 1.3).[42] Larger institutions (by instructional FTE) tend to employ learning-focused language more frequently.[43] There are no other statistically significant differences by MSI nor women's college status, CTL age, nor time of coding.

Because learning-focused aims are so prominent, I also coded 11 variations in how this goal was expressed. Most frequently, this aspiration was written as a *general focus on student learning* (30%). An example is given by the Faculty Teaching and Learning Center at Aims Community College in Colorado, which "is dedicated to our common mission to help students learn."[44] Also common—especially among associate's institutions—were aspirations to support *student success* (16%), such as the Center for Teaching and Learning at Scottsdale Community College in Arizona, which provides "opportunities for faculty professional development to promote innovation and excellence in teaching and learning to enable student success."[45] More than 1 in 10 CTLs sought to create effective *learning environments* (12%) or cultivate more *student- or learning-centered* approaches (8%). To illustrate, the Faculty Center for Excellence in Teaching and Learning at California State University, Stanislaus is "dedicated to building a learning-centered community."[46]

Other sub-themes of learning-focused goals and missions include:

- Promoting *student learning outcomes* (6%): For example, Mills College's Center for Faculty Excellence in California indicated that a key purpose was "to promote equitable outcomes for our students."[47]
- *Transformative learning* (4%): The Faculty Center for the Advancement of Teaching and Learning at Lewis University in Illinois aimed "to help faculty members create a rich and transformative learning environment."[48]
- *Student-faculty partnerships* (3%): "Providing opportunities for faculty and students to collaborate in the search for truth and academic excellence" was a goal of Albertus Magnus College's Center for Teaching and Learning Excellence in Connecticut.[49]
- *Student lifelong learning* (2%): An example of this aim was found in the mission of the Center for Excellence in Teaching and Learning at Monmouth University in New Jersey: "to advance . . . important capacities for successful engagement in life beyond our campus community."[50]

In addition to these themes, 11% of centers had other types of learning- or student-centered foci, such as:

- Assisting students in becoming "leaders and visionaries who positively impact society" (Center for Innovative and Transformative Instruction, Winston-Salem State University, North Carolina)[51]
- Preparing students to be "agents of change"[52] (Center for Teaching and Learning, Marquette University, Wisconsin)[53]

- Helping students develop as "whole persons" (Center for Teaching and Learning, Lenoir-Rhyne University, North Carolina)[54]

The emphasis on learners and learning is not new to CTLs, but the theme may be more recently amplified. Schroeder commented on the implications of this trend in its early forms: "The language used [in mission statements] may also reflect migration from a teaching-centered paradigm that was more prevalent when [CTLs] were first emerging. . . . Learner-centered institutional missions may open the door for broader center mission statements that extend the reach of [CTLs]."[55] These learning-focused aims, which often point to leadership of institutional initiatives such as student success or assessment, signal a broader campus role for centers.

Instructor Outcomes

Historically, Centers for Teaching and Learning began by addressing faculty development or initiatives that focused on the individual instructor, such as consultations on teaching, support for scholarly writing, or programs on well-being and holistic development.[56] However, because of Schroeder's argument that the field is pivoting to organizational development, I questioned if this aim has declined in emphasis over time. In her earlier study of CTL missions, almost a quarter (22%) of statements addressed this aim. Beach, Sorcinelli, Austin, and Rivard's survey data also suggested that educational developers placed much less priority on support for individual faculty members' professional development goals when compared to 10 years earlier.[57] Both of these studies would suggest a decrease in instructor-focused aims in 2020.

However, 2020 CTL missions show substantial presence of goals related to instructors' professional learning. Instructor-related outcomes are the second-most frequent aim overall, described in half (50%) of center purpose statements. At medical school and other health profession–related contexts, this purpose was even more dominant, as well as at mid-sized and large institutions.[58] There are no other statistically significant differences by MSI or women's college status, time of coding, nor CTL age.

Instructor- or faculty-related outcomes are represented in three key ways. First, seen in almost a third (32%) of statements overall is a desire to support professional development for the purposes of *lifelong learning or growth*. For example, the University of Illinois at Urbana-Champaign's Center for Innovation in Teaching and Learning displays on its website the core value "Expanding Scholarship, Lifelong Learning and Career Potential."[59] In many of these cases, faculty are the key constituency, but some examples were more inclusive of instructional communities at large. For example, in Ohio, Youngstown State University's Institute for Teaching and Learning "seeks to support the professional development of all faculty (full-time and part-time, tenure and non-tenure track, graduate teaching assistants) across all career stages in the areas of teaching, research, service, and work/life balance."[60]

Second, a quarter (25%) of statements express an aim to impact some aspect of instructors' *behaviors or dispositions*, such as well-being or scholarly productivity. Illustrations include a goal to create a "professional, well-educated faculty" (e.g., Office of Faculty Development, Marine Corps University, Virginia)[61] or to support "teaching excellence, clinical skills, research development, leadership enhancement and technological implementation" (Office of Faculty Affairs and Development, Morehouse School of Medicine, Georgia).[62] Most frequently, these goals relate to developing good teachers as illustrated in this statement from Michigan's Lansing Community College: "The mission of the Center for Teaching Excellence is to inspire and enable faculty to enhance teaching potential and effectiveness."[63] Similarly, Angelo State University in Texas noted, "The mission of the Faculty Learning Commons (FLC) is to support and develop faculty members in their role as teachers."[64] Developing faculty as scholars, encouraging holistic career development, and fostering professional well-being are components of many centers' aims as well.

A final instructor-related outcome, but in only 2% of all missions, is *engagement*. Just as centers aspire to promote student involvement, "engaged faculty" is a desired outcome. For example, at the University of

Berea College's (KY) **Center for Teaching and Learning** Director Leslie Ortquist-Ahrens describes one CTL goal as being "in that liminal space between faculty and administration, the 'betwixt and between.' I want to be responsive to both and I'm interested in change at the grassroots level that is responsive to declared needs, but also to institutional needs and strategy. I'm interested in having those two things talk to each other."

Southern Maine, one of the Center for Collaboration and Development's key goals was to "Create an Engaged Teaching Community," while the Faculty Development Program at the Medical College of Wisconsin described its mission as "to design and implement innovative programs which foster engagement and job satisfaction among faculty."[65]

The continued focus on professional learning by CTLs is wise because faculty who perceive that they develop teaching-related knowledge or skills also report a more positive sense of colleagueship, satisfaction, career agency, productivity, and intent to stay at the institution.[66] Additionally, from the perspective of organizational change, which happens on multiple levels, it is important to maintain a connection to both faculty development and organizational development.[67]

Change and Innovation

In her study of CTL missions about 15 years prior, Schroeder found that nearly a quarter (22%) of statements described an aim to promote change or innovation. This emphasis appears to intensify in 2020, with over a third (37%) of centers advancing the aim of change or innovation. CTLs at doctoral and larger institutions express change/innovation goals slightly more frequently, but there were no other statistically significant differences by CTL age, time of coding, nor MSI or women's college status.[68]

Change and innovation are related concepts;[69] but interestingly, prior survey data suggest that CTL directors think about them orthogonally. In 2016, while a robust proportion (29%) of CTL staff wanted their centers "to act as a change agent within the institution," a much smaller percentage (12%) hoped "to position the institution at the forefront of educational innovation."[70]

This may be because "innovation" is often coded to mean "technology" or "digital learning." Certainly, that idea was represented in CTL statements, such as the Center for Excellence in Teaching and Learning at the University of the Virgin Islands, which aspires to "enhance the learning experience and environment with innovative technologies."[71] However, there is no statistically significant difference in the presence of the change/innovation theme when comparing CTLs that have digital staff and those without (see appendix 1 for definition of "digital staff").

Instead, we largely observe innovation represented in broader strokes, signaling commitment to transformation or institutional change even if the center embeds technology. A key example is the Center for Excellence in Learning and Teaching at King's College in Pennsylvania, which had no instructional technology staff at the time I visited the center website, but the center still hoped to serve "as a catalyst to stimulate innovations in teaching and learning."[72] In contrast, the University of Iowa's Office of Teaching, Learning and Technology, which had a strong digital focus, aspired to "challenge the institution, the faculty, and ourselves by supporting change agents and transformational ideas."[73] Other examples include the Center for Teaching and Learning (now the Peter J. Golden Teaching and Learning Center) at Sandhills Community College in North Carolina, which values "change that is based on research and evaluation"[74] as well as the University of San Diego's Center for Educational Excellence, which seeks to be "an institutional change agent supporting the transformation of the university into an inclusive community of learners."[75] These statements seem to blur the idea of change and innovation more than previous surveys would indicate.

Kim and Maloney described the rise of innovation-focused units, noting, "While maintaining the traditional CTL portfolio of responsibilities around faculty and graduate student development, course redesign, and a community of practice for campus educators, CTLs have also taken new roles as change agents for learning innovation."[76] This approach also appears to be reflected in CTL aims, whether digitally focused or not.

Culture

Organizational culture is generally defined as collective meaning-making, such as "shared understandings"[77] or "shared assumptions."[78] Therefore, a center's aim to impact organizational culture reflects its most collective aspirations.

Surveys of educational developers consistently indicate that a top goal is to create a culture of teaching (72% in 2006 and 75% in 2016).[79] In contrast, previous studies of center missions suggested that aspirations to impact an institution's culture were relatively low (12%).[80]

Here, it does appear that missions are catching up to individual aspirations with over one in five (22%) statements of purpose referencing cultural, climate, or environmental impacts. While certainly related to other themes, such as innovation (e.g., "to create a culture of educational innovation" at Washtenaw Community College's Teaching and Learning Center in Michigan)[81] or learning (e.g., to "foster an institutional culture where learning is our central focus" at Middlesex County College's Center for the Enrichment of Learning and Teaching in New Jersey)[82], the breadth and collaborative character of this theme is distinct. There are no statistically significant differences in prevalence of this theme by institutional type, time of coding, CTL age, institutional size, nor MSI or women's college status.

Scholarly and Creative Work

Educational development is often associated with teaching and learning, but the original faculty development tactic is thought to be the research sabbatical, which was first offered in 1810 at Harvard University.[83] Similarly, the first CTL in the United States, the Center for Research on Learning and Teaching at the University of Michigan–Ann Arbor, originated in 1962 because a faculty committee recommended that the university establish a center to research effective instruction.[84]

Therefore, in light of this history of the field, it should not be surprising that a substantial proportion (20%) of centers include research development in their aims, that is, fostering scholarly and creative work on their campuses. Medical/health-focused contexts express this aim most frequently, which is consistent with their focus on faculty/instructor outcomes.[85] However, master's institutions also described this goal at a high rate, perhaps to support instructors in contexts where research aspirations have risen while teaching expectations also remain high.[86] There are no other statistically significant differences in prevalence of this theme by institutional size, time of coding, CTL age, nor MSI or women's college status.

This finding suggests a possible hourglass effect observed in centers that had their roots in research, then contracted this aim in the last century as they moved to focus on teaching and learning, and now appear to be expanding their work in this area. This trend is explained further in chapter 4.

Diversity, Equity, and Inclusion

Another emergent theme, seen in about one in five (19%) of all CTLs' aims, are goals to support ideals of diversity, equity, justice, inclusion, and/or culturally responsive teaching (here referred to in shorthand as "DEI"). The purpose statements of CTLs at larger institutions have a higher prevalence of this theme,[87] which may be because larger institutions tend to have higher student body diversity.[88] Interestingly, centers in existence for 30 or more years tend to express DEI-related aims at the highest rate (40%), which may signal a developmental trajectory of a center's work, as well as the political challenges of this change goal for a less-established CTL.[89] However, while more established CTLs are most likely to express this goal, it is also the case that the newest centers, those with zero to nine years' experience, are second most likely (34%), which may be an early predictor of its rise. There are no other statistically significant differences in prevalence of this theme by institutional type, control, time of coding, nor MSI or women's college status.

Because ideals of diversity, equity, justice, inclusion, and culturally responsive teaching suggest distinct outcomes and change strategies, it is important to disaggregate these ideas. McNair, Bensimon, and

Malcolm-Piquex, writing for the American Association of Colleges and Universities, distinguished these approaches:

> Diversity is an understanding of how individual and group differences contribute to the diverse thoughts, knowledge, and experiences that are the foundation of a high-quality liberal education. Inclusion is an active, intentional, and ongoing engagement with diversity across the curriculum, and our communities to increase awareness, content knowledge, cognitive sophistication, and empathetic understanding of the complex ways individuals interact within systems and institutions. Equity prioritizes the creation of opportunities for minoritized students to have equal outcomes and participation in educational programs that can close the achievement gaps in student success and completion.[90]

Using these definitions, ideas of *diversity and inclusion* are named most frequently (17% of statements). For example, Virginia's College of William and Mary Studio for Teaching and Learning Innovation hopes "to sustain an inclusive and vibrant learning community for faculty, students, and staff across the university,"[91] and multiple centers aimed to create "learning environments in which diverse students and instructors can excel" (Center for Research on Learning and Teaching, University of Michigan; Office of Teaching and Learning Excellence, Montana State University–Northern; and Teaching and Learning Center, Kansas State University). Ideas of *universal design and accessibility* are also identified. For example, the Center for the Advancement of Faculty Excellence at California State Polytechnic University, Pomona, when referencing their value of universal design for learning, indicated that they "strive to incorporate legal accessibility solutions throughout a project."[92]

Outcomes pertaining to *equity or justice* are infrequently referenced across CTLs, making up 5% of all purpose statements. CTLs take an equity lens by "championing social justice through engaged and experiential learning" (De La Salle Institute for Advanced Teaching and Learning, La Salle University, Pennsylvania),[93] supporting "social justice through critical, inclusive, and embodied practices" (Center for Teaching and Learning, Pratt Institute, New York),[94] or championing "transformative practices through educational risk-taking for an equi-

The **Faculty Center for Teaching and Learning** (FCTL) at the Community College of Philadelphia, Pennsylvania, was formed in the early 1980s and recently completed its 2020–25 strategic plan. However, in recent discussions, Stephanie Scordia (currently Title III Professional Learning Coordinator), noted that those involved with the center realized "that commitment to equitable teaching and inclusive teaching really needs to be front and center in our mission and in our work." Girija Nagaswami, currently FCTL Facilitator, added, "There are departments right now actively engaged in equity-centered initiatives and as FCTL, we felt we have to complement what they're doing and offer professional growth, so the faculty can take advantage."

table and just world" (University of Washington Bothell, Teaching and Learning Center).[95]

In many cases, however, centers drew on both the inclusion and equity paradigms to describe their aspirations. To illustrate, the California State University, Long Beach's Faculty Center describes a vision for "promoting and embracing equitable and inclusive practices,"[96] and the School of Medicine Faculty Development unit at the University of California, Riverside seeks to "foster a culture that promotes excellence in teaching, advances inclusion, equality, and equity."[97]

It is important to note that my coding took place over the course of 2020 amid a year of COVID-19 and national calls for racial equity. There is not a statistically significant difference in time of coding for prevalence of this aim in missions, as one might expect. However, I anticipate that DEI aims will—and should—take more prominence in the years to follow and hope future researchers will examine this trend.

Support of Institutional Mission, Strategic Plan, or Goals

Interestingly, in surveys of CTL staff, support of institutional aims does not appear to be a high priority. In a 2016 study, only 15% noted that a top goal was "to respond to critical needs as defined by the institution," and 12% reported that a priority was "to help the institution respond to accreditation, quality enhancement plans." These low proportions are striking in comparison to Schroeder's analysis of organizational missions in which the top articulated purpose (28% of statements) was one that supported a broad, institution-wide aim, such as support of a college or university mission.[98]

My 2020 analysis of missions, visions, and goals is in closer alignment with educational developers' views. Interestingly, if comparing the two analyses, support of institutional mission, strategic plan, or goals is one of the few aims that declined in frequency over the decade, from 28% to 18% across CTLs (table 1.2).

This is not to say that such a theme was nonexistent. Examples can be seen with University of Cincinnati's (OH) Center for the Enhancement of Teaching and Learning by "advancing university initiatives in student learning,"[99] as well as Valparaiso University's (IN) Institute for Teaching and Learning, which indicated that one of its key goals was to "play a key role in university strategic planning with respect to academic initiatives."[100] These two examples clearly signal a center's intent to play a role in supporting key institutional aims.

However, there is a qualitative sense of challenge in some of the statements that espoused institutional aims. In some cases, while expressing support for an institutional mission, a center's purpose seemed to exist in dynamic tension with the institution, suggesting more of a change or advocacy role. An example of how a center can espouse an activist role while also being responsive to a university's mission can be seen in the purpose statement for the Institute for Learning and Teaching Excellence at Indiana University Southeast, which seeks to "place student learning, intellectual persistence, and attainment at the center of the university's mission by advocating for enhanced student learning."[101] Additionally, DEI change aims were sometimes positioned alongside institutional mission-focused ones. To illustrate, the Center for Teaching and Learning at American River College in California "supports professional development that helps the college fulfill its mission, values, and commitment to social justice and equity and to achieve its strategic goals."[102] As Land argued, even institutionally focused orientations can be located on a continuum from "domesticating" (e.g., support of institutional accreditation) to "liberating."[103]

Teaching Effectiveness and Excellence

The most popular name for centers for teaching and learning is, predictably, *Center for Teaching and Learning*, with 195 examples. (Named centers are also included in this count.) Common variants include Teaching and Learning Center (58), Center for Teaching (16), Center for Learning and Teaching (7), and Learning and Teaching Center (4). Based on individual word counts, *Excellence* is also prominent as the fourth-most frequently occurring word (295 mentions, tied with *Faculty* and after *Center*, *Teaching*, and *Learning*) (figure 1.1).

Therefore, what is unexpected is that the goal of promoting teaching excellence or effectiveness did not arise more frequently. In fact, it is one of the lesser-named goals with slightly under a fifth (18%) of centers espousing this aim. It may be that in a field where there are many ways to teach well, there is an uneasiness to connote standard-setting through terms such as "academic quality" and "teaching effectiveness." For example, among all of the missions and goals in this dataset, there are over 200 counts of *teaching excellence* or *enhance teaching* and only two of *teaching quality*.

Still, examples are replete, such as the one from this Illinois institution: "The Teaching & Learning Center (TLC) promotes teaching excellence at John A. Logan College."[104] Not surprisingly, in light of its nomenclature, the Center for Teaching Excellence at Anna Maria College in Massachusetts named this aim in its mission: "to recognize, develop, implement, and evaluate innovative and effective teaching and learning strategies that foster student engagement."[105] Likewise, a similarly named Texas center at Lee College (now the Empirical Educator Center) viewed its mission as "to inspire and enable faculty to enhance teaching effectiveness."[106] There are no statistically significant differences in prevalence of this theme by institutional type, time of coding, CTL age, instructional FTE, nor MSI or women's college status.

Community Building

Ranking relatively low in Schroeder's study, "community building and collegiality" was an expressed aim in slightly over 1 in 10 (13%)

missions.[107] In 2020, this goal is also one of low priority, and the proportion of missions with community building aims decreased slightly (11%). Although still at a relatively low rate, CTLs at master's institutions expressed this goal most frequently.[108] There are no statistically significant differences in prevalence of this theme by size (instructional FTE), time of coding, CTL age, nor MSI or women's college status.

Among CTLs promoting this aim, ideas of developing a collaborative culture arose frequently. For example, the American Public University System's Center for Teaching and Learning in West Virginia notes that its vision is to build "communities of lifelong learners and practice in selected disciplines."[109] Another illustration is the Center for Teaching and Learning at Miami University Middletown, which offered, "The role of the CTL is to foster a sense of collaboration among all campus educators—full- and part-time faculty, staff, and administrators—and all students as a means of fulfilling that mission."[110] Others noted how a community-building goal can be an important intermediary step to achieve other goals. To illustrate, SUNY Cortland's Faculty Development Committee aimed to build "among its faculty a sense of community, where communication about professional activities is easy and open, so that individuals can explore with others new ways of being more effective teachers and scholars."[111]

It is surprising that community-building goals did not occur with more frequency in light of the importance of collegiality for faculty satisfaction and productivity[112] as well as CTLs' own articulation of having a "hub" role on their campuses (chapters 2 and 3). However, as we will see in the next chapter, it may instead be that educational developers at those institutions viewed collaboration and community building as a change strategy rather than as a goal *per se*.

Conclusion

In the preceding sections, I compare several sources of data about CTL constituencies and aims:

- A 2006 analysis of 100 center mission statements
- Surveys of educational developers that were published in 2006 and 2016
- My own 2020 analysis of 1,209 CTL names as well as 1,105 statements of purpose (missions, goals, visions, and values)

The first section documents a small increase in the mean number of named constituencies, from an average of 1.18 in mission statements collected in 2006 to 1.50 audiences among purpose statements analyzed in 2020. We see continuing emphases on work with faculty, staff, and administrators as well as an expansion into aims of serving student learners, academic units, and external communities.

Along with this broadening of constituency base, this chapter documents a change in CTL aims. Schroeder's hypothesis that the greater breadth of constituencies in mission statements signals a changing mission of centers seems to be coming to fruition. In 2020, the majority of centers include student learning as an aim (with medical/health-related centers as a key exception), marking one of the most significant increases over the decade. The rise of student learning aims, alongside the maintenance of faculty professional learning goals, is consistent with key understandings of the field of educational development. Despite a diversity of career paths and practices in CTLs, all educational development aims to support learning, whether of students, faculty, or staff.[113]

In 2020, the vast majority (94%) of CTLs listed at least one of the key aims shown in tables 1.2 and 1.3; three-quarters (75%) listed more than one. There is also some indication that the number of CTL aims has also increased in recent years.[114] We also gain some sense of the expansiveness of center goals through CTL names like those of Roger Williams University's Center for Scholarship, Assessment, Learning, Teaching and Technology (now Center for Teaching, Learning and Scholarship) in Rhode Island, as well as center missions like the Center for Teaching and Learning Excellence and Faculty Success at Virginia Commonwealth University, which supports "faculty success with a well-rounded 360-degree view of all things faculty must do to thrive throughout their careers . . . [including] supporting faculty in teaching, scholarship,

TABLE 1.3. Most frequent CTL aims, by Carnegie type, 2020 (in percentages)

Aim	All (N = 1105)	Doctoral (n = 324)	Master's (n = 290)	Associate's (n = 206)	Baccalaureate (n = 167)	Medical/ health (n = 90)	Other special focus (n = 27)
Student learning	65	71	72	62	64	39	52
Faculty learning	50	49	54	42	50	69	26
Change or innovation	37	43	35	39	37	23	26
Culture, climate, and environment	22	22	27	21	17	17	22
Scholarly and creative work	20	19	29	8	19	31	7
Diversity, equity, and inclusion	19	24	19	16	15	18	15
Support of institutional mission, strategic plan, or goals	18	20	19	20	14	17	4
Teaching effectiveness and excellence	18	21	16	18	16	9	22
Community building	11	10	17	7	11	6	0

NOTES: Statements of purpose could include more than one aim. Percentages are presented for unique Carnegie type. (See appendix 1 for methodology.) One institution is missing Carnegie classification information.

writing, performance and creative arts, career goal planning, leadership development, mentoring, balance and well-being, and so much more."[115]

While we see Schroeder's prediction coming true—that the stated aims of CTLs have changed and even expanded over time—the forecast has not exactly followed anticipated trends. CTL goals that support institutional missions have decreased in frequency. In contrast, we see a rising emphasis on compelling home institutions to change, and ideas about supporting student success and changing culture have certainly increased. Although not previously measured, other change emphases included promoting diversity, equity, and inclusion. Finally, despite the field's turn to organizational development, individually focused outcomes continued to be strong, including instructional development, scholarly support, and holistic development.

On the one hand, the decline of institutional alignment may be problematic for CTLs. In Schroeder's analysis, she argued that this primary theme signaled an increasing organizational development role for centers, or a "coming in from the margins."[116] Alongside others, I have also argued that responsiveness to institutional priorities is one key factor in CTL effectiveness.[117] This may lead us to believe that centers are returning to the periphery and rejecting organizational development.

Another interpretation, however, is that CTLs are instead declaring their own path, defining a distinctive approach to change leadership in a postsecondary context. Indeed, almost 30 years ago, William Bergquist described the tensions between the academy's developmental culture, in which CTLs traditionally have situated themselves, and the managerial culture with links to academic administration and power.[118] Others have written about the challenges of aligning with administrative aims, reinforcing that "academic developers are power-holders linked to expertise, institutional management, and policies."[119] An additional challenge is the increasing frequency of administrative leadership changes and visions in higher education today,[120] and therefore, a close alignment with institutional priorities may actually make one more vulnerable to transition when new priorities are established.

The University of Denver's **Office of Teaching and Learning** (OTL) was founded in 1999. Interestingly, the OTL's stated mission code in 2020 was relatively brief ("to foster innovation and strengthen practices in teaching, course design and curriculum development to improve learning across the university"). However, in 2018, the OTL used the HITS framework (see next chapter) to identify its theories of change on micro, meso, and macro levels, and it later developed an expanded statement of purpose. Kate Willink, Vice Provost of Faculty Affairs, noted that this process was a way to think about how "even individual transformative learning can be amplified through networks and how different levels of change might engage different modes."

I argue that what we are seeing is a conversation among educational developers about ways to be situated, but also pushing for change, within their academic institutions. For example, faculty-focused outcomes continue to be strong because trust and relationships with individual instructors are critical for a CTL to move forward large change strategies.[121] Connecting professional learning with institutional priorities and goals is considered by some to be a core principle supporting learner-centered change.[122] In other words, instead of seeing the field as maturing from instructional to organizational development,[123] it appears that both of these approaches are necessary for the change aspirations of CTLs. From a change strategy approach, there are multiple scales of engagement, from the individual to the ecosystem.[124] With any of these orientations, however, CTLs are increasingly positioning themselves as organizational change agents.[125]

I am grateful for the foundational work of Connie Schroeder's *Coming in from the Margins*, on which much of this chapter is based. Schroeder astutely predicted a broadening of constituencies and a change in missions. While the latter finding appears to be becoming more complicated over time, my 2020 analysis suggests that centers continue to pursue change-related aims. However, they are defining them in ways that align with the values of the profession, such as student learning,

---

The **Professor Magda Vasillov Center for Teaching and Learning** (CTL) at CUNY Hostos Community College (NY) was founded in 2003. Carlos Guevara, Co-Director of the CTL, noted, "I like to use systems thinking and organizational change theories. We look at change and we look at resistance and how those two forces are competing. We have to be focusing on the innovators and how we recognize them and how we make sure that they are empowered and motivated. Then, they become your best allies and messengers to faculty, resonating with other faculty. If I bring the message, as the co-director of the Center, it is not going to resonate as much if you have another colleague and other faculty. I call it the 'Innovations Web.'"*

* See also Carlos Guevara, "Leading above the Fray: Turning Challenges into Opportunities," in *Developing Educational Technology at an Urban Community College*, edited by Kate S. Wolfe, Kate Lyons, and Carlos Guevara (Cham, Switzerland: Palgrave Macmillan, 2019), 11–19.

inclusion, and equity. At the center of CTL work is change, inherent even in the name of the field (e.g., faculty development or educational development).[126]

Elsewhere in her book, Schroeder noted that center missions help facilitate their "place at the table." However, she does not examine in detail *why* an articulated sense of purpose helps CTLs navigate change. In the next chapter, I examine a possible rationale for this link, arguing that they serve as theories of change.

CHAPTER 2

How Do We Get There?

CTL Theories of Change

UNDERSTANDING IN ORDER to facilitate change, then, is an absolute priority."[1] Here, Peter Ashworth, the director of a UK learning and teaching institute, notes the importance of having educational developers identify the object and process of their change efforts. One way that educational developers can make intentional their change efforts is through a theory of change. While the previous chapter identified the aspirations, or end goals, identified in CTL purpose statements, this chapter focuses on how CTLs determine they will achieve those aims through the lens of theories of change. It is necessary to understand these theories because centers are a key site for affecting individual and organizational transformation in higher education, particularly around teaching and learning.[2]

One definition of *theory of change* is that it is "a series of hypotheses about how change will occur," explaining a driving mechanism that goes beyond a single initiative.[3] Others helpfully elaborate, "*A theory of change is a predictive assumption about the desired changes and the actions that may produce those changes. Putting it another way, 'If I do x, then I expect y to occur, and for these reasons*'" (italics in original).[4]

Many educational grants require statements of theories of change, and for good reason. The presence of explicit theories of change is critical for enabling the process of organizational transformation.[5] By articulating the end goals (e.g., student success) and the key vehicles hypothesized to best get to that aim (e.g., a course design institute), CTLs are more likely to affect change. While many in higher education are familiar with CTL programs and services, such as workshops or learning communities, few may be conversant with their change strategies. What are key strategies used by centers to affect change?

The previous chapter examined nine key CTL aims and argued that these suggest a distinctive change vision that balances individual and organizational change aspirations. This chapter focuses on strategy, or how centers theorize—also through statements of purpose—that they can reach their stated aims. Further, it analyzes why an articulated sense of purpose can facilitate organizational change efforts and examines CTL theories of change, which I also term "strategies" because they offer an intended plan for achieving any given aim.

This chapter adopts a sociological lens to group these strategies. In 2008, sociologists Mitchell Stevens, Elizabeth Armstrong, and Richard Arum authored a literature review that served as a "critical integration" on the scholarship around the sociology of higher education, clustering understandings of higher education into four metaphorical categories: Hub, Incubator, Temple, Sieve.[6] In 2017, I gave a presidential address at the annual POD Network Conference, which adapted this metaphorical framework to the work of CTLs.

A year later, I had the privilege of collaborating with 15 other educational developers across multiple countries and US institutional types to develop these ideas further through a guide entitled *Defining What Matters*, which was eventually distributed by the POD Network.[7] Although we originally conceptualized *Defining What Matters* as a tool for centers to evaluate their work (and it is applied in this way in Chapter 5), I have heard anecdotally that it has been most widely used for strategic planning purposes. I believe the guide is useful for strategic planning because it articulates four theories of change, or strategic ways that centers can align programs through a contextually situated belief about how change happens on their campuses.

The guide and this chapter define four key typical CTL strategies, or the HITS framework.

1. Hub. In a Hub role, centers promote connection, sponsor collaborative initiatives, and bring people together in learning communities. Additional Hub functions include coordination and consolidation of resources—in other words, the "centering" function of Centers for Teaching and Learning. At the time of my 2017 POD address, I invited participants to submit written responses to the prompt, "What are you most proud of [in your center's work]?" Hub-related responses were most prevalent. Similarly, when a 2016 survey of educational developers asked about the top approaches used to provide services, those that bring people together and centralize resources were named most frequently.[8]

2. Incubator. In universities, the idea of a "tech incubator" is commonly expressed, but CTLs also play these roles for both people and ideas. Commonly, an Incubator approach might take the shape of programs that support individual growth and development, such as new faculty orientation or a mentoring program for chairs. A center can also seed and incubate initiatives, digital innovations, or teaching approaches. Historically, an Incubator role has been a key priority of CTLs in terms of services provided. For example, new faculty development was identified as the top signature service in two North American surveys (2006 and 2016) of educational developers, suggesting that "centers remain attuned and responsive to the need to create a welcoming environment for a new, more diverse generation of faculty."[9] Other Incubator approaches (e.g., grants) seed ideas or focus on student support. Although these may seem like strange bedfellows, by looking at the approaches as an Incubator strategy, how might we better understand their common role in CTL portfolios?

3. Temple. As defined by educational developers, CTLs play secular Temple roles by offering sanctuary and sites for legitimation. As noted in *Defining What Matters*, "The Temple function of CTLs establishes teaching as an ongoing scholarly endeavor, worthy of professional development. Second, the Temple is a sanctuary, a space where campus teaching and learning communities can find hope and inspiration, as well as an institutionally-sanctioned space for exploring pedagogy."[10] The key aim for a Temple strategy is to elevate the value of teaching, learning, and educational development by providing spaces and opportunities for recognition and reward of these endeavors. Other studies have shown contradictory findings regarding use of Temple-associated approaches by CTLs. For example, in both 2006 and 2016, the top goal for educational developers in North America was "to create or sustain a culture of teaching excellence," while the least popular goal was "to provide recognition and reward for excellence in teaching."[11]

4. Sieve. This role of CTL work is rooted in the value of evidence-based practice and therefore often reflects vetting, curational, or research-related endeavors.[12] While an Incubator strategy might seek to expand and grow an idea, a Sieve strategy takes the opposite approach: to ensure that actions are carefully aligned with "best practices" or research. Initiatives like assessment, evaluation, quality standards, disciplinary-based education research (DBER), and the scholarship of teaching and learning (SoTL) reflect Sieve-like strategies for a CTL. At the time of my 2017 address, Sieve-related responses were named least frequently by the POD Network members in the audience. In *Defining What Matters*, we speculated that this role was selected less often "perhaps because of the hesitancy many CTLs have in taking on an evaluative role, or difficulty saying 'no.'"[13] However, in other venues, we get a different perspective on Sieve strategies among CTLs. For example, Beach, Sorcinelli, Austin, and Rivard found that directors predict an increase in prioritization of services to promote SoTL and course/curricular evaluation compared to a decade earlier. Similarly, across institutional types, assessment of student learning was named by CTL directors as the top issue faculty development should address in the next five years.[14]

The Hub-Incubator-Temple-Sieve (HITS) framework represents four general strategies or theories of change. In this way, the strategies mirror Land's twelve orientations to educational development practice (e.g., managerial, reflective practitioner, or entrepreneurial), but they take an organizational, or center-wide, perspective rather than an individual one.[15] Another difference from Land's model of academic developer orientations is that HITS categories are not mutually exclusive. To illustrate, this is evident in goals set at St. Edward's University, Texas (HITS orientations added):

> The Center for Teaching Excellence focuses on a variety of activities designed to support our mission, which include: [. . .]
> - Facilitating a culture of continuous teaching improvement [Sieve]
> - Building communities of teaching and learning across campus [Hub]
> - Providing support for faculty at all stages of their St. Edward's teaching career [Incubator]
> - Recognizing excellence in teaching [Temple][16]

In this case, all four HITS strategies are named.

Although the HITS framework has been recommended elsewhere for CTL strategic planning,[17] to my knowledge, no one has conducted an empirical analysis. Similar to the last chapter, this section examines 1,105 purpose statements, combining missions, visions, goals, and values/guidelines. Just as in the last chapter, while most of the center names and statements have stayed the same (from 2020 to 2022), there have been some changes, which are noted in the text or notes.

Four key questions about these strategies are examined. First, I document the extent to which these strategies are reflected in CTLs, in aggregate and by institutional characteristics, such as Carnegie classification, control, CTL age, institution size by instructional FTE, minority-serving institution (MSI) status, time of coding, and women's college status. (See appendix 1 for definitions of these variables and the statistical methodology.)

Second, the chapter associates the HITS strategies with key CTL aims identified in the previous chapter. A third dimension involves language associated with each strategy. How might the language we use to describe these strategies to stakeholders vary, such as the verbs employed? In answering this last question, I compare an analysis of key action verbs that were most frequently used in a sample of 100 CTL mission statements a decade earlier.[18] Finally, I examine strengths and cautions for use of each strategy as derived from the literature on change in higher education.

Hub: Organizational Connector

The Hub function of CTL work focuses on developing inclusive communities, connecting constituencies across campus, and building collaborations toward a common aim. Some describe this as a CTL orientation toward collegiality and structured relationship building.[19] Because collaboration and inclusion are expressed values in educational development,[20] in the previous chapter, it was surprising to see goals such as community building and DEI occurring relatively infrequently. However, as a change strategy to achieve aims, a Hub approach is one of the most frequently documented. Four centers even named their organizational unit as a "Hub," such as the University of Portland's Teaching and Learning Hub.

As operationalized here, there are four key ways that centers express a Hub-related approach: (1) promoting dialogue and collaboration, (2) playing a coordinating role, and offering centralized (3) programs or (4) campus resources. Over two-thirds of CTLs (70%) described at least one Hub-related strategy, and over one-third (35%) described more than one.

The Teaching and Learning Center at Camden County College in New Jersey is an example of a center that employs all four Hub strategies in its purpose statement. With Hub elements emphasized in bold, its statement in full follows.

> The Teaching and Learning Center (TLC) at Camden County College inspires and enables faculty to enhance teaching potential and effectiveness so that students are more likely to achieve their desired learning outcomes. The Teaching and Learning Center **serves as a focal point for college-wide efforts to support the improvement of teaching and learning**.
>
> The Teaching and Learning Center:
>
> (1) Supports the continuing improvement of instruction by **offering programs and resources** related to the individual professional development needs of faculty.
> (2) Encourages teaching innovations.

(3) Enhances faculty dialogue and promotes cooperation and information sharing across the disciplines.

(4) Supports the integration of technology as a tool for improving teaching and learning.

(5) Collaborates with other institutions, organizations, and individuals to exchange information and share resources.[21]

By serving as a "focal point," encouraging both faculty dialogue and organizational collaboration, and offering programs and resources, this CTL very much demonstrates a Hub theory of change.

The most frequently identified CTL Hub approach is bringing together members of the teaching and learning community for dialogue and collaboration. This strategy was articulated in over a third (36%) of all CTL purpose statements. Examples include the following:

A campus locus for conversations about learning and teaching in the liberal arts.
—Center for Innovation in the Liberal Arts, St. Olaf College (MN)[22]

Connectiveness: We are part of an interconnected, interdependent whole: we build relationships, and connect, bridge, and support communities of practice to invigorate teaching and learning at Cornell.
—Center for Teaching Innovation, Cornell University (NY)[23]

Connecting people and units across the campus in an effort to elevate our work and ensure institutional success (*Kauhale*).
—Office of Professional Development and Academic Support, University of Hawai'i–West O'ahu[24]

All of our programs connect faculty to each other so innovations and passion for teaching can spread throughout ACC.
—Faculty Center for Teaching and Learning (now Teaching and Learning Excellence Division), Austin Community College (TX)[25]

A second frequently noted strategy involves offering centralized programs and services for the campus (42%) or resources and information (26%). A related approach is centralization or coordination of initiatives, appearing in slightly more than 1 in 10 statements (14%). These three approaches are embodied in the very idea of a "center"—to help instructors and students connect "distributed resources as campuses navigate a de-centered educational landscape."[26]

Hub statements in this vein often included specific direct reference to the metaphor:

> The Center is an information and support "hub" for all faculty development needs and interests all in one central location.
> —Center for Teaching and Learning Excellence, Medgar Evers College (NY)[27]

> The Center for Teaching and Learning is a professional development resource hub that promotes learning-centeredness and leverages technical and experiential expertise to further the College's mission.
> —Center for Teaching and Learning, Cincinnati State Technical and Community College (OH)[28]

> . . . a hub for promoting teaching excellence and innovation. Housing the staff from Digital Learning and Teaching Excellence, the Center is a one-stop destination for all George Mason faculty and graduate students seeking to explore and test new ideas for teaching methods and techniques including online course delivery and integrated instructional design.
> —Stearns Center for Teaching and Learning at George Mason University (VA)[29]

Hub is the most frequently named change strategy across CTL and institutional types (table 2.1). There are no statistically significant differences by Carnegie classification, control, CTL age, institution size, time of coding, nor MSI or women's college status.

Articulating a Hub Approach

Now, I turn to how CTLs express a Hub strategy. This understanding can aid others who might wish to refine their own purpose statement and aids in the ongoing comparison with Schroeder's prior study. Because a Hub strategy often includes centralized provision of programs, services, and resources, the verb *provide* is prevalent. Although *provide* is frequently used in many statements (48% of all), it is mentioned in over half (58%) of all Hub-related purpose statements, and it is most highly correlated with a Hub strategy ($r = .30$, $p < .001$) as compared to Incubator, Temple, or Sieve. Actions like *connect* or *bring together* are noted in 4% of all Hub statements (3% of all statements), and these terms are most strongly associated with Hub ($r = .10$, $p < .01$), as are *coordinate* or *oversees* (5% of all Hub statements, 3% of all, $r = .11$, $p < .001$).

Unexpected actions related to a Hub strategy are *explore*, *examine*, or *investigate* (4% of Hub, 3% of all). While I anticipated that these would be related to a Sieve strategy due to its focus on quality improvement and research, these verbs were most strongly associated with a Hub approach ($r = .08$, $p < .01$). Although these relationships are not strong, they do signal the interplay between the four HITS change strategies. Examples of this interrelationship include the goals from University of South Florida's (Saint Petersburg Campus) Center for Innovative Teaching and Learning, which "provides resources and an environment to explore new and innovative ways to engage in learning and scholarship through open dialogue, research, feedback and reflection."[30]

Schroeder's analysis of 100 mission statements found use of *provide* but much less frequently (26%). Schroeder noted few mentions of *coordinate* (3%), but other action concepts linked to integration and connection roles were not documented at that time. By this metric, a Hub approach appears to have grown sharply over the past decade.

Strengths and Cautions of Hub Change Strategies

It is not surprising that most CTLs articulate a Hub change strategy to serve as an organizational connector for people and resources. As a vehicle to achieve key CTL aims, Hub strategies are well documented in the research for their effectiveness through group-based models such as faculty learning communities and communities of practice.[31] These change approaches align with research about the need to provide a forum for deliberation to help people understand the need for change.

Social networks or learning communities can connect people with similar ideas and create moral support to sustain momentum over time, and a Hub orientation is closely aligned with diffusion of innovation models and ideas of peer influence.[32] For example, pre-tenure faculty's expectations for success in the classroom are related to their sense of supportive relationships among colleagues.[33] Additionally, teaching networks play an important role in creating a culture of teaching and are associated with positive student feedback.[34]

Models of coordination and collaboration are also good for centers. Sociologist Ron Burt theorized on the idea of "structural holes," or places where social networks are not connected to each other. Burt's research found that people who can serve as connectors to bridge these holes have, as a result, access to more diverse information, which gives them a competitive advantage for understanding an organization. Information is a powerful resource for CTLs, and having it offers structural leverage and fosters creative thinking.[35] Burt noted, "The creative spark on which serendipity depends, in short, is to see bridges where others see holes."[36] With a Hub approach, CTLs bring people together and move forward initiatives across disciplinary silos, allowing them to serve as brokers between a campus's structural holes.

However, there are also associated cautions for a Hub approach. As defined here, a Hub approach includes "Programs and Services" and "Resources and Information," but these are capacious categories. Some formats of these services are more likely to promote change than others. For example, extended programs with opportunities for ongoing interaction, like faculty learning communities and change teams, are found to be more impactful compared to short-term programs, especially for more complex goals like culture change.[37] In contrast, while short-term workshops or dissemination of websites that highlight new teaching ideas may achieve certain objectives (e.g., teaching a discrete skill, first exposure in a curriculum of interaction for instructors), they are less effective for promoting widespread adoption of new approaches.[38]

In general, Hub approaches are effective for prompting individual change. However, unless deliberately structured with larger aims, reflective communities may not effectively address larger-scale curricular or organizational challenges.[39] Because of their focus on community building, this strategy may not be as aligned with organizational change ambitions.[40] For example, one study of faculty reflective approaches suggested that a focus on challenges with curriculum and instruction (a common emphasis of CTL learning communities) most frequently results in "instrumental reflection" or having faculty make small-scale changes to teaching.[41] According to these education researchers, to have impact on organizational change or DEI-related aims, groups would need to intentionally engage in a more critical process of reflection on social structure. Support of department change teams or action teams, as described in chapter 3, may be additional models to further organizational impact.[42] Others have also described intentional approaches to forefront change through communities of transformation, or "communities that create and foster innovative spaces that envision and embody a new paradigm of practice."[43]

Incubator: Growth of Individuals and Ideas

An Incubator function focuses on growth and encouragement. The popularity of this strategy can be seen in the common names for the field itself, such as educational development, academic development, and faculty development. Although there is debate about which initial descriptor is best, what joins them all is an incubation perspective in the word *development*. As defined here, Incubator also highlights an orientation toward reflective practice as lever for individual change.[44]

In all, over one-third (37%) of all CTLs noted at least one Incubator change strategy, and 10% listed multiple strategies. Approaches that were also coded as associated with an Incubator change strategy included:

- Consultations with individuals, often faculty (13% of centers).
- Explicit use of the word *Incubator* or description of mechanisms with an orientation to promoting growth and development. (Examples of this are St. Petersburg College's Center for Excellence for Teaching and Learning [FL] goal statement, "to serve as an incubator for innovative teaching and learning strategies,"[45] and Cornerstone University's Center for Excellence in Learning and Teaching [MI], which hoped to "develop our

faculty into better disciples of their life and work, as well as the cultivation of their students."[46]) This was seen in 10% of statements.

- Programs that were explicitly articulated as having a mentoring or orienting goal, such as New Faculty Orientation (10%).
- Initiatives to promote reflection, to help individuals find their own direction (8%).
- Approaches to invest in and grow ideas or initiatives, such as grants or other incentives to initiate, scale, or sustain projects (5%).
- Direct student support, such as advising or tutoring (3%).

With the exception of direct student support, many of these strategies are among the most traditional in the educational development portfolio— the "bread and butter" of CTL programs with a focus on developmental approaches to foster growth in people and ideas. For example, going back to Centra's original survey of the field, one of the most frequent types of programs offered were those "to acquaint faculty with goals of the institution and types of students enrolled,"[47] and later surveys found that educational developers perceived new faculty orientation and development as the top "issue" for which their units offered services.[48]

Other examples of Incubator strategies in CTL purpose statements include the following:

The vision of the Center for Teaching and Learning is to be recognized by the IUPUI community and beyond for fostering teaching and learning excellence and serving as an Incubator for teaching innovation.
—Center for Teaching and Learning, Indiana University–Purdue University Indianapolis[49]

Reflection is crucial to effective teaching, to Ignatian pedagogy, and to deep learning. The Center promotes reflection by integrating reflective activities into our services and programs; by helping faculty design effective reflection activities for students; and by reflecting deeply on our own practices so that we can make continuous improvements.
—Paul C. Reinert, S. J. Center for Transformative Teaching and Learning, Saint Louis University (MO)[50]

Berea College's (KY) Center for Teaching and Learning (CTL)

Berea's CTL opened in 2002 as the Center for Learning, Teaching, Communication, and Research, with roots in writing and reading labs that were established in 1970. The center demonstrates one of the strongest Incubator orientations in this study. In full, its mission reads (with Incubator elements added in bold):

> The Center for Teaching and Learning exists to **equip and empower members of the Berea College student, faculty, and staff community** to become effective, well-informed, and confident thinkers, writers, learners, and teachers through **individual consultations, mentoring**, workshops, and communities of practice. Together these programs enhance participants' knowledge and skills and **contribute to humanizing** and historicizing traditional classroom practices, norms, and assumptions for the purpose of creating greater equity in higher education.

Incubator-associated programs include a new faculty orientation, a student-faculty partnerships program, a teaching assistant and tutor certification program, midterm assessment of teaching, and student writing support. (Because of institutional budgeting structures, the center does not offer grants.) Director Leslie Ortquist-Ahrens notes that what unites faculty and student development is "conceiving of students as teachers and faculty as learners and offering programming where part of the power is blurring the traditional hierarchy."

By institutional type, there is some variation in the proportion that supports at least one Incubator strategy. This strategy is most common at master's universities and baccalaureates; however, this theory of change is less frequently expressed at community colleges.[51] Incubator strategies also appear more frequently in CTL purpose statements at private not-for-profits compared to other control types.[52] In both of these cases, institutional resources may account for these differences. Many Incubator approaches are highly relational and resource dependent. For example, consultations are difficult to scale if a CTL has few staff or if an institution is large, and grants certainly require a degree of financial stability or a strong development office.

Interestingly, CTLs coded in the latter part of 2020 have lower presence of Incubator strategies compared to those in the early months of the year.[53] While unlikely that many statements of purpose would have been rewritten in response to the effects of COVID, this may demonstrate the immediate impact of the pandemic on some centers' "About" statements as they suddenly needed to pivot resources and work at scale. There are no other statistically significant differences by institutional characteristic, but CTLs with digital staff are slightly *less* likely to articulate an Incubator orientation.[54] This is notable because digitally integrated centers are more likely to offer Incubator-related programs such as consultations (chapter 3), but it could be that these types of services are more skills based than reflective.

Articulating an Incubator Approach

Besides the articulation of these strategies, CTLs convey an Incubator approach through the action verbs they use. Those having the strongest association with the presence of an Incubator approach, compared to other change strategies, include *help*, *assist*, or *aid*, occurring in 18% of Incubator statements (13% overall) ($r = .10$, $p < .001$), as well as *develop* or *establish*, which occur in 15% of statements (10% overall) ($r = .12$, $p < .001$). The terms *sustain*, *maintain*, or *reinforce* appear in 10% of Incubator statements (6% overall) and have the strongest association with this strategy ($r = 0.14$, $p < .001$). *Empower* occurs in 6% of statements (4% overall) and is also most strongly correlated with an Incubator approach ($r = .10$, $p < .001$).

In comparison with Schroeder's analysis, the use of Incubator-associated actions appears to be slightly higher in 2020. For example, in 2006, 12 missions (out of 100) used *help/assist/aid*, 5 employed *develop*, 3 utilized *maintain*, and 1 *sustain*. However, there were no documented instances of the stronger *empower*.

Strengths and Cautions of Incubator Change Strategies

Other CTL surveys suggest that Incubator-related services are quite familiar. In the 2016 *Faculty Development in the Age of Evidence*, individual consultations were reported as the second most frequently offered service and new faculty orientation/development was the most frequently addressed "issue."[55] In addition to the consideration of alignment with aims, why and when might a CTL wish to utilize this approach?

While different models and terms are used, an Incubator approach primarily focuses on prompting transformational change among individual instructors. The role of the change agent with this approach is to motivate transformation by exposure to new ideas about teaching, or beliefs about teaching, which at times trouble existing frameworks.[56] Critically reflective change or reflection-in-action are guiding threads woven through many of these approaches.[57] These include tactics discussed in more detail in chapter 3, such as consultations and Small Group Instructional Diagnosis.[58]

There are also compelling reasons to implement orientation and mentoring approaches. New faculty initiatives tap into principles of anticipatory socialization.[59] For example, a welcoming experience to the culture of teaching can take place before the new faculty member becomes enmeshed in other cultural frameworks (e.g., research, in the case of doctoral universities). Additionally, there are well-documented and rigorously studied examples about the impact of longer-term new faculty programs on outcomes such as sense of preparation for teaching, student evaluations of teaching, ongoing engagement with the CTL, and equitable outcomes for student learning.[60] Some new faculty programs are very short orientations (see chapter 3), and there is limited evidence of the effectiveness of these brief formats. CTL mentoring programs, whether one-on-one or group-based, can also have an impact. As with orientation initiatives, outcomes are highly dependent on structure and implementation, and most studies are based on self-selection, complicating the evaluation.[61]

Turning to grants, the key drawback is the most obvious: resources needed to offer funds and to administer them fairly. Resource constraints may be the most significant reason that grants are not more frequently employed because, in general, they offer promise as a change strategy, named by one educational researcher as "one of the most pragmatic, and potentially productive, ways of honoring teaching."[62] Teaching grants, especially when they are paired with CTL support to carry out the grant project, are valuable for helping faculty develop new teaching skills and expertise.[63] They may be effective because the incentive motivates future behaviors, unlike a teaching award, which recognizes past achievements.

A final approach, although infrequently found here, is the integration of instructor and student support. This model is relatively new but can be found at a wide-ranging set of institutions such as Berea College (cited above), University of Dayton in Ohio, Northeast Alabama Community College, Princeton University, Tulane University, Yale University, and the center that I currently direct at Brown University. Some centers are even now working with high school students, such as the University of Connecticut's Center for Excellence in Teaching and Learning's Office of Early College Programs. Although the newness of this approach means there is limited research about it, my own observations are that there are key affordances as a change strategy. First, the intergenerational approach (i.e., involving faculty, staff, graduate students, undergraduates) that many of these centers employ can very powerfully effect change, whether though "students-as-partners" or as more traditional research assistants in SoTL projects.[64] Additionally, I find that our student support practice informs our educational development practice. For example, when working directly with students on writing or tutoring, we learn about patterns in challenges (or successes) across courses. This can allow for broader systemic viewpoint, helpful for CTL change. However, balancing the needs of multiple constituencies is challenging work! Without ample staffing, some centers may experience the broadened mandate as mission creep.

Temple: Recognition and Reward

Now, we turn to the least-expressed theory of change in CTL purpose statements: Temple. The key aim for a Temple strategy is to elevate the value of teaching, learning, and educational development by providing spaces and opportunities for recognition and reward of these endeavors. Approximately one in five centers (19%) employ at least one Temple strategy, and a very small proportion (2%) use more than one.

Promoting recognition and reward is the most frequently used approach to carry out a Temple strategy (13%), whether it involves teaching, learning, technology, or even the work of the center itself. Common examples of a "recognition and reward" approach include teaching awards, other celebrations of faculty achievements, and efforts to develop processes that value teaching or SoTL through hiring, promotion, and tenure.

A second Temple approach is deceptively simple: demarcate a symbolic or physical space (6%). Although a dedicated space allows for programs and community building to take place, it is also representative of a larger vision. To illustrate, Michigan's Kalamazoo College Teaching Commons notes that it provides "a physical and virtual place of possibility"[65] and Massachusetts's Curry College Faculty Center's vision is to "offer a 'third place' where achieving strategic objectives though new curricula and fostering learning go hand-in-hand."[66] While there are examples of virtual CTLs in this dataset and the literature, physical spaces have both functional and symbolic implications, and discussion of them is evident in many educational development discussions and publications. Space is also tied to the value that the CTL and related activities hold on campus because of the perception that "the more central your location, the more you signal to your campus stakeholders that faculty development is a priority of the institution."[67]

Finally, although mentioned infrequently, advocacy (2%) is a Temple strategy. This approach increases the value of certain endeavors that may otherwise be marginalized in the academy. These areas include advocacy "for the appropriate use of technology" (Center for Excellence in Teaching and Learning, University of the Virgin Islands),[68] placing "student learning, intellectual persistence, and attainment at the center of the university's mission" (Institute for Learning and Teaching Excellence, Indiana University Southeast),[69] and the desire to "advocate for including ongoing instructional improvement and the study of pedagogical practices as an expectation for all faculty and a factor of significant weight in the Promotion and Tenure process" (Central Connecticut State University, Center for Teaching and Faculty Development).[70]

The 2020 purpose statement for Michigan's Davenport University Center for Teaching Excellence (now Center for Excellence in Teaching and Learning) offered multiple examples of a Temple strategy (bold font added for emphasis).

> Our Mission states that the Center for Teaching Excellence supports, develops and **recognizes excellence in teaching, service and scholarship** by enhancing faculty skills, knowledge, and behaviors in support of student success. . . . The Vision for the Center for Teaching Excellence is to **provide a physical and virtual collaborative community** designed to facilitate and encourage faculty participation in the scholarship of teaching and learning. Welcome to our virtual community—we're glad you're here, and we look forward to learning with you![71]

Other examples of Temple strategies in 2020 CTL purpose statements include the following:

> The Commons is conceived as an institutional space where faculty can cultivate practices and develop tools that will give all students the chance to excel and to meet the Six Expectations of an Evergreen graduate.
> —The Learning and Teaching Commons, The Evergreen State College, Washington[72]

> Our aim is to promote teaching as a scholarly practice that is integral to the University's values.
> —Chicago Center for Teaching (now the Chicago Center for Teaching and Learning), The University of Chicago, Illinois[73]

> Elevates and amplifies the work of all educational developers at the university.
> —Michael V. Drake Institute for Teaching and Learning, The Ohio State University[74]

CTLs at master's and doctoral institutions show the highest presence of Temple strategies.[75] Master's institutions' emphases on a Temple strategy may be reflective of the ratcheting up of research expectations in this context, possibly signaling to CTLs that they need to carve out a space to maintain the institutional value of teaching.[76] Similarly, CTL work at a doctoral university may require a countervailing emphasis on supporting the value of teaching due to typical reward structures at these institutions. There are no other statistically significant differences by institutional or CTL characteristics nor time of coding.

Articulating a Temple Approach

In CTLs' descriptions of their Temple strategies, four key actions came into play. Of the verbs most strongly associated with a Temple approach, *recognize* or *celebrate* appears most frequently. These definitional features of a Temple approach are found in 30% of Temple statements (8% overall), and they are much more strongly associated with a Temple approach ($r = .41$, $p < .001$) compared to other orientations. *Cultivate* or *nurture* is found in 19% of Temple statements (8% overall), and these terms also had the strongest correlation with this change strategy ($r = .19$, $p < .001$) compared with Hub, Incubator, or Sieve. Reflecting the affective nature of a Temple strategy, *encourage* is seen in 26% of all Temple-associated purpose statements (13% overall), and this verb has the strongest association with the presence of a Temple approach ($r = .19$, $p < .001$). *Champion* or *advocate* is also most strongly correlated ($r = .17$, $p < .001$), in line with the advocacy approach of this strategy, and they appear in 10% of Temple statements (3% overall).

Most of these verbs—*encourage, cultivate, nurture, celebrate, advocate*—are documented in Schroeder's analysis, with only slightly greater frequency in 2020. In 2006, *encourage* was also seen in the same proportion (13%) of missions, while *cultivate* (2%), *nurture* (2%), *celebrate* (1%), and *reform advocate* (1%) are found in slightly fewer. In other words, if signaled only by the verbs associated with its approach, Temple does not appear to be a quickly growing change strategy compared to 15 years earlier.

Strengths and Cautions of Temple Change Strategies

A Temple strategy is the least common change approach articulated in CTL purpose statements. Comparison with Schroeder's semantic analysis suggests that it is not increasing in popularity, which is corroborated by other scholarship on centers. Why is this the case?

Temple is a difficult strategy to pull off, particularly if seeking to move the needle on recognition and reward structures. As others have noted:

> Providing rewards for teaching is related to the recognition of teaching effectiveness in personnel decisions such as tenure, promotion, and merit. These rewards are primarily located at the department level and are further related to an institution's valuation of teaching. If such values are not embedded in institutional culture—from departments to the provost's office—it is difficult for the teaching center to provide meaningful recognition of rewards for teaching.[77]

Because recognition and reward approaches are more frequently described in doctoral and master's institutions, where research has more primacy in personnel-related decisions, this change strategy may take a long time to come to fruition. With some exceptions, tenure and promotion structures have remained remarkably intractable over the past century.[78]

Possible outcomes for teaching awards might be affirmation of good teachers, rewarding effective teaching, improving teaching, enhancing learning, and developing campus climate for teaching. Yet, while teaching awards may be very popular on campuses, there is little research about their impact on these or other outcomes. Therefore, the limited evidence basis for Temple change strategies presents another barrier to their use.[79]

Recognition can still be a powerful motivational strategy, particularly if it is to help faculty, academic staff, and students feel that their contributions are valued. This approach to recognition reframes the question away from, as Jon Wergin noted, "How should we change the reward system?" and more to, "How do we create environments most conducive to productive faculty [and staff and student] life?"[80] In many ways, recognition-rich approaches draw on ideas of appreciative inquiry or positive change, which "begins with an inquiry into the positive core— what works well when the organization or community is at its best."[81] Other more systemic recognition strategies are discussed in more detail in the next chapter but include newer programs in CTLs that shift approaches away from evaluative mechanisms like teaching awards and toward more invitational approaches, which spotlight faculty innovations and open up classrooms to colleagues.

Although less commonly noted, advocacy and space are two approaches that CTLs may want to consider more frequently as change approaches. Resources such as space are associated with climate for instructional improvement.[82] However, intertwined with an advocacy approach, CTL spaces can also take on much larger meaning. Educational developer Laura Cruz wrote, "CTLs are intended to provide safe havens . . . to emphasize teaching and learning as ongoing—and very much intellectual—processes; and to recognize and reward multiple pathways of development."[83] For DEI aims, a space-based approach can help to provide models for different ways of being. Educational developer Peter Felten, borrowing from Melanie Walker, noted that educational developers can occupy "as if" spaces to "behave the way we want to live."[84] Although space has been previously conceptualized as a CTL signal of status and prominence (see the fantastically titled article "The Role of Educational Developers in Institutional Change: From the Basement Office to the Front Office" as an example) it is also helpful to understand how it can be employed as a change approach for CTLs.[85]

Sieve: Evidence and Expertise

Sieves function to sift, screen, and filter out, and a CTL Sieve change strategy takes a similar tack. With this approach, centers vet ideas to select those that are most evidence based, and they employ their expertise to shape policies and standards. A Sieve change strategy is the second most common approach in CTL orientation. Two-fifths of centers (40%) describe at least one Sieve strategy in their purpose statements, and 12% describe multiple.

The purpose statement for Oregon Health and Science University's Teaching and Learning Center offered multiple examples of a Sieve strategy in 2020 (bold emphases added).

(1) Collaborate with faculty and staff to **develop, improve and implement best practices** in teaching and course design. (2) Provide high-quality academic support services to OHSU's diverse learners to promote student success. (3) **Provide educational expertise and evaluation data to help**

programs measure and improve student learning outcomes. (4) Advise programs on curricular development for continuous program improvement. (5) Contribute to a culture of scholarship and innovation to promote educational excellence.[86]

As described below, this statement characterizes a Sieve approach because of its emphasis on best practices, expertise, evaluation and research, and quality improvement.

As defined here, six components compose a Sieve strategy. First, and most popularly (26%), centers indicate in their purpose statements that they foster the Scholarship of Teaching and Learning (SoTL) or use the science of learning to inform teaching design and facilitation (evidence-based teaching). As a "catalyst for thought and action," SoTL has been defined as an inquiry about student learning made public, which is open to critique and in a form on which others can build.[87] While SoTL activity often involves instructors creating and generating new knowledge, scholarly teaching or evidence-based teaching applies research to one's teaching practice or implementation of "educational practices derived from empirical data that show a well-established association with improved course grade, student feedback, and course-driven learning goals."[88]

An example of a CTL that employs this approach is Georgia Southwestern State University's Center for Teaching and Learning (changed to the Office of Teaching and Learning in 2021), which states that its mission "is to provide faculty with opportunities for development so that they may continue to investigate pedagogical strategies, discuss and debate issues relative to the scholarship of teaching and learning, and pursue areas research interests [*sic*] within their disciplines."[89] Another illustration of this, found in its guiding principles, is the CTL at Yale University in Connecticut: "The Poorvu Center values research-based decisions about teaching and learning and partners with instructors, departments, and programs to measure and evaluate impact."[90]

A second approach in the Sieve repertoire is assessment and evaluation, described in 14% of purpose statements. Like SoTL, this approach involves a systematic public inquiry about student learning and experiences but often with a broader scope across courses, curricula, and institutions.[91] Here, *assessment* is defined as "inquiry into student learning as a systemic and systematic core process of institutional learning—to improve educational practices and, thus, student learning," and *evaluation* is "information used for local decision making, which can also make a CTL's work visible on campus"[92] Although assessment has traditionally been seen as the domain of centralized institutional research or assessment offices, recent studies of CTL directors identify assessment as a top area in which the field will move in five years, and chapter 4 discusses assessment-infused centers in more detail.[93]

An example of an assessment focus can be seen in the mission of the Center for Teaching Excellence, at Anna Maria College in Massachusetts, which "values reflective practices that result in systematic assessment, quality improvement, and openness to growth."[94] As a change strategy, assessment can help to move forward several key CTL aims, including bridging work across communities and institutional levels, student learning, and diversity, equity, and inclusion.[95]

Third, although teaching and learning are focal activities for CTLs, centers also suggest that their direct engagement in research is a change strategy (6%). With this approach, rather than foster the activity in which others engage, CTLs define the conversation by doing the research themselves. The University of Iowa's Office of Teaching, Learning, and Technology seeks to "influence the national conversation through presentations, publications,"[96] and Georgetown University's Center for New Designs in Learning and Scholarship was "proud to have participated in a variety of projects that successfully uncover students' learning processes."[97]

While the three approaches named above describe specific programmatic initiatives, a fourth Sieve-based approach is the presentation of values or cultures that embody the idea of promoting only "the best." Several centers (4%) indicate in their purpose statements that they support ideas of quality improvement, academic rigor, and "best practices." An excellent example of this is the Office of Academic Effectiveness at St. Augustine College (IL), which promotes:

(1) A culture of quality assurance, continuous institutional improvement, systematic assessment, and sustained excellence across academic programs consistent with local and international standards,

(2) Quality processes of teaching and learning,

(3) Systematic evaluation of the effectiveness of all aspects of College operations and academic programs, and

(4) A cyclical monitoring function to ensure policy and accreditation compliance.[98]

Other examples include the Teaching and Learning Center at the University of Florida Warrington College of Business that was "dedicated to the support and enhancement of quality in the college's courses and degree programs"[99] and the University of Pennsylvania's Center for Teaching and Learning, which sought in 2020 "to increase the quality of education at Penn."[100]

Fifth, although infrequent (3%), some centers describe a role in setting or disseminating policies and standards, particularly around teaching. For example, in 2020, California's College of the Canyons Center for Excellence in Learning and Teaching noted that it "influences policy

---

The University of North Carolina Asheville's **Center for Teaching and Learning** (CTL) was founded in 1994–95 as a result of a declaration by the UNC Board of Governors that every state university should allocate a budget toward faculty development. Melissa Himelein, professor of psychology and the director of the CTL from 2010 to 2020, helped to draft the center's current mission, to "assist faculty with their use of evidence-based instructional strategies, encourage the integration of innovative educational technologies, and foster the university's commitment to academic rigor and student success." Himelein recounted, "When I started in the CTL, we were finishing up a SACSCOC [Southern Association of Colleges and Schools Commission on Colleges] reaffirmation and initiating our first Quality Enhancement Plan (QEP). Across campus, everybody was starting to recognize the importance of assessment, which also became a critical component of the QEP. I became deeply involved with the QEP, which focused on teaching critical thinking, collaborating closely with its director, and the CTL supported faculty who were part of the QEP through extensive programming. That work in particular helped to solidify the CTL's standing across campus."

discussions in ways that encourages the development of an excellent teaching and learning environment"[101] and Arizona's Grand Canyon University Center for Innovation in Research and Teaching listed as one of its goals, "Facilitate dissemination of evidence-based principles, strategies, and educational policy."[102]

The last and most infrequent approach is demonstrating expertise (3%). In some cases, this involves offering programs to "invite colleagues to learn from experts," as expressed by the University of Wisconsin–Whitewater's Learning Enhancement, Assessment and Research Network (LEARN) Center.[103] However, in other cases, the CTL is positioned as the locus of expertise. For example, the mission of Kentucky's University of Louisville Delphi Center for Teaching and Learning ends with this statement: "We deliver expertise, leadership, and resources to become the first-choice partner for fostering educational excellence."[104]

By institutional type, there are some clear variations when using a Sieve strategy. CTLs at doctoral institutions express the strategy most frequently.[105] Most of the doctoral institutions in this group are those with high research activity, and many Sieve strategies align with this character of work. Because most doctoral institutions are situated in the highest instructional FTE quartile, this may also be why larger institutions tend to employ a Sieve theory of change at a higher rate compared to those with fewer instructional FTEs.[106] Interestingly, CTLs with digital learning staff are more likely to have a purpose statement that names a Sieve approach compared to those that did not.[107] Possible reasons for this pairing, in strategy and tactic, are elaborated in chapter 3.

Articulating a Sieve Approach

For those seeking to describe a Sieve approach, options were replete. Verbs found to be most correlated with this change strategy, compared to Hub, Incubator, or Temple, include:

- Support (57% in Sieve, 47% overall)
- Promote (47%, 36%)
- Foster (30%, 21%)
- Collaborate/Partner (19%, 13%)

- Advance/Drive/Catalyze (17%, 11%)
- Conduct (16%, 10%)
- Engage (10%, 6%)
- Lead/Instigate/Initiate (8%, 5%)
- Serve (7%, 5%)
- Disseminate/Distribute (5%, 3%)
- Use/Apply/Implement (5%, 3%)
- Integrate (4%, 2%)
- Evaluate (3%, 2%)

All of these actions demonstrate a statistically significant association with a Sieve approach.[108]

In comparison to Schroeder's analysis of mission statements, Sieve-associated actions continue to be among those most frequently named and are growing in popularity. Schroeder's research found that *support* was the most frequently used verb (35% of statements), and it was also the most common verb in my 2020 analysis, used in almost half of all purpose statements. Schroeder's third- and fourth most frequently observed actions—*promote* (26%) and *foster* (14%)—are more frequently utilized in 2020. Stronger actions connoting a more powerful organizational development position are also increasing in use. The agentic *advance* (4%) and *lead* (1 mention of "take a leadership role" in 2006) are more common today than over a decade earlier.

Discourse analyses of statements associated with educational development professional associations, such as the POD Network, Higher Education Research and Development Society of Australasia, and Canada's Society for Teaching and Learning in Higher Education, point to the care-orientation of such language "focused, as it is, on measuring educational developers' success by the successes of those they serve."[109] Researchers noted that this service- or care-orientation is an important function and one that draws many (often female-identified) practitioners to the field. However, Bernhagen and Gravett cautioned that these gendered representations can "result in a diminished status for that labor and the professionals who perform it" and advised "that educational developers be selective and strategic, based on a rich understanding of their contexts, about using this kind of language—in CTL mission statements, in job ads, even when introducing themselves to others—instead of seemingly defaulting to a service model simply because it is the norm."[110]

Bernhagen and Gravett's call for strategic intentionality is well-placed. In both Schroeder's 2010 analysis and today, *support* is one of the most frequently used—and likely overused—verb phrases. (*Support* occurred in 35% of 2006 missions, and the verb is seen in 47% of statements of purpose in 2020.)

It is helpful for centers to consider stronger, more agentic language—such as *promote*, *advance*, or *lead*—but it is equally useful to consider how language might be contextualized. While use of *support* is significantly associated with the presence of Hub (r = .07, p < .05), Incubator (r = .08, p < .05), and Temple strategies (r = .12, p < .001), it is most strongly associated with Sieve (r = .15, p < .001). With Sieve's emphasis on expertise, this may shed a different light on the field's heavy use of *support* to describe the work.

Strengths and Cautions of Sieve Change Strategies

With six approaches, the Sieve change strategy is capacious; therefore, effective utilization depends on which aspect is most highlighted. Between 2010 and 2017, teams of STEM education researchers laid out a persuasive argument about the various degrees of success that one might anticipate with different facets of a Sieve approach. In 2010, STEM education researchers Charles Henderson, Noah Finkelstein, and Andrea Beach introduced four change strategies from their analysis of approximately 200 articles in the STEM change literature. These are: (1) disseminating curriculum and pedagogy, (2) developing reflective teachers, (3) developing policy, and (4) developing shared vision. In 2011, the same authors aligned these strategies with the STEM educational researchers' self-reports about whether the intended aim was achieved.

Category 1, with its focus on dissemination (a word found to be most strongly associated with a Sieve strategy) had one of the lower rates of success. In 2017, Henderson and others critiqued this "dissemination paradigm," which holds that collecting strong data about an educational innovation will create a compelling case for its adoption, convincing instructors to change their teaching. They wrote, "The underlying assumption of the dissemination paradigm is that a potential adopter who becomes aware of an innovation that solves an instructional problem and sees that it 'works' (that is, there is sufficient evidence for efficacy of the innovation) will decide to try the innovation."[111] This pitfall was narrated by Nobel Prize physicist, turned educational change agent, Carl Weiman when describing the activities of his Science Education Initiative (SEI) and how he was unsuccessful at convincing his colleagues with "objective data":

> The goal of the SEI was to change the teaching culture, but to carry out that change in a way that relies heavily on the values and practices of the research culture. . . . Essentially, this model would have the self-identity of faculty members of scientists expand to include their identities as teachers of science. However, this requires that their teaching practices and measures of success be based on research, empirically grounded principles, and objective data. Although this was the original design concept for the SEI, I learned that it gave too much emphasis to faculty as scientists and the belief that their "scientific thinking" would transfer over to how they thought about teaching. In reality, while there was a complex mixture of reactions, teaching was generally viewed more as a personal, emotion-based activity than as a scientific, evidence-based activity.[112]

In other words, a Sieve strategy that focuses simply on data gathering, analysis, and dissemination, without being attendant to the affective, cultural, and organizational complexities of change, will likely fail.

Category 3, with a focus on policy, is also clearly a Sieve-oriented approach. In this category, Borrego and Henderson grouped quality assurance protocols, another Sieve process. Unfortunately, policy was found to be the least successful at effectively prompting change.[113] They noted that the downside of this approach is that faculty can resist or subvert policies, and top-down initiatives can be complicated in the loose coupling of a university environment. While found to be helpful for addressing "a specific charge, such as a new curriculum or system for advising or evaluating faculty members," the authors suggested readers turn to other change strategies for "changing the culture for supporting teaching improvement."[114]

Because of these potential pitfalls, can a Sieve strategy ever be impactful? Certainly, yes. The other two categories of change strategies, reflective practice and shared vision, had better outcomes and can also be consistent with a Sieve approach. For example, Henderson, Finkelstein, and Beach found that many reflective practice articles used SoTL or action research approaches, a successful strategy that was also consistent with Sieve.[115] To have the greatest impact, however, it will be important to pair a Sieve strategy with another approach, such as reflection (Incubator) or dialogue and collaboration (Hub) because "how real people think about and use teaching-related data is a complex and idiosyncratic process shaped by a host of cognitive, cultural, and contextual factors."[116]

Conclusion

The HITS framework offers four broad change strategies for CTLs to employ in guiding their key aims. Hub strategies, which are most frequently used across institutional type (table 2.1), rely on promoting dialogue and collaboration, playing a coordinating or centralizing role, and offering centralized programs or campus resources. Incubator strategies are the third most frequently employed and use consultations, mentoring and orienting programs, reflective approaches, grants, and direct student support. The least articulated strategy, Temple, draws on approaches that emphasize advocacy, dedicated space, and recognition and reward. Finally, Sieve approaches, the second most frequently used overall, place an emphasis on facilitating SoTL and evidence-based teaching, conducting research, engaging in assessment and evaluation, maintaining quality control, offering expertise, and developing policies and standards. In comparison with Schroeder's semantic analysis of missions collected in 2006, aspirations to advance Hub and Sieve strategies appear to be growing while Incubator and Temple are relatively stable.

The vast majority (84%) of CTL purpose statements apply at least one HITS strategy, over half (52%) employ multiple, and some (6%) use all

TABLE 2.1. CTL change strategy by institutional type, 2020 (in percentages)

	All (N = 1105)	Doctoral (n = 324)	Master's (n = 290)	Associate's (n = 206)	Baccalaureate (n = 167)	Medical/ health (n = 90)	Other special focus (n = 27)
Hub (*Connector*)	**70**	69	73	68	69	71	78
Sieve (*Evidence*)	**40**	47	41	29	37	39	41
Incubator (*Growth*)	**37**	34	44	26	43	34	41
Temple (*Recognition*)	**19**	22	24	16	12	13	19

NOTES: Percentages are presented for unique Carnegie type. (See appendix 1 for methodology.) One institution is missing Carnegie classification information.

four. What does this mean for the small proportion (16%) of CTLs that did not document any change strategy listed in table 2.1? Possible explanations include that there was a change strategy but one that fell outside of the HITS framework or one that was articulated outside of a mission, vision, goal, or values statement. However, it is also the case that some of these statements are brief or provide aims with approaches that were difficult to categorize. In almost a *Mad Libs* fashion, CTL staff may wish to examine their purpose statements by filling the Connolly and Seymour variables in their definition of a theory of change: "If I do x, then I expect y to occur, *and for these reasons*."[117] If there are gaps, it may signal a time to revise our purpose statements.

When revising or developing a new center, which approach(es) should a CTL employ? There is not a quick answer to this question, and this chapter offers several nuances by organizational characteristics and evidence basis. It is also the case that these strategies are not mutually exclusive, and a "multi-theory" approach to change makes it more likely to succeed at the intended aim.[118] When looking at correlations among the strategies, all have small positive but statistically significant associations with each other.[119] However, two overriding considerations are important in making this choice: (1) institutional context and (2) alignment with aims.

First, institutional type matters. Although there are some variations, in most cases, the key driver of statistically significant differences is the Carnegie classification type. Across all institutional types, the top strategy is Hub and the least-used strategy is Temple, as seen in table 2.1. While Incubator is ranked number two for baccalaureates and master's institutions, Sieve is next most commonly referenced for CTLs in associate's and doctoral institutions, as well as medical/health contexts. (Incubator and Sieve are equally frequent for other special focus contexts.)

Second, this chapter began with the premise that by articulating end goals and the means to those aims, it will be more likely that CTLs can affect change. In line with this thesis, CTL staff may wish to examine the change strategies most articulated by other centers to achieve key goals. The approach most frequently associated with the nine CTL aims identified in the previous chapter is presented in table 2.2. In other words, of CTL statements of purpose that name a specific goal, what percentage also co-locate a particular change strategy?

Table 2.2 illustrates that there appear to be signature strategies across CTLs. These include promoting dialogue and collaboration, designing and offering programs and services, and in one case, facilitating the Scholarship of Teaching and Learning and evidence-based teaching. In other words, returning to the premise established at the beginning of this chapter, core theories of change for educational development work are dialogue and collaboration, programs and services, and SoTL. Making

TABLE 2.2. Most frequently applied theory of change by CTL aim, 2020

CTL aim	Theory of change
Student learning	Hub: Dialogue and collaboration (39%)
	Hub: Programs and services (39%)
Instructor outcome	Hub: Programs and services (46%)
Change or innovation	Hub: Dialogue and collaboration (50%)
Culture, climate, and environment	Hub: Dialogue and collaboration (44%)
Scholarly and creative work	Hub: Programs and services (49%)
Diversity, equity, and inclusion	Sieve: SoTL and evidence-based teaching (50%)
Institutional mission	Hub: Programs and services (43%)
Teaching effectiveness and excellence	Hub: Programs and services (49%)
Community building	Hub: Dialogue and collaboration (52%)

these approaches explicit will enable CTLs to more powerfully enact their change aims.

Each of these signature strategies is very broad. For example, what specific kind of programs and services do CTLs offer (e.g., workshops, course design institutes, learning communities), what topics do they address, and how do these vary by organizational characteristics? The next chapter outlines these tactics in more detail to help CTLs align their resources with greatest impact.

CHAPTER 3

What Tactics Do We Employ?

Signature CTL Programs and Services

N 2010, US educational developer Virginia Lee offered, "Like a chameleon, the distinctive coloration, shadings, and features of the programs offered by teaching and learning centers have changed . . . at the same time that the underlying structures and basic spheres of activity have remained true to the origins of the field."[1] How much have CTL programs changed over time, and what are the most frequently offered program types today?

The last chapter examined CTL theories of change as narrated in purpose statements. In this chapter, I examine the *tactics* that CTLs employ or the specific initiatives that they use to carry out their work. There are three key reasons why CTL tactics matter, drawing from both external and internal depictions of the field, as well as a return to thinking about centers as agents of change. First, external viewpoints about the programs and services that CTLs offer contribute to perceptions of the field. For example, one 2020 *Inside Higher Education* article argued, "It's time to replace teaching centers with centers for educational innovation, evaluation and research," basing this premise on the claim that the CTL "approach tends to be pretty uniform, consisting largely of teaching consultations, workshops and classroom observations."[2] In scholarly journals, we also see suggestions that CTL work is characterized by change strategies that focus primarily on individual-level or workshop-based approaches.[3] When examining the programs and services that CTLs actually offer, are these depictions accurate?

Second, an understanding of CTL work helps enhance internal understandings of the field. Educational development is not traditionally defined as an area of study but rather as a field of practice that draws professionals from many different academic backgrounds.[4] Indeed, a commonly used definition of educational development, presented in the introduction, denotes the field through the work practitioners do rather than the backgrounds or epistemologies we hold: "helping colleges and universities function effectively as teaching and learning communities."[5] Yet, is there enough coherence in our functions to adequately describe the practices as "a field"? For example, British educational developer Graham Gibbs made this observation of his work in the UK: "Over the past 40 years, I have engaged in such a wide variety of 'change tactics,' with the broad intention of improving teaching and learning, that it is sometimes difficult to encompass them all under a banner like 'educational development' without feeling that the term is being stretched a little."[6] Therefore, a comprehensive understanding of the practices of Centers for Teaching and Learning helps shape understandings of the field of educational development in the US, including knowledge of its fractures or coherence.

Finally, this chapter continues the thread of CTLs as agents of change. While chapter 1 examined aims and chapter 2 explored strategies, this chapter analyzes tactics or particular approaches CTLs take to (perhaps unintentionally) enact a strategy or achieve an aim. In chapters 1 and 2, I analyzed CTL names and their statements of purpose. Here, I look at other sections of CTL websites to understand what programs were currently advertised and what initiatives were highlighted. In this chapter, I use for this analysis all CTL websites ($N = 1,196$), which represent 340 CTLs at doctoral institutions (28% of dataset), 308 master's institutions (26%), 233 associate's colleges (20%), 181 baccalaureates (15%), 104 medical / health-related contexts (9%), 29 other special focus contexts (2%), and 1 institution missing classification information (< 1%). I explore how occurrence may vary by institutional and CTL characteristics, as well as the time the site was visited. (These variables are defined in appendix 1.) The chapter also examines the degree to which strategies and tactics align.

Just as theories of change are grouped into four main categories, I cluster tactics into the Hub-Incubator-Temple-Sieve framework (table 3.1), with an attempt to locate the program in its primary orientation. In some cases, programs cross categories. For example, workshops are located in a Hub orientation, because these are primarily group-based activities, often interdisciplinary, premised on social learning (i.e., involving connection and collaboration). However, workshops on SoTL are also discussed as a Sieve tactic. It may be the case that any single program type might be used by an individual CTL in a different orientation, and I imagine that readers will have their own arguments about which program type goes where. Even in this exercise, my hope is to promote intentionality around strategy and tactics.

Most of the initiatives in table 3.1 are derived from program types noted in prior scholarship of educational development.[7] I also use an inductive approach by including newer initiatives that appeared on CTL sites in 2020. It is clear that tactics have grown substantially since Centra's 1976 study, which described only six groups of practice: instructional

TABLE 3.1. CTL change tactics, 2020

Hub	Incubator
Small-group programs (workshops, series, certificates, and courses) Course transformation initiatives Institution-wide events Dialogue and collaboration communities (book groups, CoPs, learning communities, teaching circles, affinity groups, change teams) Resources	Consultative approaches (consultations, observations, SGIDs, open classrooms, SCoT, and SaLT) Orientations and new instructor programs Mentoring programs Grants Direct academic support
Temple	Sieve
Teaching awards Recognition-based approaches Teaching academies Advocacy	Scholarship of teaching and learning Assessment and evaluation Policy and standards Quality assurance Educational research and scholarship of educational development

assistance, workshops and seminars, grants, assessment, traditional teaching practices, and publicity.[8]

To understand how the field has moved over time in the United States, I compare 2020 frequencies with a number of prior studies. First, I use Centra's 1976 study, as well as the 2012 survey of educational developers completed by Andrea Beach, Mary Deane Sorcinelli, Ann Austin, and Jaclyn Rivard (published in 2016). For graduate student professional development, I rely on a 2009 survey of all US research universities (283 institutions, 95% response rate) conducted by a team of US educational developers.[9] According to educational developer Michael Palmer's analysis, in 2009, most (83%) doctoral institutions offered one or more structured professional development programs for graduate students, with a range of 63% at doctoral/research universities and 99% at universities with very high research activity.

As in the previous chapters, any organizational changes, such as a CTL name change from 2020 to 2022, are noted. However, unlike a center name or statement of purpose, this chapter assumes that a CTL will update its program offerings relatively frequently. Therefore, updates to a referenced CTL's 2020 programs and services are not separately noted here. Variations in tactical approaches that are analyzed here include institutional contexts (Carnegie classification, institutional size by instructional FTE, MSI status, women's college status, control), CTL characteristics (age, staffing size), and time of coding. (See appendix 1 for definitions.)

Hub: Organizational Connector

As seen in the prior chapter, a Hub strategy is one of the most frequent approaches for Centers for Teaching and Learning to describe how they achieve their aims. As operationalized here, key tactical ways that centers express a Hub-related approach are by offering programs that advance community building and coordination:

1. Small-group interactive programs (workshops, series, certificates, or courses)
2. Course transformation initiatives

3. Institution-wide events
4. Communities that promote dialogue and collaboration (book groups and journal clubs, communities of practice, learning communities, teaching circles, faculty interest groups, affinity groups, change teams)
5. Resources

In 2020, the vast majority (82%) of CTL websites suggested that they used one or more of these Hub approaches. This section explores in more detail the programs, services, and resources that CTLs with a Hub strategy can employ. (Although consolidation and centralization are other key Hub tactics, this is often a larger organizational strategic approach and is covered separately in chapter 4.)

Programs

As identified in statements of purpose, one of the most common CTL theories of change is the development and provision of programs. As seen in the previous chapter, 42% of all center purpose statements suggested this strategy.

From their survey of educational developers, Beach, Sorcinelli, Austin, and Rivard noted that across institutional types, brief programs (specifically one- to three-hour workshops) were the top approach used by CTLs in aggregate. They observed that this approach may be used most frequently because it is "responsive to the hectic schedules of faculty members."[10] Accordingly, program types involving more time and involvement, such as multiday course transformation initiatives or faculty learning communities, were less frequently named by respondents as part of their CTLs' repertoires. In the intervening decade, it is clear that a key challenge for CTLs has been how to balance the tension between the efficiency and effectiveness of programs. To develop a broad reach with instructors, time-efficient programs are attractive, but short-term workshops tend to have less impact on adoption of new teaching approaches.[11]

A decade later, interactive programs continue to be frequently offered by CTLs, and across Carnegie types, workshops are the most frequent Hub-related tactic, offered at nearly all centers. However, there is a growing number of efforts to promote change with offerings of longer duration (e.g., series, certificates, or courses) or scope (institution-wide events). As an example, Jennifer Friberg, director at Illinois State University's Center for Teaching, Learning, and Technology (now the Center for Integrated Professional Development), noted, "We really want to optimize the professional development that we have that we offer and so we've made a transition from having one-time workshops, where people leave with really good intentions of making changes in our teaching, to doing what we refer to as 'deep dives' into topics where part of the professional development is actually applying it to your class and studying the impacts on your students' learning." Additionally, several centers are engaged in programs that move the focus of change away from the individual to course-based transformation.

Workshops, Series, Certificates, and Courses

A decade earlier, "hands-on workshops (1–3 hours)" were the most frequent program type to be reported by CTL directors across all institutional types except community colleges.[12] (For community colleges, individual consultations were indicated to be most used, with workshops as a close 2nd.) Out of 15 possibilities, longer-term programs with multiple commitments were ranked 6th, and "institutes/retreats (2–3 full days)" were 9th, signaling the predominance of brevity. Even more intriguingly, webinars ranked 13th, and asynchronous online programs were in last place, also highlighting the importance of face-to-face programming 10 years ago. Although they may be the most maligned CTL program type, workshops certainly can be effective if they are designed well: offering interactivity, involving peer facilitation, allowing practice and feedback, being grounded in a theoretical framework, addressing concrete takeaways relevant to the instructor's context, and focusing on specific skill or knowledge acquisition.[13]

Today, interactive workshops continue to be a heavily used tactic by CTLs. Over two-thirds of centers (72%) list one or more specific program of this type.[14] Workshops are listed most frequently on the websites of centers at doctoral and medical/health-focused institutions, with least presence in baccalaureates.[15] Larger institutions and CTLs also provide workshops more commonly, which may be related to CTL capacity and resources.[16] There are no statistically significant differences by control, MSI or women's college status, age of center, nor time of coding.

For this study, over 5,000 small-group program listings were analyzed by type (i.e., workshops, series, or certificates) and topic. (Many thanks to Emmajane Rhodenhiser, a Brown University junior at the time, who coded most of these workshops.[17])

Within the group of centers that listed workshop programs, over a third (35%) note a program type with the expectation that an instructor would attend multiple sessions over time, potentially with a deliverable. Over one in five (23%) offered a **workshop series**, or a themed set of workshops that allow instructors the option of engaging in a topic through multiple perspectives, spaced over time. Series typically involve a sequence of brief workshops around a theme. Examples include the four-part "Actionable Equity Faculty Professional Development" series offered by California's American River College Center for Teaching and Learning, designed to help faculty and academic leaders make data-informed, equitable decisions. Another illustration is California State University, Fresno's Center for Faculty Excellence (now consolidated with the Office of Innovation and Digital Excellence for Academic Success), which offered a Universal Design for Learning series to focus on the science of learning, design of high-impact practices, and assessment.

Almost one in five CTLs (19%) offered a **certificate, course, or badged program**. These initiatives are similar to a series in that they are multipart, but they add a credential that often involves demonstration of attendance and, frequently, requires a deliverable. Examples include Idaho's Boise State Uniting for Inclusion and Leadership in Diversity (BUILD) program offered by its Center for Teaching and Learning. With objectives such as increased critical awareness around one's positionality and enhanced understanding of patterns of marginalization and systems of oppression, participants were required to submit a final reflection after attending 10 sessions, which were customized from a menu of workshops, faculty learning communities, book circles, and dialogues. In turn, California State University's Office of the Chancellor offered a

Certificate Program in Student Success Analytics, which provided "cross-divisional teams of higher education faculty, staff, and administrators the opportunity to improve student success on their campus" through a data action project and engagement in 8 sessions. To support environmental sustainability, two District of Columbia centers offered a Green Teaching Certificate Program (Howard University's Center for Excellence in Teaching, Learning, and Assessment; and American University's Center for Teaching, Research and Learning).

Unlike educational development contexts in other global regions, it is customary for US CTL programs to be optional and sometimes incentivized with a certificate and/or payment upon completion. However, there are indications that some institutions require engagement. For example, the University of the District of Columbia's Center for the Advancement of Learning offered two certifications: Online Teaching Certification, required for teaching online or hybrid courses, and Online Build Certification, required for building courses in these modalities. Similarly, the Iowa State University Senior Vice President and Provost Office required faculty attendance at an annual Inclusive Classroom training facilitated by its Center for Excellence in Learning and Teaching. However, these requirements appear to be relatively rare.

Certificates or courses were also a common professional development offering for graduate students. In 2009, almost a quarter (23%) of institutions offered a graduate certificate open to students from all disciplines.[18] In their 2010 study, Schönwetter, Ellis, Taylor, and Koop found 131 courses for graduate students on college/university teaching, representing 17% of the US higher education institutions in their study, with CTLs being one of the most frequent homes for these initiatives.[19] (Other common locations were colleges of education or graduate schools.) Some CTL websites (7%) in this 2020 study note courses or certificate programs tailored to graduate students. For example, the University of California, Berkeley's Graduate Student Instructor Teaching and Resource Center offered two credit-bearing courses: Becoming an Effective Mentor, and Teaching and Learning in Higher Education.

Medical residents and postdoctoral scholars are other constituencies for whom longer-term programs were customized. The University of

Central Florida School of Medicine's Faculty Development Programs offered "Resident as Teacher" to provide professional learning around teaching skills such as writing narrative evaluations, and the Texas College of Osteopathic Medicine's Faculty Development Center sponsored the seven-session Graduate Certificate in Academic Medicine. The University of Michigan–Ann Arbor's Center for Research on Learning and Teaching developed a "Postdoctoral Shortcourse on College Teaching in STEM," which engaged participants in drafting a syllabus, writing a statement of teaching philosophy, and facilitating a practice teaching session

Topics of workshops, series, courses, and certificates have a wide range. While many focus on teaching, others address wellness, community building, and career development for faculty. In his 1976 study of the field, Centra examined 10 types of workshops and seminars, helpfully noting the variety of objectives these brief programs can have: examining pedagogical approaches, developing curricula, improving research and scholarship capacities, enhancing organizational development, exploring educational trends, and developing faculty's interpersonal skills in working effectively with others or groups. At that time, Centra found that programs "that explore various methods or techniques of instruction" were reported to be most utilized and most effective, while those that "help faculty improve their research and scholarly skills" were perceived to be least used and effective.[20]

Almost 50 years later, to understand the range of topics that CTL programs are addressing, 5,135 small-group program listings were coded according to 32 topics. Most frequently (36% of centers offering a workshop, series, certificate, or course), these programs addressed general teaching and learning issues that are difficult to specify by title alone (e.g., "Pedagogy Discussion," "Talk about Teaching"). However, among more specified **topics in relation to teaching and learning**, those that arose most frequently were:

- Digital teaching and learning tools and approaches (36% of centers)
- Diversity, equity, and inclusion (33%)

- Assessment, grading, and feedback (28%)
- Online/hybrid/remote course design (26%)
- Engagement and active learning (24%)
- Course and curriculum design (23%)

Moderately applied topics include:

- Wellness (16%)
- Accessibility and Universal Design for Learning (14%)
- Writing and communication (11%)
- Science of learning (10%)
- Advising and mentoring (10%)
- Difficult or challenging moments in the classroom (9%)
- Service learning and community engagement (8%)
- Open educational resources (7%)
- Discussions (7%)
- Collaborative learning (6%)
- Academic integrity (6%)

Least-applied topics include:

- Scholarship of teaching and learning (5%)
- Teaching improvement (4%)
- Critical thinking and information literacy (4%)
- Trauma-informed teaching (3%)
- Global learning (3%)
- Sustainability (2%)
- Affective dimensions of teaching, such as the role of emotions in teaching and learning (2%)
- Teaching large classes (2%)
- Education grand rounds (2% overall, but 14% of medical / health science schools)
- Undergraduate research (1%)

(An additional 11% of centers offered programs on other topics. Percentages total more than 100% because many centers offered programs on multiple topics.)

Centra found that faculty development topics (i.e., addressing the growth and development of the individual instructor) and organizational development topics (i.e., addressing ways to improve functioning of the institution) were not offered as much as those addressing instructional approaches.[21] This still generally holds true, with non-pedagogical programs offered with moderate degrees of frequency. **Community building** was represented by 11% of centers offering workshops, with examples like the University of Wisconsin–Madison's Collaborative for Engineering Education and Teaching Effectiveness sessions on "Coffee and Conversations," the Columbus State University (GA) Faculty Center for the Enhancement of Teaching and Learning's "Grading Marathon," or the fully online Purdue University Global Center for Teaching and Learning's "Faculty WorkOUT," which connected remote faculty who were located in the same area to work together and network. **Career development–related topics** were seen in 10% of CTLs that offered workshops, such as the Appalachian State University (NC) Center for Academic Excellence (now Center for Excellence in Teaching and Learning for Student Success), "Mid-Career Faculty: Managing Energy, Not Time" session, or the University of Central Florida College of Medicine's Faculty Development Programs workshop on "Documenting for Success: A Workshop on Promotion Dossiers."

Finally, sessions on **organizational development and policy change** were offered by 4% of centers. Examples included the Fort Hays State University (KS) Faculty Development Lunch and Learn that focused on faculty senate work, the University of Wyoming Ellbogen Center for Teaching and Learning's session on "How to Develop a Faculty-Directed Education Abroad Program," and the La Salle University (PA) De La Salle Institute for Advanced Teaching and Learning Explorer Café, which examined mission-centered questions such as "What Does It Mean to Be Lasallian?"

Beginning in March 2020, the COVID-19 pandemic had a profound impact on the work of CTLs generally and on the modality of programs specifically. However, the pandemic appears not to have also introduced topical changes in programs, to the degree that one might expect. While there was an increase in offerings pertaining to remote, online, and hybrid teaching, an analysis by Wright and Rhodenhiser suggests that it was not the topic that increased the most.[22] Topics showing the greatest positive change were those at the "core" of CTL work: engagement and active learning; diversity, equity, and inclusion; and course and curriculum design. These topics also reflect that the pandemic was not the only challenge that centers needed to address in supporting campus efforts toward resiliency. Many seismic events of 2020 (including not just the COVID-19 pandemic but also calls for racial equity and the US election) appear to have influenced center offerings.

Although modality was not coded separately, because nearly all colleges and universities moved to online, remote, or hybrid instruction for a portion of 2020, it is safe to assume that program formats shifted dramatically at CTLs, deepening permeation into both synchronous and asynchronous online initiatives. One example of this is the Emory University (GA) Center for Faculty Development and Excellence, which included a variety of modalities among its offerings: face-to-face programs, such as a two-day Alan Alda Science Communication workshop and a "Reimagining Retirement" luncheon; asynchronous learning management system (LMS) modules on topics such as "Teaching with Video"; webinars on subjects like "Getting Started with Group Work and Research Projects Online"; a Coursera-based teach-out on "Making Progress"; and a five-part asynchronous and badged "Foundations for Teaching Online" course. It remains to be seen what the stickiness of multimodal approaches will be, although there are preliminary reports that CTLs will continue to add remote and asynchronous participation formats to their permanent repertoire to structure greater flexibility to engagement.[23]

Course Transformation Initiatives

While individuals are the target focus for many workshops, series, and certificates, the course transformation initiative shifts the lens to a different unit of analysis: the academic class. Most frequently, this takes the shape of a Course Design Institute (CDI), defined as "multiday programs that consist of presentations, workshops, roundtables, consultation blocks, as well as opportunities to work individually or in groups to complete a set task, such as the design or redesign of a course."[24] Published and well-known examples included Purdue University Center for Instructional Excellence's IMPACT, which connects cross-campus teams to engage in course redesign over a term, guided by self-determination theory.[25] The University of Virginia's Center for Teaching Excellence weeklong Course Design Institute is also a widely distributed model with documented impact on learning-focused syllabi and confidence to enact teaching practices.[26]

Multiday, intensive initiatives were not frequently reported in previous surveys of CTLs, possibly due to concerns about time.[27] Indeed, a study of one institute at James Madison University found the CDI resulted in a higher perceived value of teaching among faculty participants, as well as an increased sense of the costs of teaching (e.g., time and stress required to teach a redesigned course).[28] Despite these concerns, however, this tactic appears with more frequency compared to reports from a decade earlier. Over 200 centers (18%) describe one or more course transformation initiative on their websites. However, there appears to be a wide degree of variation in occurrence of this tactic by institutional type. While over a third of doctoral institutions list such a program, this proportion drops considerably for all other institutional types.[29]

CDIs appear to be a tactic related to scale and, potentially, access to resources needed to carry out a multiday program. Smaller centers and institutions, as well as CTLs at MSIs, less frequently offer course transformation initiatives.[30] There are no other statistically significant differences by institutional characteristics, CTL features, nor time of coding. Though many institutes appeared to be created in response to 2020's academic continuity needs, this was already a trend in motion.

Course transformation programs are an incredibly flexible tactic. For example, at Brown University's Sheridan Center for Teaching and Learning, we have held a Problem-Solving Course Design Institute, a Writing across the Curriculum Seminar, a Capstone Course Design Institute, a Data Science Course Design Institute, the Launch weeklong course design institute for new faculty, the semester-long Seminar for Transformation around Anti-Racist Teaching (START), and the Anchor Course Design Institute to support resilient teaching during the pandemic. What is common to this tactic is a focus on intentional course design and an extended format.

In many cases, CDIs support institutional initiatives. For example, Princeton's (NJ) McGraw Center for Teaching and Learning used this approach to support faculty in redesigning junior methods courses, and Auburn's (AL) Biggio Center collaborated with faculty to teach in active learning classrooms. California State University, San Marcos's Faculty Center recently offered programs to allow participants to "include more Chicano/Latino related content and assignments" and a second program to design a course to meet the university's diversity and equity requirement. Some focus on constituency, such as the University of Michigan's Center for Research on Learning and Teaching's academies for new faculty, and others on certain disciplines, like the University of California, Berkeley's Center for Teaching and Learning's Transforming STEM Teaching Faculty Learning Program. Elon University's (NC) Center for the Advancement of Teaching and Learning also had an innovative model by offering both Course Design Working Groups, which focused on designing a new course or rethinking an existing class, and Assignment Alignment Working Groups, which focused more specifically on alignment of assessments with learning goals.

While there is a wide range of course transformation models, a 2021 survey of 61 course design institutes found that most address the following core concepts, principles, or theories:

- Active learning, assessment of learning, equity and inclusivity, and learning goals and objectives (92% each)
- Assignment design, formative feedback (87% each)
- Alignment, backward-integrated design (85% each)
- Syllabus design, Universal Design for Learning (84%)
- Learning theories (75%)
- Scaffolding (74%)
- Learning taxonomies (72%)
- Sense of belonging (70%)
- Science of learning principles (67%)
- Transparency (64%)[31]

Unlike the wide range in workshop topics, this analysis suggests a high level of consensus around key concepts that should be addressed in institutes.

While most institutes support faculty, there are a few examples of programs that support other constituencies. For example, Purdue University Center for Instructional Excellence's Summer Course Design Institute offered a 6-day program for faculty and postdoctoral scholars. Additionally, although not termed "institutes," several CTLs offered courses or certificates around course design, such as Rutgers University (NJ) School of Graduate Studies TA Project's 12-week "Design Your Own Course" non–credit bearing class and the University of California, Irvine's Division of Teaching Excellence and Innovation's "Course Design for Instructors of Record" credit-bearing offering.

Institution–Wide Events

While course transformation initiatives are known for their focus and depth, institution-wide events are designed for breadth. Featured by a third of centers (33%), these are large conference-like events that are intended to draw large numbers of participants. Examples of CTL events with an institutional reach include those with both a pedagogical and a holistic focus. For example, Virginia Commonwealth University's Center for Teaching and Learning Excellence organized both a Faculty Wellness Day and a Teaching Excellence Symposium. Several centers offered weeklong programs, like California Institute of Technology's Center for Teaching, Learning, and Outreach, which coordinated "TeachWeek," featuring a keynote speaker, open class sessions and discussion, multiple presentations, and a reception and teaching awards ceremony. Similarly, Tarleton State University's (TX) Center for Instructional Innovation (now the Center for Educational Excellence) hosted a "Celebrate Teaching Week" with a 2020 theme of "Curiosity." This program also featured a keynote speaker, faculty panels, and teaching awards ceremony as well as a 30-minute boxing workout!

Institution-wide events are most likely to be offered at doctoral, associate's, and master's institutions.[32] Like other Hub tactics, this one also appears to be related to scale, with larger CTLs and institutions posting these types of programs more frequently.[33] Additionally, CTLs at private, for-profit institutions and at public institutions, which tend to be larger, were more likely to feature this program type compared to those at private not-for-profits.[34] There are not any other statistically significant differences by institutional or CTL characteristic nor date of coding.

Dialogue and Collaboration Communities

A decade ago, as noted in one study, CTL staff did not report offering "faculty and professional learning communities (i.e., full semester or academic year, regular meetings)" with great frequency, although this approach was top of the list of those to expand in the future.[35] In 2020, over a third (36%) of centers alluded to a strategy of using dialogue and collaboration in their purpose statements, and a sizable proportion (41%) of all centers listed a program of this type on their websites. CTL program types that align with a dialogical approach include reading groups, communities of practice and professional learning communities, teaching circles, faculty interest groups, affinity groups, and change teams.

Dialogue and collaboration communities are offered most frequently at doctoral, master's, and baccalaureate institutions.[36] As with many of the other Hub tactics, CTL size is a factor, with larger organizations offering this approach more frequently.[37] There are no other statistically significant differences by institution or CTL feature nor time of coding.

Although similar in aim—to promote dialogue and collaboration—this tactic unites several similar types of programs:

Book groups and journal clubs are a common type of these approaches, often centered on discussion of a text. As an example, Faculty Development at Texas State University offered "Bookchats" for non-tenure-line faculty. Michigan's Grand Valley State University Robert and Mary Pew Faculty Teaching and Learning Center featured two programs each term, one on foundational progressive educational pedagogy texts (e.g., bell hooks, John Dewey) and the other on more contemporary pedagogical writings. Several centers offered podcast-based discussion groups, such as Cuyahoga Community College District–East Campus's

(OH) Center for Learning Excellence and Southwestern University's (TX) Center for Teaching, Learning, and Scholarship. Others used them to bring together different constituencies. For example, Kentucky's Morehead State University Faculty Center for Teaching and Learning offered its "Book Reads" to faculty, staff, and students.

A **community of practice** (CoP) is "a group of people who share a concern or a passion for something they do and learn how to do it as they interact regularly," often with the goals of networking and exchanging knowledge.[38] Boise State University's (ID) Center for Teaching and Learning offered three CoPs pertaining to pedagogical approaches: Process-Oriented Guided Inquiry Learning (POGIL), service learning, and team-based learning. This approach was also applied by centers for their leadership development aims, such as the Chairs' Community of Practice offered by Seattle University's (WA) Center for Faculty Development and the University of Nebraska Omaha Center for Faculty Excellence's Faculty Leadership Forums.

As a subset of CoPs, **learning communities** are a similar approach used by many centers. As defined on the center website at which this approach was initiated, "A *faculty learning community* (FLC) is a specifically structured learning community of faculty and staff in higher education that includes the goals of building community, engaging in scholarly practice, and developing the scholarship of teaching and learning (SoTL)" (Center for Teaching Excellence, Miami University, Ohio).[39] (Although "faculty learning communities" is the most commonly used term, I prefer the term "professional learning communities," which acknowledges that staff and students can be full members of these groups as well, with Heffernan and Wright offering an example of a faculty–athletic coaches learning community at Brown University.)[40] Michigan State University's Academic Advancement Network (now the Office of Faculty and Staff Development) offered over 20 topics, including Anti-Racist Strategies for Teaching, Learning and Faculty Development Efforts; Department of Animal Science Teaching and Learning Community; Digital Humanities Pedagogy Learning Community; Mindful Teaching and Learning in Higher Education; and Restorative Justice. Many FLCs addressed institutional initiatives, such as Northern

Arizona University's Faculty Professional Development Program (now Teaching and Learning Center), which offered a "Becoming a Hispanic-Serving Institution" topic, and the University of Oregon's Teaching Engagement Program, which supported the development of Diversity, Inequality, and Agency courses through a group that develops learning goals and a syllabus statement for these classes. FLCs are also supported through digital tools, such as Bellevue College (WA) Faculty Commons "Climate Justice in Action" asynchronous learning community to support faculty who want to develop and implement a climate justice–focused student project within a local community.

Less formal options include **teaching circles** or **faculty interest groups**, which bring together participants for an extended time around a particular topic or strategy, but often with a little less time or structure compared to FLCs or CoPs. Teaching circles originated at the University of Nebraska and, accordingly, its Center for Transformative Teaching offered a group on teamwork.[41] As another example, to develop shared community around teaching, the John Crosland Jr. Center for Teaching and Learning at Davidson College in North Carolina bought lunch for up to eight faculty who wished to talk about teaching in its "Experimenting As Teachers (EAT) Lunches" program. In Virginia, Shenandoah University's Center for Teaching, Learning and Technology offered "Pop-Up Pilots," which were short-term gatherings for faculty or staff who were interested in using a particular tool in their teaching. Finally, the Center for New Designs in Learning and Scholarship at Georgetown University in the District of Columbia facilitated a teaching circle on "Engaging Georgetown's History of Slaveholding in the Classroom."

Affinity groups offer a space for inclusion, particularly for instructors from groups historically excluded from higher education, bringing together participants for an extended time around a shared lived experience. To illustrate examples from two New York institutions, the Center for Leadership, Teaching and Learning at Skidmore College offered a Faculty Women of Color Coaching Group, and the Columbia University Center for Teaching developed a "Teaching Hour" series to initiate networks for underrepresented and diverse faculty. Appalachian State University's (NC) Center for Academic Excellence (now Center for

Excellence in Teaching and Learning for Student Success) offered an "Academics for Black Survival and Wellness: The Rewind and Remix" to offer spaces for Black academics to focus on wellness and for non-Black academics "to honor the toll of racial trauma on Black people, resist anti-Blackness and white supremacy, and facilitate accountability and collective action."

Change or **Action Teams** are a growing model. In both cases, a small group of faculty, staff, and/or students meets to improve some aspect of the teaching and learning environment. One review of research on the impact of team-based professional development in higher education found that this approach could have positive effects on members' critical reflection about teaching, approaches to teaching, pedagogical knowledge, identity as a teacher, and sense of collegiality.[42] As one example, the University of Oregon's Teaching Engagement Program offered "Communities Accelerating the Impact of Teaching" to revise and test teaching evaluation instruments and dashboards. At Berkeley City College's Teaching and Learning Center, faculty participated in a Focused Inquiry Group to ask a teaching and learning-related research question, gather data, and make recommendations, and then in "Action Plan Projects for Learning Excellence" they acted on their plan. Finally, "Ideas to Action" at the Center for Teaching Excellence at the University of Kansas supported department teams to "explore questions, challenges, and opportunities in their programs and develop a vision for evidence-informed changes."

Across all of these models, a sizable proportion (41%) of CTLs offered one or more communities to foster dialogue and collaboration (i.e., one or more book groups, journal clubs, communities of practice, learning communities, teaching circles, faculty interest groups, affinity groups, or change or action teams). On average, among CTLs that offer such a program, there is a mean of four groups per center.

The 1,300+ topics of these groups were coded by CTL aim (see chapter 1). Of the CTLs that offered at least one community, teaching enhancement and DEI were the most frequently represented topics. This may be because individual transformation is most likely in environments that are fostered by communities that are based on respect, openness,

SQxP4dpk5P

Your order of August 12, 2024 (Order ID 113-0829319-4465052)

Qty.	Item	Item Price	Total
	Centers for Teaching and Learning: The New Landscape in Higher Education	$39.26	$39.26
	Wright, Mary C. --- Hardcover		
	1421447002		
	1421447002 9781421447001		

We've sent this part of your order to ensure quicker service. The other items will ship separately.

Subtotal		$39.26
Shipment Total		$39.26
Paid via credit/debit		$56.26

Return or replace your item
Visit Amazon.com/returns

QxP4dpk5P/-1 of 1-//LGA5-TWI/next-1dc/0/0812-23:00/0812-18:58

A2-30

challenge, empowerment, and trust.[43] Educational developers Leslie Ortquist-Ahrens and Roben Torosyan observed that professional learning communities "depend for their success on countering the individualism and alienation of the academy with a balancing spirit of appreciation for the collective, acceptance of others, support for all members' growth, and willingness to engage in genuine collaboration."[44]

Of CTLs offering a dialogue and collaboration community, moderate to small numbers align them around these key center aims:

- Teaching effectiveness and enhancement (34%)
- Diversity, equity, and inclusion (32%)
- Student learning (28%)
- Community building and collegiality (16%)
- Instructor outcome (most commonly faculty learning) (12%)
- Change and innovation (8%)
- Institutional mission (6%)
- Scholarly and creative work (6%)
- Culture (< 1%)

In addition to the nine primary CTL aims, other common topics include:

- Digital and online learning (20%)
- SoTL and evidence-based teaching (12%)
- Community engagement (7%)
- Assessment (7%)
- Service (< 1%)

(Percentages total more than 100% because many centers offered programs on multiple topics.)

The previous chapter noted that purpose statements that espouse certain aims—namely, student learning, change and innovation, culture, and community building—also tended to list "dialogue and collaboration" more frequently as a change strategy. (Additionally, although not most frequently identified, "dialogue and collaboration" was commonly employed alongside equity and inclusion aims.) Therefore, it is interesting that, in some ways, there is strong alignment in change strategies and change practice. A significant proportion of these groups did support student learning and equity and inclusion, as well as community-building goals. However, in other areas, there appeared to be misalignment, such as very few programs on culture and climate, or on change and innovation.

Resources

A decade ago, web-based resources were listed as one of the top three approaches used to provide services, although this approach did not rank especially high as an area directors wished to expand.[45] Web resources are characteristic of nearly all of the CTLs in this book (this being a website-based study), and many sites compile links to institutional policies, awards, and supports around teaching and learning. (At the time of writing, COVID-19 and teaching continuity resources continue to remain on many centers' pages.) However, centers also develop their own useful content. Rich examples include the University of Southern California's Center for Excellence in Teaching and its definition of excellence in teaching,[46] the University of Maryland's Teaching and Learning Transformation Center and its evidence-based model of effective courses,[47] and New Jersey's Montclair State University Office for Faculty Engagement and Advancement (now Office for Faculty Excellence), which compiled a list of teaching exercises around contemplative pedagogy.[48]

Podcasts are another resource developed by multiple CTLs. Recent examples include the *FIT to Teach* podcast (Florida Institute of Technology, Florida Tech Teaching Council), *Playing in the Sandbox: Conversations in Pedagogy* (Trinity University, Texas, Collaborative for Teaching and Learning), *Teaching Commons Podcast* (University of North Texas, Center for Learning, Experimentation, Application, and Research), *CFI Teaching Podcast* (James Madison University, Virginia, Center for Faculty Innovation), *Moving the Needle* (University of Maryland, Baltimore, Faculty Center for Teaching and Learning) and *Leading Lines* (Tennessee's Vanderbilt University Center for Teaching).

Finally, centers create tools and resources, which develop or synthesize knowledge about a subject. For example, in Massachusetts, Babson College's Center for Engaged Learning and Teaching developed and distributed business cases. Rice University's Center for Teaching Excellence in Texas developed two interactive web interfaces, including a course "Workload Estimator" based on research about the time it takes students to complete tasks related to reading and writing and to study for exams.

Hub Summary

In the previous chapter, we saw that nearly three-quarters of CTLs (70%) articulated a Hub strategy in their statement of purpose by indicating that they used at least one of the following change approaches: (1) promoting dialogue and collaboration, (2) playing a coordinating or centralizing role, and offering (3) centralized programs, or (4) campus resources. When analyzing the programs that CTLs offer, an even higher proportion (82%) list at least one Hub tactic: small-group program, dialogue community, course transformation initiative, and/or university-wide event. (Resources were not added to this calculation because every CTL in this study has a website.) A small group of CTLs (7%) present all four Hub tactics. In short, Hub strategies and tactics are by far the most frequently used change approaches by US Centers for Teaching and Learning.

By Carnegie classification, there are statistically significant differences by presence of at least one Hub tactic, with doctoral institutions listing them most commonly and other special focus contexts least frequently.[49] Larger CTLs and institutions show higher frequencies of deployment.[50] However, in every category, including "centers of one," over three-quarters of centers employ one or more Hub tactics. (There are no other statistically significant differences by institutional or CTL characteristic nor time of coding.)

Across most Carnegie types, short-term workshops are the most frequently used Hub tactic, ranging from 38% in other special focus institutions to 52% in baccalaureates. (The exception is doctoral institutions, for which dialogue and collaboration communities were most frequent at 54%.) Although CTLs continue to offer short-term workshops with frequency, longer-term Hub programs are also very prominent. Among centers offering any Hub program, a majority (69%) offer longer-term

Faculty Center for Teaching and Learning (FCTL) at the Community College of Philadelphia (PA)

FCTL illustrates a Hub role in both its mission and programs. Its statement of purpose suggests that a key goal is to promote "interdisciplinary exchange and collegiality." Girija Nagaswami, currently FCTL Facilitator, reflected, "Our intention is to bring faculty from across the College together." In 2020, the center offered an extensive array of professional learning opportunities: brief workshops, certificates, faculty learning communities, spring/fall professional development weeks, and a course design institute. (See below for an example of the programs captured in 2020.) Professional Learning Coordinator Stephanie Scordia noted, "It's very much a place for collegiality, for connecting faculty. . . . We say that the FCTL is the hub of professional learning at the College."

Sample Faculty Center for Teaching and Learning Programs, 2020

Faculty learning communities: Online Discussions Learning Community; Curriculum Design for the 21st Century Learner; Teaching Intensive and Accelerated Courses: Instruction that Motivates Learning; White Privilege and Its Role in Racism; Open Educational Resources: A Cost-Effective Alternative to Textbooks; Teaching Dual Enrollment Students; Trauma-Informed Teaching Circle

Certificates: Learning Certificates (5 sessions); Diversity Certificate (Bronze Certificate—4 training events; Silver Certificate—8 training events; Gold Certificate—12 training events, plus a diversity project and a capstone interview)

Series:
White Privilege Session 1: What Is White Privilege?
White Privilege Session 2: White Supremacy Culture
White Privilege Session 3: White Fragility
White Privilege Session 4: Liberatory Consciousness and Anti-racist Identity
That's the Human in You: Restorative Practices for Real Connections
    Introductory Session
That's the Human in You: Restorative Practices for Real Connections Session 2
That's the Human in You: Restorative Practices for Real Connections Session 3

Workshops:
Racism 101
Transgender 101
Race Talk Series: Macroaggressions and the Workplace—Creating Safe Spaces
    for Faculty of Color
Allyship 101
LGTBQ 101

I'm More than Just a Label: Clarifying Misconceptions about What It Means to
  Be Muslim
Latinx 101: The Latin American Diaspora in the United States
How To Have Courageous Conversations with Your Child: The Importance of
  Parental Diversity Dialogues
Race Talk: Black Rage and White Fragility: Creating a Path for Change
A Diverse City, Divided
The Impact of Philadelphia's Racial Residential Segregation in Our Classrooms
  and Beyond
Race Talk: Racial Trauma and the Student Experience
Call Out Culture and Tone Policing
Gun Violence in Philadelphia and the College Classroom
White Fragility 101
Open Educational Resources (OER) and EDI (Equity, Diversity, and Inclusion)

University-wide:
Fall/Spring PD Weeks

initiatives such as a course transformation initiative, courses, series, a
certificate, or a learning community. There is a significant research
basis behind longer-term program types, especially for promoting
change (whether of the individual, the course, or the organization),
making this an evidence-based strategy for CTLs.[51] In summary, CTLs
are wisely allocating resources to approaches that research suggests will
best help them serve their goals for enhancing our postsecondary
teaching and learning communities.

In enhancing CTL change strategies, there could be more alignment
with aims. While learning-related goals are most common among CTLs,
we will see in the next chapter that many centers have in their mandate
other important functions of our higher educational institutions. Although Hub strategies can also be used to advance non–teaching and
learning aims, fewer program offerings addressed these topics. For example, a small proportion of learning communities were focused on topics related to change and innovation, even though groups to promote
dialogue and collaboration are ideally positioned to help people understand the need for a change, customize an innovation to a campus, connect people with similar ideas, and create moral support to sustain an
initiative over time.[52]

Incubator

The Incubator function of CTLs focuses on growth and encouragement, whether of people or ideas. Within an Incubator strategy, key tactics are:

1. Consultative approaches to support individual reflection, including one-on-one meetings, observations, Small Group Instructional Diagnoses (SGIDs), open classroom initiatives, and student partnership–based programs
2. Orientations and new instructor programs
3. Mentoring initiatives
4. Grants
5. Direct academic support for students

(Another Incubator approach is career and leadership development, which is addressed in more detail in chapter 4.) On their websites, the vast majority (78%) of CTLs suggest that they use one or more of these approaches. This section explores in more detail the programs, services, and resources that CTLs with an Incubator strategy can employ.

Consultations and Observations

Individual consultations and observations are one of the oldest strategies in the CTL playbook, possibly because they can be so flexibly employed to co-identify solutions, offer technological resources, foster personal growth, or confront an instructor about discrepancies between goals and practice.[53] Centra's 1976 survey asked about at least six types of consultations, including use of "formal assessments by colleagues for teaching or course improvement (i.e., visitations or use of assessment form)" as well as "analysis of in-class video tapes to improve instruction."[54] A metanalysis of the approach finds that "use of consultative feedback as an effective teaching improvement strategy has received much empirical support."[55]

In Beach, Sorcinelli, Austin, and Rivard's study, consultations were the most frequently named approach used by community college CTLs, and they were second for all other US institutional types. The authors theorized that consultations are "efficient for busy faculty [and] . . . highly valued by developers and faculty for their confidential, relational, and focused nature."[56] Related services, such as "teaching observation and feedback with a trained consultant," peer observations of teaching, and Small Group Instructional Diagnoses were not reported to be as frequently offered, although "peer observation of teaching with feedback" was in the top three services that directors wished to expand.[57]

In chapter 2, only a small proportion (13%) of centers identified consultations in their statements of purpose, and even fewer (8%) indicated reflective approaches. These small aspirational proportions stand in contrast to the large proportion of centers that actually list some form of this tactic. According to program listings on CTL websites, almost half (44%) offer some form of consultation.

Comparing Carnegie types, doctoral institutions most frequently offered consultative services on their websites.[58] However, among all tactics in the Incubator toolkit, consultations and observations are the one offered most frequently by centers in doctoral (62%), master's (42%), other special focus (41%), and baccalaureate (40%) contexts. Because one-on-one approaches do not scale readily,[59] consultations are more easily accomplished in CTLs with more staff or resources, and MSI status and smaller organization size are associated with less frequency.[60] Numerous centers offered consultations on online courses and programs; indeed, consultations were more frequent at CTLs that had digital staff compared to those that did not.[61] There are no other statistically significant differences by CTL or institution characteristic nor time of coding.

Consultations involve a one-on-one meeting, often, but not exclusively, around a teaching issue (e.g., syllabus design, challenges to authority, student course feedback). This is the most frequently offered reflective approach, highlighted by a third (33%) of centers. While research on consultations finds them effective for issues related to teaching and learning, such as improving student course feedback, this service is extremely flexible and able to adapt not only to the issue brought by the instructor but also to the mission of the center.[62] For example, the Center for Innovation in Research and Teaching at Grand Canyon

University (CO) offered research consultations to assist with research proposals, methodology, or data analysis, while the Faculty Development Center at University of Maryland, Baltimore County spotlighted opportunities to discuss writing, communication, career development, and SoTL. The Center for Teaching and Learning at California State University, Sacramento advertised consultations on Open Educational Resources, and in Vermont, the Middlebury College Center for Teaching, Learning and Research highlighted digital liberal arts.

Blurring an Incubator and Hub approach, consultations are also used by centers for organizational development. Jonathan Torres, the current director of Quinnipiac University's (CT) Center for Teaching and Learning notes, "Individual and departmental consultations are the primary methods of engagement for the CTL. I help deans/chairs with curriculum mapping, faculty with instructional design, and I work with each school to create 'faculty development days' specific to their disciplines and fields."

Observations invite an educational developer or trained faculty or student into a class to observe classroom dynamics.[63] This type of service typically involves at least two consultations: first, before the observation to establish trust, logistics of the observation, and focal questions, and second, after the observation, to debrief notes or a recording. Generally, the addition of observational data into a consultation carries more benefits than a consultation alone because it offers a "better picture of teaching behaviors to be discussed in the consultation session."[64] In 2020, 14% of CTLs offered observations specifically, while an additional 3% of centers publicized **peer observation training**, or development of standards for instructors to do this work on their own with colleagues.

Even though observations are promoted by a small proportion of CTLs, there are a wide array of approaches listed. Three CTLs advertised a very structured approach, training their staff in use of the COPUS (Classroom Observation Protocol for Undergraduate STEM).[65] Other centers promoted formative peer observations, such as Dartmouth Center for the Advancement of Learning's (NH) funding for faculty to have lunch while they discuss reciprocal observations. Several CTLs offered geometric versions of this program depending on the number of instructors involved, such as Iowa's Kirkwood Community College Center for Excellence in Learning and Teaching's teaching squares and triangles. In California, Stanford University's Center for Teaching and Learning offered a "Teaching Practice Adventure" that formed small groups to engage in mutual observations and to develop a plan for incorporating the teaching strategy into their own course. Finally, the Center for Teaching at Sewanee: The University of the South (TN) employed its "Back to School" grants to fund faculty to audit a colleague's course with goals to "increase awareness of the learner's experience, to enhance reflection on teaching through engagement in a colleague's classroom, and to develop new skills and interests that could complement one's professional development."[66] Many CTLs take the stance that their observations are for formative purposes only.

First developed at the University of Washington's CTL in the early 1980s, **Small Group Instructional Diagnoses (SGIDs)** bring together consultations, observations, and formative student feedback collected through guided discussion.[67] (Other common names for similar approaches include Midterm Student Feedback or Quick Course Diagnoses.) A study in one doctoral university involving random assignment to treatments found that the SGID method produces the greatest benefits in terms of gains on course feedback and reported changes to teaching practice, compared to video feedback or consultation alone.[68] Another study of a learner-centered SGID (LC-SGID), which asks students to reflect on their contributions to the learning process, demonstrated gains in students' enthusiasm, motivation to succeed, and perceptions of interactions with classmates.[69] Educational development research in a Canadian context suggests that early feedback works so well because it aligns with principles for good practice in higher education, such as communicating high expectations and developing environments that foster reciprocity and cooperation.[70] Yet, perhaps because of time involved in implementing SGIDs or LC-SGIDs, they were relatively infrequently highlighted and observed on only 11% of center sites.

Open classrooms are a growing approach to promoting reflection and sharing in teaching. Almost 1 in 10 CTLs (9%) offered such an initiative. Emergent in the mid-2000s, these events are designed to encourage peer observations at scale. Faculty volunteers agree to have visitors in their classrooms for a day, allowing other instructors the opportunity to gain a window into their teaching. As one example, San Francisco State University (CA) Center for Equity and Excellence in Teaching and Learning's open classroom program was titled "Teaching as a Spectator Sport," culminating in an ice cream social.

Another new initiative, although still listed by very few centers (4%), is the **Students as Learners and Teachers (SaLT)** or **Students Consulting on Teaching (SCoT)** models. The former was developed at Bryn Mawr College's Teaching and Learning Institute in 2006 to engage students as pedagogical partners. Student consultants visit their faculty partner's classroom weekly and meet to discuss what they observed. As Alison Cook-Sather, the director of this CTL, explains, SaLT creates a "liminal space" for faculty and students to build community and "aims to change the culture on campus to one in which dialogue about teaching and learning among faculty and students is a common, desired, and desirable practice."[71] In contrast with SaLT, which is an ongoing relationship, the SCoT program works with students in shorter-term roles. Developed in 1992 at Brigham Young University's Center for Teaching and Learning, ScoT offers multiple possibilities for the student consultant role, including notetaker (as if the student were in the class), observer, or SGID facilitator.[72] In many ways, this approach doubles down on an Incubator change strategy by supporting the pedagogical development of both faculty and students. Students gain interpersonal skills, learn to give constructive feedback, and develop empathy for the work of their instructors.

Orientations

In two previous surveys of educational developers, new faculty orientation and development was identified by CTL directors as the leading "issue" their unit needed to address.[73] Fast-forward to 2020, only 10% of CTLs described a mentoring or orienting strategy in their statements of purpose, but nearly half (43%) listed at least one orienting program. A large CTL at a public, doctoral university is most likely to highlight this tactic when compared to centers of other sizes, Carnegie types, or control contexts.[74] However, considering all Incubator tactics, the orientation is the most frequent one employed by CTLs at associate's colleges (36%).

Ideally held before the commencement of teaching, **orientations and new instructor programs** provide a socialization experience to the institution. Although the literature on the effectiveness of such programs is limited, Ann Stes, Liesje Coertjens, and Peter Van Petegem demonstrated a small impact of a yearlong program for new faculty on student-focused approaches to teaching.[75] Other literature has established organizational impacts from such programs. A study of the University of Michigan–Ann Arbor's Center for Research on Learning and Teaching's yearlong academy for new faculty used a quasi-experimental design to establish its impact on student reports of their experience of the course and continued engagement with the CTL.[76]

A sizable proportion of CTLs (39%) offered a new instructor orientation event, but some smaller colleges took a more personalized approach. For example, California's Art College of Design's website indicated that the director of the Office of Faculty Development meets with each new instructor. Similarly, the site at Wisconsin's Saint Norbert College Office of Faculty Development highlighted that the director meets with all job candidates and attends the teaching demonstration to begin assessing strengths and growth areas for each instructor.

For those with a new faculty orientation, agendas suggest that events typically focus on the teaching and research responsibilities of new instructors as well as procedurals (e.g., benefits and parking). However, development of community and a sense of belonging in the institution are also clear goals at many institutions. For example, the Biggio Center for the Enhancement of Teaching and Learning at Auburn University (AL) sponsored a new faculty run/walk, and the faculty working with the Edward D. Smith Center for Teaching and Learning at Brigham Young University–Hawaii participated in a tour of the area "to help faculty gain an 'assurance that God has had his hand over this entire valley' by visiting some of the sacred spiritual places in our community and becoming familiar with its people and culture."[77]

Among the 270 CTLs that listed a duration of their new faculty program, the most frequent length was more than a week (39%). The next most common length was one day (21%). Duration varies by institutional type, depending on teaching focus. At baccalaureates (67%), associate's (51%), and master's institutions (34%), initiatives that are longer than one week are most common. However, at doctoral institutions, one day is most frequently noted (32%), and at medical / health-focused CTLs, the most common format is less than a day (46%).

An orientation might be planned over a six-year time span at some liberal arts colleges. One example includes Pennsylvania's Bucknell University Teaching and Learning Center, which offered a "New(ish) Faculty Learning Series," open to instructors in their second to fourth years. While less frequent, there are also examples of more extensive programs at research universities. Oregon State University's Center for Teaching and Learning offered a three-year certificate program, "New2OSU," which provides a great deal of flexibility in terms of modality of engagement. Year one includes "Tuesday Teaching + Tech Talks" (face-to-face or online/synchronous), year two involves an LMS Academy (online/asynchronous), year three engages participants in mutual mentoring (flipped hybrid), and the capstone is a teaching ePortfolio.

In Beach, Sorcinelli, Austin, and Rivard's 2016 study, "new faculty orientation/development" was named as a top issue, but orientation and support for part-time, adjunct, or fixed-term faculty ranked among the lower priorities.[78] Although it could be the case that all faculty are welcome at a centralized orientation, 73 centers (6%) publicized a customized orientation for adjuncts or part-time faculty. For CTLs that noted any specialized programs for adjuncts, new faculty orientations were the most common approach.

For graduate students or residents, 80 CTLs (7%)—nearly all at doctoral universities—indicated they offered a new graduate teaching assistant (GTA) orientation.[79] The goals of GTA orientations are typically to provide new instructors with concrete teaching skills, prepare them for classroom management issues, introduce policies and campus resources, encourage engagement in additional professional development, and provide tools for grading, lecturing, and facilitating discussions.[80] They are generally brief, but one study of two Canadian universities' GTA orientations suggested that they could still effectively achieve affective outcomes such as increasing confidence when performing GTA responsibilities and heightening a sense of preparedness for teaching.[81] In 2020, one day was the most common (52%) duration for new graduate teaching assistant orientations (perhaps because courses or certificate programs were more common for graduate student offerings), but at the time of this writing, many graduate student orientations are being offered asynchronously online.

Recognizing the role that undergraduates play at many institutions as teachers or curricular peer mentors (e.g., undergraduate teaching assistants, peer learning assistants, tutors), 12 institutions offered undergraduate preparation programs. Four also indicated that they lead orientation programs for incoming undergraduate or graduate students, which focus on academic adjustment more generally.

Although infrequent, some CTLs offer orientations for staff in addition to faculty. These included New Mexico Highlands University (Center for Teaching Excellence), Kirkwood Community College (Center for Excellence in Learning and Teaching, Iowa), The University of Texas at El Paso (Center for Faculty Leadership and Development), and SUNY at Fredonia (Professional Development Center). Morehead State University's (KY) Faculty Center for Teaching and Learning offered a new faculty and staff regional tour. Although some CTLs offer customized programs for postdoctoral scholars, I was not able to find any examples of teaching orientation programs tailored to this constituency.

Mentoring

Generally, postsecondary formal mentoring programs are offered most frequently for undergraduates, compared to other constituencies in higher education.[82] However, CTL data suggest opposite patterns. In 2020, about a quarter (23%) of centers offered mentoring programs, most frequently for faculty. This tactic was most common at medical / health-focused CTLs and least common at centers in other special focus contexts.[83] In fact, among all Incubator tactics, mentoring is the one most frequently offered by centers located in medical/health contexts (35%). Medium-sized (2–3 individuals) and larger CTLs (7+ personnel), as well as centers at larger institutions, also describe mentoring tactics more frequently.[84] There are no other statistically significant differences by CTL or institutional characteristic nor time of coding.

Recent models of faculty mentoring suggest that group and networked approaches are effective ways to support faculty thriving, and CTLs are well-positioned to support these types of programs. The Mutual Mentoring Initiative, developed at the University of Massachusetts Amherst's Center for Teaching and Learning, offers small grants to faculty for proposals to develop mentoring teams, including themes such as "Supporting Women of Color through Tenure and Beyond," a group of academic mothers, and mentoring teaching in physics. Their assessment data show gains in the perception of the value of mentoring as well as outcomes such as publications.[85]

Other examples include Iowa State University's Center for Excellence in Learning and Teaching (CELT), which used its Teaching Partners Program to supplement department mentoring by pairing a new instructor and an experienced instructor to visit each other's classrooms and attend a CELT event together. Other supportive roles that CTLs play include review of department mentoring plans, a service provided by the Medical University of South Carolina's Faculty Development Program. Several centers organized mentoring programs for lecturers or adjuncts, including University of Nevada, Las Vegas (Faculty Center), Bristol Community College (Lash Center for Teaching and Learning, Rhode Island), Leeward Community College (Innovation Center for Teaching and Learning, Hawaii), Middlesex County College (Center for the Enrichment of Learning and Teaching, New Jersey), and Shippensburg University of Pennsylvania (Center for Faculty Excellence in Scholarship and Teaching).

For graduate students, research suggests that there are numerous benefits of effective mentoring, including self-efficacy and degree completion.[86] In 2011, Laura Schram (now Director of Professional Development and Engagement at the University of Michigan's graduate school) and I identified 46 graduate student development mentorship programs, defined as "those that cultivate faculty-graduate student relationships around teaching and foster professional development beyond the functional requirements of supporting a teaching assistant role."[87] However, in 2020, only a few CTLs used their websites to showcase programs to coordinate graduate student mentorships. One exception is Notre Dame's Kaneb Center in Indiana, which offered the Graduate Student Teaching Apprenticeship Program to support a mentored advanced teaching experience in the department. Another example is the CUNY Graduate School and University Teaching and Learning Center, which offered a program to place doctoral students at LaGuardia Community College.

Instead, the mentoring initiatives of most CTLs focused on supporting faculty to become better mentors of students. Examples of this emphasis include the University of California, Berkeley's Graduate Student Instructor (GSI) Teaching and Resource Center's Annual Faculty Seminar on Teaching with GSIs, a one-day program that addressed issues such as strategies for mentoring and collaborating with graduate students. In the District of Columbia, Georgetown University Medical Center's Teaching Resources sponsored an interesting program that accomplishes both aims. *Cura Personalis* Fellows meet over four years to engage in physician professional identity formation and serve as coaches to a cohort of 10 first-year medical students. For undergraduates, there are limited examples, but one was the Faculty Mentoring Program at California State University, San Marcos's Faculty Center, which served first-generation and economically disadvantaged students.

Grants

Teaching grants, especially when they are paired with teaching and learning center staff support to carry out the grant project, are valuable for helping faculty develop new teaching skills and expertise. As part of an Incubator strategy, grants support individual growth, but they can also have a structural impact by catalyzing course-level and institutional initiatives. One interesting evaluation study of a small-grant program at a Canadian university noted how this tactic can have institutional impacts, documenting "ripple effects" and the connection between projects and institutional strategic plans.[88]

In their aspirational strategies, a very small fraction (5%) of CTLs point to grants. In contrast, over a quarter (29%) of CTL websites indicated that they coordinate at least one grant program through the center. (Grant programs offered by other campus units but listed on a CTL website were not factored into this analysis.) Doctoral universities offer grants most frequently, and CTLs in medical and health science contexts promoted them the least.[89] Organizational characteristics also matter: older and larger institutions have higher prevalence of this tactic.[90] There were no other significant differences by institutional characteristic nor time.

There was a wide range of focus for these financial incentives, including the Beckman Humor Grant at the University of Portland's (OR) Teaching and Learning Hub to "harness the power of humor to transform the world" and $10,000 for a faculty member at Art Center College of Design (CA) Office of Faculty Development to create work related to Taiwan.[91] However, grants typically were allocated to seven main purposes. (The sum of these proportions is more than 100% because many CTLs had multiple grants and a grant could have multiple aims.) Among the 313 CTLs that had incentives that could be identified, the most frequent focus is one that is *teaching and learning–related* (55%). These projects ranged from large course redesign to engagement in institutional strategic priorities. In particular, the creation of open educational resources (OER) was incentivized by 17 programs.

Faculty professional learning was a focus for 31% of centers, including funding for conference travel or professional development. *Research, scholarly, and creative work* was incentivized by 26%, with an additional 10% focused on *SoTL*. The fourth most frequent category was *innovation-related grants* (18%), and *technology-related initiatives* were targeted by an additional 8%. *Diversity, equity, and inclusion–related activities* were addressed by 5% of programs. *Community building* was the ambition of 5% of all grants, and *assessment-focused incentives* made up 4%. *Community engagement* was the focus of only 3% of grants.

Interesting examples of CTL grants in these categories included:

- A. T. Still University of Health Sciences (MO) Teaching and Learning Center hosted a "Spark Tank" event allowing a team ten minutes to pitch its idea to support the university's "mission as a learning-centered institution preparing highly competent healthcare professionals through innovative teaching and learning practices and activities."[92]
- Grinnell College (IA) Center for Teaching, Learning and Assessment's Innovation Fund was open to faculty, staff, and students and supported ideas for new approaches to teaching and scholarship or that bring innovations to campus life and learning.
- University of California, Los Angeles Center for the Advancement of Teaching managed the Provost's Grants to Increase Access and Reduce Disparities. This program funded research and interventions to close demographic disparities in time-to-degree and graduation rates, with both planning grants and "Get It Done Quick" grants.
- The "Work Culture" grant at Augsburg University (MN) Center for Teaching and Learning awarded $250 to encourage the creation of learning communities, working groups, and other collaborative efforts among faculty and staff.
- Berkeley City College (CA) Teaching and Learning Center awarded several small grants, ranging from $200 to $400, to incentivize engagement in dialogue and collaboration–related groups, such as a lesson study group, a faculty interest group, or a pedagogy for equity reading group.
- Muhlenberg College (PA) Center for Teaching and Learning funded small groups to work on projects that would enhance teaching and learning on its campus.

Among the 163 centers that listed monetary amounts, the range of possible funding spanned from $100 to $95,000. Based on data about the highest amount available in each center's grant portfolio, the median amount of grant funding was $3,000. Smaller amounts were typically allocated to funding of learning communities, while larger sums generally supported technology-related innovations.

Direct Academic Support

Over half of centers have the word *learning* in their names. Although faculty development impacts student learning, this is a tertiary effect, moving from the achieved outcomes of the educational development program, to implementation of ideas in the classroom, and finally, to fostering intended student learning outcomes.[93] Therefore, it was interesting that only a small minority (3%) of CTLs suggest direct student support as a change strategy in their statements of purpose, which would tighten the link between interventions and student learning outcomes. Reflecting on CTL program offerings, double the proportion (6%) made public this tactic. A direct student support approach was most common at CTLs in baccalaureates.[94] CTL organization type is also related to this tactic, with larger units more frequently offering these programs, which makes sense because specialized staff are often needed (e.g., writing center directors, learning assistant coordinators) to do the work effectively.[95] There are no other statistically significant differences by CTL or institutional characteristic nor time.

On an organizational level, direct student support integrates units, involving centers within centers. While this approach is discussed in more detail in chapter 4, examples include Florida Atlantic University's Center for Teaching and Learning, which housed a math learning center, writing center, speaking center, supplemental instruction, and the Office for Undergraduate Research and Inquiry. The University of Dayton's (OH) Ryan C. Harris Learning Teaching Center combined Academic Coaching, Tutoring, WritePlace (a writing center), Supplemental Instruction, Disability Services, and a first-year transition program. While tutoring, writing, and undergraduate research are the most frequently integrated units, other examples include multilingual learning, undergraduate research, fellowship advising, intergroup dialogue, first-year experience, makerspaces, technology support, financial advising, and TRIO (federal educational opportunity outreach programs).

This is also a fluid space for CTLs. For example, in 2020, the University of Washington Bothell Campus's Teaching and Learning Center housed the Writing and Communication Center, the Quantitative Skills Center, the Office of Community-Based Learning and Research, and Global Initiatives (study abroad advising). Since I visited the website, the Writing and Communication Center and the Quantitative Skills Center were relocated to the Office of Student Academic Success, and the other units were included in the Office of Connected Learning. A close reader will note a few other similar changes in the notes for other chapters.

Although many CTLs are administrative units, some centers offer curricular or co-curricular programs. The University of Connecticut's Center for Excellence in Teaching and Learning managed the Catalyst Learning Community, a three-term, nonresidential learning community for second-year students, and Benedictine University's (IL) Center for Teaching and Learning Excellence directed the Emerging Scholars Learning Community Program. Cameron University's (OK) Office of Teaching and Learning offered student success courses as well as two degrees: an AS and a BS in interdisciplinary studies.

There are limited cases of CTLs offering direct academic support for graduate students. Examples, however, primarily address multilingual learning. For instance, the Georgia Institute of Technology's Center for Teaching and Learning offered three courses for international graduate students: Academic Writing, Oral Communication, and Presentation Skills.

Incubator Summary

Over a third of CTLs (37%) espoused an Incubator strategy in their statements of purpose, but over two-thirds (78%) listed at least one Incubator tactic and over half (56%) offered multiple approaches. As a suite of tactics, an Incubator approach is characterized by one or more of the following: (1) consultative services to promote reflection, (2) orienting programs, (3) mentoring initiatives, (4) grants, and (5) direct student support. In statements of purpose, Incubator strategies are somewhat more common at master's and baccalaureate institutions. Analyzed as CTL tactics, or the actual programs and services that centers listed, Incubator approaches are much more common at doctoral universities and medical/health contexts compared to other institutional types—but even so, the vast majority of centers at every institutional type used an Incubator tactic.[96] Size also has an impact, with larger institutions and CTLs showing more use of these tactics.[97] Interestingly, CTLs with digital staff also show a higher presence of this tactical type.[98] There are no other statistically significant differences by institutional or CTL characteristic nor time of coding.

Among the individual tactics in the Incubator repertoire, the oldest educational development approaches continue to be used the most: consultative services designed to promote reflective growth (44%) and orientations (43%). Grants (29%) or mentoring programs (23%) factor into the work of about a quarter of centers. Direct student academic support is offered least frequently (6%).

For orientations, most are of longer duration, usually a week or more. While orientations most frequently serve new faculty, many institutions also recognize the range of constituencies who contribute to the teaching mission, with many examples of customized programs for adjuncts, graduate students, and undergraduate teachers. This is also the most frequent Incubator tactic offered by centers at associate's colleges (and it is a very close second for those at doctoral institutions).

Mentoring is the most frequent Incubator tactic offered by centers located in medical and health contexts. Most frequently, CTLs offered mentoring to faculty constituencies. New models of faculty mentoring use group and networked approaches.

Consultations and observations are the most frequent Incubator tactics offered by centers at other special focus, baccalaureate, master's, and doctoral contexts. Consultations and observations are a long-standing service in the field of educational development with roots in individual conversation to promote growth. However, there are new models of this approach, such as the use of student consultants to invigorate and scale the tactic.

Temple: Recognition and Reward

Temple strategies elevate the value of teaching, learning, and educational development. Chapter 2 suggested that Temple was the least-used change strategy, with fewer than one in five (19%) CTLs articulating it in their statement of purpose. However, a greater proportion (27%) apply a Temple approach by using at least one tactic, and 5% utilize multiple approaches. Temple-focused tactics include:

1. Opportunities for recognition and reward, such as teaching awards, recognition-focused approaches, and teaching academies
2. Advocacy-focused approaches

An emphasis on symbolic and physical space is another prong of a Temple strategy named by a small percentage of CTLs. However, space is not tallied as a tactic here because it is difficult to operationalize how this is actively employed. Most center sites reference a physical space, but in 2020, online spaces became more salient, and all of the CTLs in this study had a web presence.

Recognition and Reward

A small proportion (13%) of centers named recognition and reward-related change strategies in their statements of purpose. A slightly higher proportion (18%) listed tactics such as teaching awards, teaching academies, and non-evaluative approaches to recognize the value of teaching. While teaching awards are most common, CTLs are also exploring ways to develop recognition-rich environments through non-evaluative initiatives.

Teaching Awards

The most frequent tactic used in a recognition approach is awards. First initiated in 1930 at the University of Chicago with some controversy, teaching awards became more common in the 1960s.[99] Teaching awards can be offered at a number of institutional locations; therefore, the awards that appeared on a CTL's website as coordinated or sponsored by

In January 2021, I spoke to Dr. Carolyn Meltzer, then executive associate dean at Emory University Medical School's (GA) **Office of Faculty Academic Advancement, Leadership and Inclusion** (OFAALI). This unit was founded in 2019 and originated from a dean's request to Dr. Meltzer (then an associate dean for research) to rethink the School of Medicine's faculty affairs unit. OFAALI originated to focus on four pillars of practice—faculty affairs, professional and leadership development, DEI, and wellness—and at the time, its vision included being "a place where faculty feel valued and empowered to engage in the [School of Medicine] journey from excellence to eminence." Although the OFAALI featured all four of the change strategies named in this book, as its vision suggests, it has a strong Temple orientation to its work. In addition to an academy, OFAALI offered several awards (e.g., distinguished services, mentoring, diversity and inclusion, innovation) and opportunities for broader recognition (e.g., Educator Appreciation Day, Research Appreciation Day)—some of which predate the founding of the office. It also had a strong advocacy orientation by making its own work visible in an annual report, but particularly in its leadership around promotion guidelines to support academic success of all faculty. Spearheaded by the associate dean for faculty affairs and professional development, all faculty are now tenure-eligible through flexible tracks. For example, these guidelines established a new path at the associate professor level for faculty who contributed extensively to institutional mission.

In 2021, the unit split to an Office of Equity and Inclusion and an **Office of Faculty Academic Affairs and Professional Development** after Dr. Meltzer took a position at another university. The current focus of the Office of Faculty Academic Affairs and Professional Development is on providing professional development in teaching, research, patient care, and leadership, as well as handling appointments and promotions. The unit is currently led by Dr. Kathy Griendling, R. Wayne Alexander Professor of Medicine and Executive Associate Dean for Faculty Affairs and Professional Development in the School of Medicine.

the center give some sense of the degree to which it promotes this approach.

A relatively small proportion (15%) of CTLs coordinate or sponsor one or more awards. Of these, the most frequent constituency of the awardee is faculty:

- 93% of CTLs giving awards have one or more for faculty.
- 17% have a specific award for adjunct, lecturer, or non-tenure-track faculty.

- 13% make the award to a graduate student.
- 4% designate an academic unit, such as a department, as the awardee.
- 3% recognize undergraduate instructors.
- 3% make awards to staff.

For the focus of the award, not surprisingly, *teaching* is the most frequent emphasis (79%). Examples of the breadth of this category included "Green Teacher of the Year," awarded by American University's (DC) Center for Teaching, Research and Learning for commitment to sustainable teaching, as well as Eastern Michigan University's Bruce K. Nelson Faculty Development Center's "Liggit Family and Friends Teaching and Learning Partnership Scholarship," which celebrated an instructor-student pair who exemplified an effective teaching and learning partnership. For graduate students, the University of California, Berkeley's Graduate Student Instructor (GSI) Teaching and Resource Center offered a "Teaching Effectiveness Award for GSIs" based on review of a one-page essay that honored GSIs who devised solutions to teaching or learning problems they identified in their classes.

There were other categories of awards as well:

- 17% of centers had an award focused on innovation.
  Florida Agricultural and Mechanical University's Teaching and Learning Center offered the Teaching Innovation Award, which recognized faculty who explored new ways of teaching critical thinking and who demonstrated "quantifiable gains" in student learning outcomes.
- 14% honored teaching with technology.
  University of Florida's Center for Teaching Excellence offered Exemplary Online Awards for courses that had 80% or more of their content online.
- 13% addressed achievements in advising or mentoring.
  For example, the University of California, Berkeley's Graduate Student Instructor Teaching and Resource Center offered a Faculty Award for Outstanding Mentorship of Graduate Student Instructors.

- 10% made an award for research, and an additional 9% focused on SoTL specifically.
  The University of Texas Health Science Center at Houston's Center for Teaching and Learning offered three Dean's Excellence Awards in the Scholarship of Application, the Scholarship of Integration, and the Scholarship of Teaching.
- 9% focused on service or contributions to the institutional mission.
  Shaw University's (NC) Professional Development offered an Excellence in Academic Service Award to staff.
- 6% honored work in community engagement or service learning.
  Indiana University Bloomington's Center for Innovative Teaching and Learning offered the Excellence in Community-Engaged Learning Student Award, a Community-Engaged Learning Partnership Award, and the ACE Award for Exceptional Facilitation of Community-Engaged Learning.
- 4% made awards for work in diversity, equity, and inclusion.
  Georgia State University's Center for Excellence in Teaching and Learning (now Center for Excellence in Teaching, Learning, and Online Education) offered a Teaching for Social Justice and Democracy Award that celebrates instructors who integrate social justice into their courses.
- 3% promoted work in assessment.
  North Dakota State University–Main Campus Office of Teaching and Learning sponsored an award for Excellence in Course Assessment (individual) and Excellence in Program Assessment (department).
- 3% made awards for contributions to professional learning of others.
  Through the Santos Innovation Award, the Center for Faculty Innovation at James Madison University recognized a faculty member who enriched the impact of the center's mission.
- 2% focused on contributions to community building.
  Examples included the James D. Clowes Award for the Advancement of Learning Communities, at the University of Washington's Center for Teaching and Learning.

In short, although awards most frequently were used to recognize contributions to teaching, there were a wide variety of approaches to spotlight other aims, such as innovation and research.

Teaching Academies

Another form of recognition, most common in the health sciences context, is the teaching academy, which was initiated in 2001 at medical schools at Harvard University and the University of California, San Francisco. A teaching academy is generally defined as "a formal organization of academic teaching faculty who have been formally (or specifically) recognized for excellence in their contributions to the education mission of the medical school, and who serve specific functions on behalf of the institution."[100] A 2010 article found 36 academies at US medical schools, while a 2012–13 survey identified 53.[101] Most frequently, faculty are selected based on letters of recommendation, application forms, CVs, and, sometimes, teaching portfolios. Although teaching academies, like awards, can be selective, one study found that a majority (69%) are criterion based. Top stated goals included stimulating educational innovation, developing faculty education skills, and providing mentoring. Teaching academy activities frequently include faculty development opportunities, networking, and mentoring.[102]

Outside of the health and medical education context, "academy" can be a relatively elastic title used to signal a longer-term program. Therefore, for the purposes of this analysis, I identified only programs that aligned with the definition presented in Charlene Dewey's seminal article about teaching academies, that is, having some selection or recognition process.[103] (For example, a "New Faculty Academy" that serves as an orientation program for all new instructors would not be considered an academy.) Using this definition, a small proportion (5%) of centers offered an academy, with nearly all in health sciences or medical schools.

Examples include the Teaching Academy at Morehouse School of Medicine's (GA) Office of Faculty Affairs and Development. Among other benefits, this academy offered "rewards for faculty who meet guidelines for excellence in teaching."[104] Similarly, the Georgetown University

Medical Center (DC) Office of Faculty and Academic Affairs indicated that the core purposes of its academy "are to nurture, recognize and reward excellent teaching at GUMC; to engage our faculty educator in ongoing professional development; and to foster educational excellent [*sic*] and scholarship in health sciences education."[105] Health science schools other than medical schools also offered academies. For example, the Washington State University College of Veterinary Medicine offered brown bag discussions, faculty development workshops, guest speakers, and a "teaching tool kit" series as part of its academy.

Although most examples of teaching academies are found in health sciences institutions, there were several illustrations of the program type outside of this context. Sinclair Community College (OH) Center for Teaching and Learning hosted a "Sinclair Teaching Excellence Academy." Only teaching award winners were eligible, and members committed to seven three-hour meetings to discuss topics such as teaching philosophies and theory. Michigan State University's Academic Advancement Network organized the "Walter and Pauline Adams Academy of Instructional Excellence and Innovation," which met monthly to discuss readings about educational theory and practice and asked participants to write a paper or make a presentation on a teaching-related topic. Twelve participants were selected based on evidence of teaching excellence (cover letter, CV, teaching philosophy, letter of support from a chair or dean). Although nearly all programs were oriented to faculty, Virginia Tech's Center for Excellence in Teaching and Learning held an "Academy for Graduate Teaching Excellence." While the first level (member) was open to all graduate students, the highest level (fellow) was more selective, requiring a letter of application, CV, letter of recommendation, and teaching portfolio.

Recognition

While teaching awards are most typically selective, newer non-evaluative programs in the CTL repertoire emphasize faculty innovations through events and initiatives. These include more invitational approaches to recognize a large number of instructors. A recognition-based program was offered by 53 CTLs (4%).

One example of this approach is the "Thank-a-Prof" initiatives offered at several institutions, which collect positive notes from students. Georgia Highlands College's Center for Excellence in Teaching and Learning offered a riff on this idea with its "Thank an Advisor" program, which invited students to send 150-word notes beginning with "Thank you for ————." Lansing Community College's (MI) Center for Teaching Excellence offered a Faculty Appreciation Day to recognize faculty contributions.

A final example is the Center for Faculty Excellence at Texas Woman's University, which organized a STAR (Students for Teaching and Assignment Recognition) Symposium. The center asked students to nominate instructors and graduate teaching assistants based on effective assignment design. Out of the over 100 nominations, 40 instructors were randomly selected to share their student-nominated assignments at a poster fair that was disseminated with the broader community.

Advocacy

In their statements of purpose, a small proportion of CTLs (2%) noted advocacy as a change approach. It was difficult to conceptualize how one might measure the full range of center initiatives related to advocacy. However, if considering advocacy for educational development and the center's work, there is one possible artifact: the annual report. In annual reports, centers often described their activities, people involved, and evaluation data. The genre spotlights the work of the center. Although CTL annual reports will be addressed in more depth in chapter 5, it is worth noting here that a small proportion—fewer than 1 in 10—of centers highlighted such a document on their websites.

Temple Summary

Over a quarter of CTLs (27%) describe one or more Temple-focused tactics. These are listed most frequently at CTLs in medical/health contexts and least frequently at associate's.[106] Additionally, CTLs at PWIs feature these tactics at a slightly higher frequency compared to those at MSIs.[107] It may be that CTLs in these institutional contexts are trying to carve out recognition systems where formal institutional rewards for teaching are not as abundant as in other higher education locations.

Institutional and CTL size are statistically significant, with larger organizations applying the tactic more frequently.[108] The anonymity of a larger institution, where faculty, staff, and students have less day-to-day familiarity because of scale, may make a recognition-focused tactic more attractive. There are no other statistically significant differences by institutional or CTL characteristic nor time of coding.

At centers in medical/health contexts, academies are the most frequently employed Temple tactic (44%). However, the Temple approach most frequently used by CTLs at all other Carnegie types is awards, primarily focused on teaching (doctoral: 24%, other special focus: 21%, master's: 11%, associate's: 10%, and baccalaureate: 9%). While CTL awards most frequently celebrate faculty and their teaching achievements specifically, there may be a growing movement to recognize other constituencies (e.g., departments or undergraduates-as-teachers) and activities. An encouraging development in this area includes initiatives to offer gratitude and recognition even more broadly by attempts to create recognition-rich environments.

Sieve: Evidence and Expertise

A Sieve strategy emphasizes standards, expertise, and evidence-based practices. This is the second most common change strategy, with 40% of CTLs describing this approach in their statements of purpose. Sieve approaches are most frequently co-located in CTL purpose statements that espouse diversity, equity, and inclusion aims. Moving to tactics, Sieve is also applied frequently, with about the same proportion promoting at least one approach (table 3.2). (Far fewer [10%] CTLs applied multiple tactics.)

While other CTL strategies may focus on being as invitational and "big tent" as possible, a Sieve strategy recognizes that there are times to take a more curational approach. As operationalized here, key Sieve-related tactics include:

1. Promoting the Scholarship of Teaching and Learning (SoTL)
2. Engaging in quality assurance processes
3. Doing research
4. Contributing to policies and standards
5. Conducting assessment and evaluation

Tactics 1–4 are described in this chapter, while assessment and evaluation is an integrative emphasis that is elaborated in chapter 4.

Scholarship of Teaching and Learning (SoTL)

In the previous sections, other change strategies have addressed SoTL, which involves making public an inquiry about student learning.[109] Felten and Chick convincingly argue that SoTL is the signature pedagogy of educational development, noting that, like CTL work, "SoTL's ultimate aim is enhanced student learning, with a proximate focus on faculty as inquirers and learners." In this conception, SoTL is an important tactic to promote culture change, or "to cultivate a generative culture of learning and teaching at our institutions and throughout higher education."[110]

The University of Denver's Office of Teaching and Learning (OTL)

OTL was founded in 1999. Since that time, the office has seen the University of Denver move into R1 status. While OTL uses tactics from all four change strategies, it demonstrated one of the strongest Sieve approaches of the centers in this study, an approach they term "curation." For example, in 2020, OTL facilitated a Scholarship of Teaching and Learning faculty learning community and organized a large group of Assessment Fellows to support reaccreditation efforts at the university.* Additionally, a staff member supported the university's assessment and accreditation work. In the policy realm, it convened a faculty-led initiative to articulate expectations for teaching excellence, examined how to create a "balanced approach" to evaluating and rewarding teaching, and supported formative professional learning activities.**

* This program was discontinued after the reaccreditation visit.
** Teaching Excellence Initiative at DU, accessed December 4, 2021, http://portfolio.du .edu/teachingexcellence.

As noted in the previous chapter, over a quarter of CTLs note in their purpose statements that they promote SoTL or evidence-based teaching.

Interestingly, of the CTLs in this study, fewer than one in five (15%) described a SoTL initiative on their website in 2020. Therefore, if SoTL is a signature pedagogy of educational development, it was not widely advertised as such, consistent also with findings from other web-based studies of SoTL activity.[111] However, of the CTLs who did sponsor this tactic:

- Most frequently, CTLs did so through a Sieve-Hub approach, such as by offering a learning community (33%). Over a quarter (28%) provided brief workshops. An additional group (19%) coordinated a longer-term initiative, such as an institute, sometimes spanning up to two years.
- Sieve-Incubator approaches were also employed. One-fifth (20%) of the CTLs offered financial incentives, and a small group (6%) publicized consultations. A small fraction (6%) of centers indicated they have staff or faculty fellows who can consult about SoTL.
- Sieve-Temple approaches were least frequently used to promote SoTL. Almost 1 in 10 (9%) recognized SoTL through awards.

If the goal of SoTL is to promote culture change, a menu of tactics will work best.[112] Georgia Southern University's Center for Teaching Excellence (now the Faculty Center) offers an excellent example of that tactical focus through multiple strategies. In addition to SoTL Learning Communities, the center promotes a SoTL Outstanding Scholar Award; a SoTL Fellows Program; and the SoTL Commons Conference. It also publishes the *International Journal for SoTL*. Another example of a center with a multipronged approach is the University of North Carolina Asheville's Center for Teaching and Learning. In addition to a workshop series and learning community, it sponsored grants and a SoTL Writer's Retreat.

In aggregate, SoTL programs are less common at two- and four-year institutions compared to doctoral universities and medical/health contexts.[113] Good examples include the United States Air Force Academy's (CO) Center for Educational Innovation, which had a SoTL-specialized staff member, offered an award, promoted a grant, and facilitated a two-year learning community to engage in SoTL research or implement evidence-based teaching. Another illustration includes Kansas City Kansas Community College's Center for Teaching Excellence, which offered the Blue Devil Faculty Academy to support the scholarship of teaching and learning. SoTL programs also appear slightly more frequently on CTL websites at PWIs and much more commonly at those of larger organizations.[114]

Policy

Policy work is relatively infrequently mentioned on CTL websites (1%), perhaps because directors may be wary of being perceived as too "top down." However, common exceptions are "umbrella" Institutional Review Board (IRB) arrangements. Because institutional approval processes for human-subjects research can be opaque to many instructors who wish to engage in SoTL projects, a negotiated agreement with the IRB can streamline engagement in research on student learning.[115] Examples of centers that highlighted such agreements included Rice University's (TX) Center for Teaching Excellence and South Dakota State University's Center for the Enhancement of Teaching and Learning.

Evaluation of teaching is another policy area that appears on CTL websites. To illustrate, the University of Kansas's Center for Teaching Excellence, funded by a National Science Foundation grant, developed benchmarks for teaching effectiveness to promote conversations in departments about what constitutes effective teaching and how it should be evaluated. Similarly, the University of California, Irvine's Division of Teaching Excellence and Innovation developed guidelines for a second piece of evidence in evaluations of teaching effectiveness.[116]

Although SoTL and evaluation of teaching are the most frequent policy topics on CTL websites, there is also a range of activity in formal bureaucratic processes of the modern higher education institution. This includes Montana State University's Center for Faculty Excellence, which offered Title IX / Mandatory Reporter Training, as well as the University of Texas Southwestern Medical Center's Faculty Diversity and Development, which conducted faculty exit interviews. In Delaware, Wilmington

University's Center for Teaching Excellence served as a human resources service center for adjunct faculty, and Emory University Medical School's Faculty Development office noted in its annual report that it advocated for changes to promotion guidelines, such as a new path at the associate professor level for faculty who contributed extensively to the institutional mission. Finally, Sonoma State University's (CA) Faculty Center (now Center for Teaching and Educational Technology) offered classroom refresh standards. Although the small numbers should be interpreted with caution, larger organizations are most likely to have such an initiative, but there are no other differences by institutional and CTL characteristic nor time of coding.[117]

Quality Assurance

Quality assurance, in regard to teaching, develops and applies standards with a focus on determining the limitations and strengths around course design or teaching effectiveness.[118] A small proportion (9%) of CTLs engage in quality assurance processes, most frequently through one of three vehicles: online course standards, engagement in accreditation, and administration of course feedback.

One of the most common ways that CTLs engage in this process is through standards for the design of online and blended courses, such as the Quality Matters (QM) Quality Assurance program. Seventy-four centers indicated that they engaged in QM, or they worked in institutions or systems that developed their own standards. (For examples of the latter, the SUNY system developed the Open SUNY Course Quality Review [OSCQR] system to address accessibility and instructional design standards, and the California State University developed the Quality Learning and Teaching [QLT] rubric.) To support application by faculty, the University of North Carolina at Charlotte Center for Teaching and Learning had several Quality Matters Faculty Fellows.

A second avenue of participation is through engagement in accreditation and its related quality assurance processes. West Virginia School of Osteopathic Medicine's Office of Assessment and Educational Development included staff who addressed accreditation and Continuous

Quality Improvement (CQI). Fifteen centers indicated that they supported their institutions' focused quality improvement processes, most frequently the QEP (Quality Enhancement Plan, for Southern Association of Colleges and Schools) but also the AQUIP (Academic Quality Improvement Program, for Higher Learning Commission). For example, the Teaching and Learning Innovation unit indicated that it supported the University of Tennessee, Knoxville's QEP for accreditation and offered workshops on assessment-related topics. Georgia's Kennesaw State University Center for Excellence in Teaching and Learning extensively supported the QEP theme, "It's about Engagement," through a workshop series, engagement-focused consultations, faculty learning communities, grants, two course design institutes, a faculty fellow who designed events, and a norming session to support assessment.

A third way CTLs engage in quality assurance around teaching is through support of student evaluations. Twenty-four centers indicated that they coordinated their campus student course feedback systems.

Although the small numbers should be interpreted with caution, quality assurance processes are most common at CTLs in master's and doctoral institutions, and least evident at baccalaureates and medical/health-focused contexts.[119] CTL size and institutional control also appear to be associated with presence.[120] There are no other statistically significant differences by CTL or institutional characteristics nor time of coding.

Research

Earlier sections of this chapter documented that many CTLs support the work of others when engaging in SoTL or faculty-student research opportunities. However, some CTL staff or affiliates do this work themselves as well (4% of CTLs). CTL-affiliated individuals produce research and spotlight this approach through listing presentations or publications. (Chapter 5 elaborates on this approach.) A second strand of work is action research or cycles of research used by a CTL to inform institutional change as well as to enhance its own work.[121]

A third approach consolidates the research as an initiative. To illustrate, New York Institute of Technology's Center for Teaching and

Learning sponsored "Operation Engage," which captured information on faculty use of student engagement pedagogies. The University of New Hampshire's Center for Excellence and Innovation in Teaching and Learning invited faculty to collaborate on several center research projects on topics such as reading assignments, test anxiety, and teaching with multimedia. In Virginia, Radford University's Center for Innovative Teaching and Learning even had a drone research program.

A fourth approach, although not very frequent, involves publishing journals on topics related to teaching and learning. (Maryland's Coppin State University Center for Excellence in Teaching and Learning listed as one of its strategic goals, "Develop a University, peer-reviewed journal."[122]) In some cases, these are peer-reviewed journals; in others, they are a vehicle to highlight student or faculty work at the institution. Examples include *Southern Dialogue* (Faculty Development, Southern Connecticut State University), *Journal on Excellence in College Teaching* and *Learning Communities Journal* (Center for Teaching Excellence, Miami University, Oxford, OH), *Journal of the Biblical Foundations of Faith and Learning* (Southern Adventist University, Center for Teaching Excellence and Biblical Foundations of Faith and Learning, TN), *Journal of Effective Teaching in Higher Education* (University of North Carolina Wilmington, the Center for Teaching Excellence), *Learning Matters* (Durham Technical Community College, Teaching-Learning Center, NC), *Journal of Instructional Research* and the *Canyon Journal of Interdisciplinary Studies* (Grand Canyon University, Center for Innovation in Research and Teaching, CO), *Perspective* (Brigham Young University–Idaho, Learning and Teaching), and *Online Journal of Distance Learning Administration* (University of West Georgia, CTL Online Faculty Development).

Not surprisingly, in alignment with their context, CTLs at doctoral institutions are most likely to highlight their research, and larger centers and institutions are even more likely to emphasize research.[123] More established CTLs are also more likely to publicize their research.[124] There are no other statistically significant differences by time of coding nor institutional characteristics.

Sieve Summary

A Sieve strategy emphasizes standards, expertise, and evidence-based practices. Sieve is the second most frequently articulated strategy in CTL purpose statements, named by a sizable proportion (40%) of centers. As a tactical approach, it was observed equally as frequently (39%) in CTL programs and initiatives listed on websites.

As defined here, key tactical ways that a center employs a Sieve strategy are through promoting or directly engaging in: (1) SoTL, (2) academic policy, (3) quality assurance processes, (4) research, and (5) assessment and evaluation (addressed in chapter 4). Sieve tactical approaches are most common at doctoral institutions, but they are also frequently employed in medical/health-related contexts and at master's institutions.[125] However, there are important variations by specific Sieve tactic. While assessment and evaluation is the most common at associate's (16%), special focus (17%), master's (20%), and doctoral institutions (38%), SoTL is the most highlighted in medical/health contexts (22%). At baccalaureates, SoTL (11%) and assessment/evaluation (12%) are about as equally prominent.

There are no significant differences in presence of a Sieve tactic by MSI or women's institutional status, CTL age, nor time of coding. By control, Sieve tactics are most frequent at CTLs situated in public institutions.[126] Larger centers and institutions tend to list Sieve approaches at a much higher frequency.[127] Additionally, CTLs that employ staff who specialize in digital teaching and learning tend to use Sieve approaches more frequently compared to those that do not have digital staffing, which makes sense in light of the quality assurance processes often used to support online teaching.[128]

Conclusion

This chapter offers over 30 Center for Teaching and Learning change tactics organized by the HITS strategic framework. The previous chapter, which examined statements of purpose, found that Hub (connector) was the most frequently articulated change strategy, followed by Sieve (evidence), Incubator (growth), and Temple (recognition). This chapter

TABLE 3.2. CTL tactics by institutional type, 2020 (in percentages)

	All (N = 1196)	Doctoral (n = 340)	Master's (n = 308)	Associate's (n = 233)	Baccalaureate (n = 181)	Medical/ health (n = 104)	Other special focus (n = 29)
Hub (*Connector*)	**82**	91	82	77	74	81	66
Incubator (*Growth*)	**78**	91	76	64	75	81	72
Sieve (*Evidence*)	**39**	58	39	24	24	42	21
Temple (*Recognition*)	**27**	45	19	14	16	52	28

NOTES: Percentages are presented for unique Carnegie type. (See appendix 1 for methodology.) One institution is missing Carnegie classification information.

analyzes programs listed on CTL websites and finds that, in aggregate, Hub is the most frequently adopted tactical approach, followed closely by Incubator, with less frequent applications of Sieve and Temple tactics (table 3.2). The vast majority (90%) of centers adopt at least one of these tactical approaches. Additionally, the extensive utilization of Hub and Incubator approaches signals a high level of coherence to practice.

Context is an important factor in CTL work.[129] Carnegie classification and CTL size frequently have an impact on how frequently these tactics are promoted, likely because of the resources available to do the work. Hub is the most frequently employed tactical type for associate's and master's institutions, while Incubator is most common among baccalaureates and other special focus contexts (table 3.2). Both Hub and Incubator approaches are used with equivalent frequency among doctoral and medical/health contexts. While CTL size certainly has an impact on presence of all tactical types, Hub approaches are most frequent, both for "centers of one" and the largest centers.

Chapter 1 introduced common aims of Centers for Teaching and Learning, expressed through centers' statements of purposes. Although there were some exceptions, Hub and Incubator tactics—learning communities, orientations, short-term workshops, and reflective consultations—most frequently align with key change aims, as noted in table 3.3. As educational

TABLE 3.3. Most frequently used tactic by CTL aim, 2020

CTL aim	Hub tactic	Incubator tactic	Temple tactic	Sieve tactic
Student learning	Workshop (brief) (47%)	**Reflective consultation** (48%)	Awards (16%)	Assessment and evaluation (28%)
Instructor outcome	Workshop (brief) (47%)	**Orientation** (48%)	Awards (16%)	Assessment and evaluation (22%)
Change or innovation	**Workshop (brief)** (52%)	Reflective consultation (48%)	Awards (16%)	Assessment and evaluation (28%)
Culture, climate, and environment	Learning communities (51%)	**Orientation** (53%)	Awards (17%)	Assessment and evaluation (27%)
Scholarly and creative work	Workshop (brief) (47%) or Learning communities (46%)	**Orientation** (48%)	Awards (16%)	Assessment and evaluation (19%)
Diversity, equity, and inclusion	Learning communities (54%)	**Orientation** (55%) or Reflective consultation (54%)	Awards (19%)	Assessment and evaluation (32%)
Institutional mission	**Learning communities** (49%)	Reflective consultation (47%) and Orientation (46%)	Awards (16%)	Assessment and evaluation (27%)
Teaching effectiveness and excellence	Learning communities (43%)	**Reflective consultation** and **Orientation** (44% apiece)	Awards (18%)	Assessment and evaluation (24%)
Community building	**Learning communities** (51%)	Reflective consultation (50%)	Awards (22%)	Assessment and evaluation (30%)

NOTE: Bold indicates the most frequently named tactic on CTL websites that also reference a given aim.

developer Laura Cruz observed, this may be because "in many ways, our events and programs serve an inherently social function; they are an opportunity for people across campus to get together and talk about a subject of shared interest—teaching and learning as *lingua franca*."[130] This understanding of the work of CTLs positions interdisciplinary dialogue, consultative reflection, and early foundational experiences (orientation) as core components of educational development work. Although less frequently made public on websites, assessment and evaluation (also discussed in chapter 4) and awards are the most frequently associated Sieve and Temple tactics.

Although some of the tactical approaches featured in this chapter, namely short-term workshops, have been criticized for their lack of evidence-based impact, most of this critique focuses on the lack of evidence for student learning outcomes. However, if the aim of the tactic is considered (e.g., is a workshop aiming to change student learning or does it have another goal?) as well as frequency of use (e.g., are workshops the most important program type to assess for student learning outcomes if consultations are actually used more to promote that aim?), our approaches to CTL evaluation shift as well. Chapter 5 focuses on this issue in more detail.

At the beginning of this chapter, Virginia Lee was quoted as describing the chameleonlike programs of CTLs and how they change while maintaining constancy in core features.[131] Indeed, most frequently, centers continue to use program types that were recorded at the start of the field about a half century ago. Small-group programs (workshops, series, certificates, and courses) continue to be the most frequently used tactic, followed by consultations and observations, orientations, and then communities to promote dialogue and collaboration. In each of these cases, however, the field has evolved to spotlight newer types of initiatives that are often longer term and more intentionally designed to promote individual, curricular, or institutional change. These initiatives include course design institutes, change teams, and feedback models that center students. Longer-term initiatives, such as certificates or learning communities, appear to be much more frequently utilized than reported by directors only a decade ago. In short, the 2020 claim that the approach of CTLs "tends to be pretty uniform, consisting largely of teaching consultations, workshops and classroom observations" is unfounded if judging by the repertoire centers present on their websites.[132] Instead, as discussed in the next chapter, in light of strains on CTL resources, a more critical project for CTLs becomes alignment of aim and theory of change to prioritize tactics.

CHAPTER 4

How Are We Organized?

CTL Leadership, Governance, Staffing, and Structures

Emory University Medical School's Office of Faculty Academic Advancement, Leadership and Inclusion *(OFAALI; now* Office of Faculty Academic Affairs and Professional Development*) in Georgia was spotlighted in chapter 3 for its strong Temple orientation. OFAALI's focus in 2020 was on four pillars of practice: faculty affairs, professional and leadership development, DEI, and wellness. At that time, the OFAALI was led by an executive associate dean, and the team included 5 assistant and associate deans (who also held faculty appointments), a director of faculty advancement and inclusion, and 17 professional staff. Leadership team meetings included the School of Medicine's head of human resources (because of the OFAALI's involvement in the faculty lifecycle) and, at times, the school's communications director and head of data visualization.*

The University of Denver's Office of Teaching and Learning (OTL) was profiled in chapter 3 for a strong Sieve emphasis, including assessment and reaccreditation work. In 2020, OTL's website indicated 11 personnel (currently, it is slightly larger) and suggested multiple faculty engagement structures: a Faculty Advisory Board, a Courseware Advisory Board, an

Assessment Groupware Committee, an Instructional Technology Advisory Committee, and several faculty fellows tied to key initiatives the OTL was leading on campus. Director Leslie Cramblet Alvarez noted, "We've tried to be very intentional about bringing in the faculty voice, because we are all staff at the OTL, so having a lot of faculty involvement is really important."

The leadership of Berea College's Center for Teaching and Learning *in Kentucky is currently Director Leslie Ortquist-Ahrens, a full professor with a 50% director appointment. In 2020, three others staffed the center: an associate director, a coordinator of teaching and learning assistant programs, and an office manager. Multiple student staff also support the center's work in the areas of writing, teaching assistant peer leaders, and office work. (Chapter 2 profiled the center's Incubator orientation, which includes direct student support.) At this time, there is not an advisory board, although the center has worked with faculty fellows in the past to lead programs and institutes.*

Chapter 2 profiled the Community College of Philadelphia in Pennsylvania Faculty Center for Teaching and Learning *(FCTL)'s "for faculty by faculty" approach, and chapter 3 highlighted FCTL's Hub orientation. FCTL's Faculty Advisory Committee selects faculty facilitator(s) to lead the unit. However, the Advisory Committee also helps support the center's extensive programming. Fran Lukacik, currently the chair of the committee, noted that the advisory body was "set up with representatives from each of the different divisions and non-teaching units, like the library—different approaches from all different sides of the college to come to support all of this programming."*

While the previous chapters analyzed Center for Teaching and Learning (CTL) strategy and tactics, this chapter turns to organizational and operational questions. The four vignettes above, featuring centers that have been profiled throughout the book, illustrate some of the organizational variations that centers embody. To understand these variations, I examine four focal questions. First, beyond teaching and learning, what other organizational mandates are CTLs now including in their portfolios? Second, in light of these mandates, what does staffing and leadership look like in terms of university role and credentialing, and third, how have these changed over time? Finally, as bridges between multiple constituencies on campus (noted in chapter 1), how are CTL governance structures organized?

Organizational Mandates

In a recent provocative article, Kathryn Sutherland, an academic developer from New Zealand, asked, "Is it time to think more broadly about the academic development project?"[1] Sutherland called for "a more holistic approach," one that acknowledges the whole of the academic role (i.e., development around all aspects of an academic career), the whole institution (i.e., strategic institutional work as well as a broadening of constituencies to include students and professional and support staff), and the whole person. Indeed, if CTLs are taking on a much broader mandate, as recent surveys and Sutherland's comments suggest, does "Center for Teaching and Learning" even continue to be an appropriate name for this type of academic unit?

Recent research on CTLs presents contradictory findings about organizational trends. *Faculty Development in the Age of Evidence*, cited extensively throughout this book, found that CTL staff reported engaging in some collaborations with other units on campus, most frequently with technology units, but these relationships were not extensive. The study also reported that "a small number" of directors observed that functions such as assessment and technology were already integrated in their centers.[2]

In contrast, a 2017 small study by Bruce Kelley, Laura Cruz, and Nancy Fire found that about half of respondents (49% of 73 completed responses) reported that they worked in a CTL that integrated with at least one other unit or college or university function. Most frequently, respondents indicated that their CTLs merged with instructional technology, assessment, or distance/online learning units. The "other" category in the survey responses was quite capacious, however, listing "service learning,

South Carolina's Coastal Carolina University **Center for Teaching Excellence to Advance Learning** well illustrates the integrative trends that many centers are experiencing. The center was formed in 2004, originally as the Center for Excellence in Teaching and Learning (CETL). Current director Jennifer Shinaberger explains the history from there: "So instructional technology was separate from the CETL, which reported to the Office of the Provost. Later, with the third director, instructional technology and the CETL were merged under one center, the Center for Teaching Excellence to Advance Learning (CeTEAL). Then we were moved into library, and we were in the library for a while. Then we reported to the Dean of the College of Education/VP for Online Learning and Teaching Excellence. Online learning and instructional technology was split apart again from CeTEAL. Now they're merging three groups of us into one department, the Office of Professional Development, Teaching and Learning. It will include what was training and development, which was for staff, then our Center and then the Office of Online Learning. Now, we will be under the College of Graduate Studies. Just a lot of moving!"

internships, disabilities support, leadership and organizational development, libraries, classroom and A/V support, student computer lab support, multimedia production, graduate studies, undergraduate research, tutoring, institutional research, diversity, research, and so forth."[3]

To examine these questions on a broader scale, I examine five organizational responsibilities that traditionally have been embedded in other institutional locations but are now incorporated in some CTL mandates. These include (1) instructional technology and online learning, (2) assessment, (3) writing, (4) service learning and community engagement, and (5) career and leadership development. Beyond their traditional teaching and learning functions, what proportions of centers are being asked to take on these broader mandates? Variations that are analyzed here are similar to chapter 3 and include institutional contexts, CTL characteristics, and time of coding. See appendix 1 for definitions.

Instructional Technology and Online Learning

Multiple studies prior to this book (and prior to COVID) suggested an increasing integration of CTL work with digital teaching and learning. Even at the time of Centra's 1976 study, most (82%) campuses offered "assistance to faculty in use of technology as a teaching aid (e.g., programmed learning or computer-assisted instruction)."[4] Published 40 years later, *Faculty Development in the Age of Evidence* listed "integrating technology into traditional teaching and learning settings (e.g., clickers)" as the most frequently offered service offered by CTLs at nearly all institutional types.[5] (This item came in at number two for community colleges.) "Blended learning approaches" and "teaching in online and distance environments" also ranked in the top five. Over three-quarters of respondents indicated that they collaborated with technology centers to a moderate or great extent. Similarly, Kelley, Cruz, and Fire's 2017 study found that instructional technology support and distance / online education / e-learning were most frequently named as units that integrated with CTLs.[6] Indeed, with the pandemic, there has been an even greater infusion of technology into the work of CTLs.

How is this made visible in CTLs in 2020? In their statements of purpose, almost a quarter (24%) of centers state that their mission includes technology, and a small fraction (8%) of statements signal support of online modalities. However, when it comes to the programs and services made visible on websites, the majority (62%) of centers describe some focus on digital or online teaching and learning (hereafter termed a *technology-infused CTL*). Almost a third (30%) have at least one staff member focused in this area (defined in appendix 1).

Of the 735 technology-infused CTLs, centers most frequently offer support for their campus's learning management system (32%). Smaller proportions provide course or media production (24%) or educational technology and classroom learning space (16%) support. Brief workshops are also frequently provided, as are longer-term offerings like certificate programs or learning communities, grants, and awards (see chapter 3).

Overall, the presence of any digital-focused program is most likely to be found in CTLs in doctoral universities and associate's and master's institutions.[7] Public institutions are also more likely to have a CTL with digital presence.[8] While nearly all larger centers have digitally infused programs, fewer than half of "centers of one" (i.e., a CTL with one FTE [full-time equivalent] or, sometimes, a fractional appointment) offer such support,

Illinois State University's center is a good example of a technology-infused CTL. According to Cross Endowed Chair in the Scholarship of Teaching and Learning and Director Jennifer Friberg, the center was formed in the early 2000s, out of a fusion of "a grassroots teaching support kind of Center and a technology support Center," which became the Center for the Advancement of Teaching, then the Center for Teaching, Learning and Technology. Now the Center for Integrated Professional Development, it offers workshops, technology short courses, LMS support, equipment checkout, Teaching with Technology small grants, workshops, and Quality Matters review. Additionally, the center offers two online course design institutes, including Design, Align, Refine, and Teach (DART) Online, a semester-long program to design a new online course, and AIM (Assess, Improve, and Modify) Online, to revise the course. Graduate students are eligible to participate in Foundations of Instructional Design, a certificate program resulting in a course plan and teaching portfolio. Faculty Prep Week also provides an all-campus event, with a series of workshops around topics such as digital accessibility and technology tools.

and in similar directions, institutional size is related to presence.[9] There are no significant differences by institutional or CTL characteristic.

By strategy, only a Sieve approach (evidence and expertise) is significantly more associated with the presence of digital learning programs.[10] (Hub and Incubator are *less* likely to be correlated with digital learning.) One reason for this emphasis may be that some technology-focused centers are involved in quality assurance processes through the review of online courses.

Although institutions' COVID response strategies may have intensified the integration and permeation of remote and online teaching into CTL work, there is no significant difference by time of coding. It may be that these changes will take longer to have impact or that trends were already in motion before the onset of the pandemic.

Holistic Professional Learning

In the mid-1970s, two groups of researchers—seemingly independently—established understandings of CTL work that continues to inform practice today. In Richard Gaff's original conceptualization, *faculty development* supported programs to "help faculty members acquire knowledge, skills, and sensitivities"; *instructional development* aligned with programs that facilitate student learning and course redesign; and *organizational development* focused on initiatives to create an effective teaching and learning environment.[11] In turn, William Bergquist and Steven Phillips argued that to address changes "at three levels: (a) attitude, (b) process, and (c) structure," an effective faculty development program needed to address personal, instructional, and organizational dimensions.[12]

These definitions have evolved over time, but the POD Network currently still denotes three realms of practice within educational development: *Faculty/Graduate Student/Postdoc Development*, which focuses on the individual (as teacher, scholar, or whole person); *Instructional Development*, which moves to the meso level to address courses and curricula; and *Organizational Development*, a structural approach addressing policies and processes such as assessment, rewards systems, and leadership capacity.[13] Beach, Sorcinelli, Austin, and Rivard's 2016 survey also found these areas continue to inform CTL directors' understandings of their work. They write that while "the teaching and learning/instructional agenda remains the most prominent focus of centers, . . . it is noteworthy that center directors identified as many areas for expansion in faculty work and career development services as they did in teaching and learning services."[14]

While a learning focus is the most common aim for CTLs (chapter 1), Beach, Sorcinelli, Austin, and Rivard's 2016 survey also found that other areas of faculty roles and responsibilities continued to inform understandings of CTL work. Although areas such as "midcareer and senior faculty development" and chair leadership development were not offered at a high rate at the time of the study, CTL directors expressed expansionary plans.[15]

As seen in chapter 1, the vast majority of CTLs include faculty or staff/administrators as key constituencies, and half of centers espouse aims to support faculty learning. Interestingly, in 2020, about the same proportion (49%) offered a programmatic initiative to support academic leaders or promote holistic professional learning (HPL) through career and scholarly development (hereafter termed an *HPL-infused CTL*). To promote faculty career development, a significant proportion (43%) of HPL-infused CTLs offered a mentoring program (chapter 3). Ample numbers (16%) of HPL-infused CTLs offered grants to support professional growth (such as travel grants), but very few (1%) sponsored an award with this focus.

In other cases, workshops, learning communities, or longer-term programs focus on dossier preparation and learning about standards for tenure and promotion. As one example, California State University, East Bay Office of Faculty Development offered a Tenure and Promotion Dossier Pizza Party as well as workshops on first- and second-year retention dossiers; roles and responsibilities for serving on tenure, promotion, or retention committees; and a professional leave workshop. However, when considering the full faculty lifecycle, it was interesting that six CTLs offered sessions on retirement. For example, Franklin and Marshall College's Faculty Center in Pennsylvania hosted a "Thinking about Retirement" session, which was listed as a "casual gathering of emeriti faculty in late April, and those of you who are beginning to think about what life might be like after leaving the classroom are encouraged to join in the conversation."

Today, we often associate educational development with teaching and learning; however, the first faculty development tactic was thought to be the research sabbatical offered in 1810 at Harvard University.[16] Of the 590 HPL-infused CTLs, the most frequent emphasis returns to the historical roots of faculty development: support for research. Over half (53%) of HPL-infused CTLs offered (non-SoTL) research support. As discussed in chapter 3, centers use consultations, workshops, grants, recognition and awards, and dialogue and collaboration to support research. Examples of these approaches in 2020 included:

- Grant Development Fellows for consultations (Salt Lake Community College Professional Development, UT)
- Author Awards to recognize faculty who have published a book of general interest and significance (California State University, Fullerton Faculty Development Center)
- A National Science Foundation CAREER writing group (Case Western Reserve University Office of Faculty Development, OH)

- Faculty Research Study Hall (University of Central Arkansas, Center for Teaching Excellence, now Center for Excellence in Teaching and Academic Leadership)
- Grant Proposal Certificate Program (California State University, Fresno Center for Faculty Excellence, now in the Office of Innovation and Digital Excellence for Academic Success)
- Manuscript Workshops, which paired a faculty member and up to three experts in their field for an intensive two-day seminar discussing and revising the faculty member's manuscript (Colorado College Crown Faculty Center)

Additionally, several centers offered university-wide events or seminar series to showcase faculty scholarship and creative work. These included salons (Mills College Center for Faculty Excellence[17]), concerts by faculty (Berklee College of Music Office of Faculty Development) and an annual campus scholarship showcase event, with four presenters (faculty, librarians, or staff) competitively selected by the Faculty Center for Teaching and Learning Advisory Committee at Westfield State University in Massachusetts.

Over one in five (22%) HPL-infused CTLs sponsor a leadership development program. Centers in medical / health-focused contexts are much more likely to have this kind of initiative, and 2020 programs included:

- Workshops such as "Leadership: Effectively Managing Teams" and "Resilient Leadership" (University of Cincinnati Medical School Faculty Affairs and Development)
- Series such as the Life and Leadership Seminar Series for Women Faculty (Texas Tech University School of Medicine Office of Faculty Affairs and Development)
- Longer-term programs such as the Graduate Medical Education Program Director Leadership Development Program (New York University School of Medicine Institute for Innovations in Medical Education)
- Academies such the Academic Career Leadership Academy in Medicine, which provided leadership development opportunities to junior faculty members, with an emphasis on those

underrepresented in medicine (University of North Carolina at Chapel Hill School of Medicine Office of Faculty Affairs and Leadership Development)

- Faculty learning communities such as the Faculty Leadership Fellows Program (East Carolina University Office of Faculty Development, now Office of Faculty Affairs and Leadership Development)
- Grants such as the Jane K. and Thomas L. Schwenk, M.D. Faculty Leadership Development Award, which encouraged and fostered leadership development for outstanding midcareer faculty in academic medical education (University of Nevada, Reno Medical School Office for Faculty)

Centers at other institutional contexts developed robust leadership offerings as well. For example, Appalachian State University's Center for Academic Excellence (now Center for Excellence in Teaching and Learning for Student Success) in North Carolina offered a New Chair Orientation; Department Chair Workshops; New Chair Mentoring Program; New Chairs Coffee and Conversations; Academic Leadership Development Program; Appalachian's Women in Leadership Series; and the Women in Educational Leadership Symposium. In California, the Pasadena City College Professional Development sponsored an innovative inter-institutional program pairing faculty who were interested in community college management with administrators from neighboring colleges.

A holistic professional learning approach is most common in centers in medical/health and doctoral contexts.[18] Midsized centers (2–6 individuals) tend to have this emphasis most frequently, as do larger institutions by faculty FTE.[19] There are no significant differences by MSI or women's college status, control, CTL age, nor time of coding.

Holistic professional learning initiatives are not significantly correlated with any strategy although they are most strongly associated with Temple and Incubator (growth of individuals and ideas) approaches.[20] The focus of these initiatives on professional growth, career development, and work on recognition and reward systems align with Incubator and Temple approaches to practice.

Assessment

A common definition of *assessment* is "inquiry into student learning as a systemic and systematic core process of institutional learning—to improve educational practices and, thus, student learning."[21] Although many institutions continue to have separate offices of institutional research or assessment, the activity is frequently becoming embedded in centers. In *Faculty Development in the Age of Evidence*, assessment of student learning outcomes was one of the top five areas of programming in CTLs. Further, when asked to identify needed directions for educational development, assessment was the most frequently identified priority, and developers also named the activity as a top area toward which the field would move in the next decade. This was also evidenced in CTL job postings where assessment was a growing area of emphasis in 2015–16.[22]

While most CTLs are engaged in assessment for improvement, or "use [of] assessment information to enhance teaching and learning," in the age of a critical public and stringent accreditation standards, some also participate in assessment for accountability "to demonstrate to policymakers and the public that the enterprise they fund is effective and worth their continuing support."[23] Many also occupy a third space between these endeavors—to engage in "assessment from an educational development approach."[24] This approach is characterized by four principles: (1) bridging work across communities and multiple institutional levels; (2) collective, collaborative ownership; (3) action-oriented focus on student-centered learning; and (4) intentionality about inclusiveness to recognize diverse experiences of participants and stakeholders.

CTL names are indicative of the pervasiveness of the endeavor in educational development today with *Center for Teaching, Learning, and Assessment* shared by CTLs at Azusa Pacific University; California State University, Monterey Bay; Chandler-Gilbert Community College; Grinnell College; Indiana University Kokomo; and Eastern Oregon University. What are the ways that these and other centers employ assessment and evaluation-focused tactics?

While a minority (14%) of CTLs note this focus in their statement of purposes, more (23%) list at least one tactical approach, and a few (7%) employ staff to directly engage in assessment, evaluation, analytics, or accreditation work. Among the 275 *assessment-infused centers*, assessment is promoted most frequently by offering programs like workshops and less frequently through learning communities, grants, or awards (see chapter 3).

Assessment and evaluation-infused CTLs are most frequently found in doctoral universities, and relatedly, larger CTLs and institutions are more likely to house assessment and evaluation functions compared to smaller ones.[25] Centers in public contexts appear to have this emphasis with the most frequency, perhaps because of higher levels of state government scrutiny for educational outcomes.[26] There are no statistically significant differences by MSI and women's college status, age of center, nor time site was visited.

Assessment and evaluation are significantly associated only with a Sieve strategy (evidence and expertise). While over a third (34%) of CTLs with a Sieve strategy named in their purpose statement also embedded some assessment and evaluation function in their work, fewer (17%) without this approach did so.[27] This strategy aligns with a Sieve approach to evidence-based practice.

In South Carolina, Coastal Carolina University's Center for Teaching Excellence to Advance Learning offers a good example of a center that uses multiple prongs of engagement around assessment. In 2020, it sponsored an assessment grant program, a writing circle, and an Assessment Institute for participants to learn about course, program, and curricular assessment. Participants were asked to complete five core sessions (e.g., Designing an Assessment Plan) and four electives (e.g., Selecting a Published Instrument) and submit a reflection plus an assessment plan, curriculum map, or assessment report. Director Jennifer Shinaberger also notes that the center has been very involved in reaccreditation efforts with the university's Quality Enhancement Plan (QEP): "All the training went through our office or we helped schedule it, whether it was using our registration system or helping build out the rubrics. Now we're on our *second* QEP and pretty heavily involved in that."

Writing

The integration of writing into educational development work is long-standing. In Kenneth Eble and William McKeachie's 1985 book about their large-scale evaluation of faculty development programs funded through the Bush Foundation, writing across the curriculum (WAC) initiatives were found to be most effective as rated by program directors. In particular, success was attributed to WAC's ability to enable faculty to assess writing more efficiently and effectively, gain writing skills themselves, facilitate more in-class active learning, and develop cross-disciplinary conversations. Additionally, early volumes of *To Improve the Academy*, POD Network's signature journal, included a section on "Student Development: Intellectual Growth and Writing." Recently, others have argued that "when we empower faculty as writers, we can also empower them as teachers of writing in their disciplines," which supports an integrative approach to faculty development and writing.[28]

However, in Beach, Sorcinelli, Austin, and Rivard's study, CTL directors reported they did not have substantial infusions of writing-related work. Respondents' centers offered writing-focused programs only "to a slight extent," including writing to learn and WAC-related initiatives, as well as support for instructors to develop as scholarly writers.[29] Additionally, only a minority of CTLs (42%) indicated they partnered with writing centers to a moderate or great extent.

Interestingly, in 2020, a scant few (1%) of CTLs referenced writing or writing support in their statements of purpose; however, over one in five (22%) embedded some writing-related program or service. Among the 265 *writing-infused centers*, the most frequent program type (57%) is longer-term support for faculty or graduate students' scholarly writing through writing groups, dissertation retreats, and writing circles. Next most frequently (37%), CTLs offered brief workshops on topics related to writing, such as effective use of rubrics or designing meaningful writing assignments,[30] often in collaboration with a campus writing center. Relatively frequently (16%), centers facilitated longer-term initiatives to support the design of effective learning environments for writing instruction, such as faculty learning communities or faculty fellows programs.

While a sizable proportion of centers offered writing-related programming, a smaller number embedded this function structurally. A small proportion of writing-infused CTLs (13%) contain a sub-unit focused on writing (e.g., a center within a center) or include staff that focus specifically on writing, communication, or multilingual learning. Additionally, nine centers (3%) maintained writing fellows programs.[31]

Overall, writing-infused CTLs are more likely to be present at doctoral universities, master's institutions, and baccalaureate colleges, as well as larger institutions.[32] Western Michigan University's Office of Faculty Development is an example of a doctoral center that included multiple approaches and constituencies in 2020. The unit offered faculty writing circles, faculty learning communities on topics like teaching writing, and a two-day institute on writing to learn / writing across the curriculum. Larger CTLs are more likely to include writing in their portfolio,[33] and women's colleges are over twice as likely to have some writing focus, compared to coeducational institutions.[34] (This dynamic is likely related to the student focus of women's colleges; see chapter 1.) For example, Simmons University's Center for Faculty Excellence in Massachusetts offered a writing retreat and planned to create structured writing groups. There are no other significant differences by CTL and institutional characteristics nor time site was visited.

By strategy, only an Incubator approach (growth of individuals and ideas) has a significant association with the presence of writing-focused programs and services. While almost a third (28%) of those with an Incubator strategy had writing-focused initiatives, fewer (20%) of those without the strategy offered this support.[35] This was likely because an Incubator strategy is aligned with direct student support and individual development, but also because the metaphor could be extended to the cultivation of writing projects.

Service Learning and Community Engagement

Service learning and community-based learning are high-impact practices with great benefits for student learning and a positive impact on faculty. For these benefits to be realized, however, instructors need to learn how to create effective learning environments that triangulate student, institutional, and community assets and needs. In both 2006 and 2016, educational developers indicated they offered these kinds of programs only to a slight extent, but they used their collaborative networks to amplify their efforts. In 2016, about half (49%) had substantive collaborations with units elsewhere on campus that address community and service learning.[36]

The recent volume *Reconceptualizing Faculty Development in Service-Learning/Community Engagement* explores the intersections of these two fields.[37] This survey of 83 service learning and community engagement professionals in the New England Resource Center for Higher Education aligns with findings from the perspective of CTL directors. Over half (55%) of respondents indicated that service learning/community engagement (S-LCE) directors take the lead for providing faculty development for S-LCE activities on their campus.[38] Tactics used were similar to those employed by CTLs (discussed in chapter 3), with most respondents using one-on-one consultations (90%) or employing workshops (86%). Topics of programs also suggested a great deal of synergy: reflection, course development, principles of community engagement, syllabus development, and assessment.

In the 2020 study presented in this book, there are few CTLs that infused service learning or community engagement in their work, as evidenced by web artifacts. Only a small proportion of CTLs referenced community engagement (3%) in their statements of purpose. Similarly, few centers (11%) offered any S-LCE programs or services, and fewer than 2% listed staff[39] or an embedded unit in their CTLs. Within these 132 *S-LCE–infused centers*, the most frequent offering was a brief workshop (52%), followed by a learning community or community of practice (26%). Small proportions offered an award (8%) or grant (7%). (See chapter 3 for examples.)

In many ways, the distribution of any program focused on service learning or community engagement demonstrates CTL responsiveness to their distinctive institutional missions. For example, public universities, with their outreach mission, tend to have S-LCE-infused centers for teaching and learning at higher rates compared to private not-for-profits and for-profits.[40] Additionally, CTLs at institutions with the Carnegie classification for community engagement status are more likely to report such work compared to other institutions.[41]

Although relatively rare, S-LCE-infused centers are more likely to be found in doctoral, master's, and associate's institutions.[42] Larger centers and institutions are more likely to have this integrative emphasis.[43] Accordingly, Iowa's Boise State Center for Teaching and Learning is an excellent example of a S-LCE-infused CTL. In 2020, it sponsored a number of related services, including consultations, multiple faculty learning communities, mini-grants, and workshops on how to incorporate service learning into a tenure and promotion portfolio. Their entry pathways (fast-track path, planner path, and deep-planner path) and staged curriculum (e.g., advanced practitioners were encouraged to participate in a faculty learning community on service learning scholarship) offered a customized approach to the work.[44] There are no other statistically significant differences by CTL feature, institutional characteristic, nor time site was visited.

Programs focused on service learning or community engagement are slightly more common among CTLs with Temple (recognition and reward) and Sieve (evidence and expertise) approaches and slightly less common among centers with Hub and Incubator approaches.[45] Although none of these differences reach statistical significance, their alignment with these educational development approaches resonates with key ideas raised in the S-LCE field, namely the importance of supporting engaged research, recognizing faculty achievements, and creating rewards systems that acknowledge service learning and community engagement work.[46]

Summary of Organizational Mandates

In the previous section, I examined organizational mandates that are infused in the work of CTLs beyond a focus on teaching and learning.

Most prominently, the majority of centers have some focus on digital or online teaching and learning, and almost half sponsor holistic professional learning with an emphasis on career development, research, or leadership. About a quarter support assessment and evaluation, and a similar proportion offer some writing-related program or service. Less frequently, CTLs infuse service learning / community engagement.

It is interesting that a Hub strategy does not have even a moderate positive association with the presence of an integrative emphasis. For example, one might expect that having a theory of change around centralization and coordination (chapter 2) might be associated with the presence of integrated units. It may be the case that practice or organizational exigency plays a stronger influence than strategy because there is a significant correlation between the presence of Hub *tactics* and having at least one integrated emphasis ($r = .4$, $p < .001$). However, as shown in the conclusion to this book, a Hub orientation may also be one of the less intentional change strategies for CTLs.

The findings in this section align with the 2017 Kelley, Cruz, and Fire study, which found that about half of their CTL respondents reported integrations with at least one other unit or college/university function, and most frequently, this was digital and online learning.[47] However, my findings differ in the scope of these integrative trends. In aggregate, according to programs and staffing listed on websites in 2020, over three-quarters (83%) of CTLs offered integrative emphases, and a majority (51%) of CTLs were infused with multiple. The following section examines how these expanding mandates may be associated with changes in organizational structures of CTLs.

Staffing and Leadership

Kelley, Cruz, and Fire's 2017 study of integrative tendencies in CTL work is also suggestive of concomitant changes in center structures and, possibly, tensions. While survey respondents reported that the change enhanced the visibility of their CTL and brought new resources, they also concluded, "It is clear that for the majority of CTLs who responded, the changes did not make for easy adjustments."[48] The following section examines CTL leadership by title (administrative and faculty) and disciplinary background. It also considers staffing levels with comparisons made to a similar study published in 2013.[49]

While this section offers helpful benchmarking information for campuses seeking to develop or pivot a CTL, it also picks up threads from the previous section and chapters. As numbers of constituencies and mandates have grown, how have CTL leadership and staffing changed? What backgrounds are now typical of a CTL leader expected to manage these complex units, strategically and operationally? If centers are to accomplish their aims, do they have the resources needed to do so?

Personnel

As a prior study of CTL staffing asserted, "Having full-time equivalent (FTE) staff is also an indicator of an institution's commitment to the permanence and sustainability of faculty development programs."[50] However, might staff also be indicative of organizational morphing of CTLs as well? For example, in light of the growth of CTL constituencies and aims (discussed in chapter 1), program types (discussed in chapter 3), and the infusion of other mandates that we see in this chapter, have CTL staffing patterns changed over the last decade?

For this study, I identify the number of individuals listed on center web pages, such as their "About Us" pages. I omit any student employees (identified as such) as well as individuals with titles that suggest they are part of faculty service (e.g., "Faculty Development Committee Chair") rather than engaged in a fully or partially compensated role at the center. My methodology allows for a broad look at center staffing patterns and focuses on 948 CTLs with any information about personnel, plus 21 centers with faculty committee leadership. Because some of these roles may be part-time, I am not able to accurately capture FTEs. Additionally, as with any aspect of a web study, a second limitation is that information not listed on a web page is not captured and information can be out of date.

Here, I align CTL personnel counts with several data sources to better understand key questions about resource allocation historically and across various contexts:

- 2020 IPEDS data about instructional and student FTE (fall 2020 full-time equivalent enrollment, or full-time plus one-third part-time)[51]
- 2018 Carnegie Foundation list of characteristics of postsecondary institutions[52]
- My web coding of CTL staff numbers, roles, credentials, and key functions

In 2020, excluding CTLs led by committee, the mean personnel size was 5.4 individuals, inclusive of the CTL leader. However, the range was sizable, 1–86, suggesting a significant variation across centers. (The standard deviation [sd] is 8.3.)

There were also significant differences by institutional type and context. While the mean personnel size of CTLs at doctoral institutions was 9.8 (sd = 12.7), this drops substantially for CTLs at other institutional types: 5.3 (sd = 8.6) for other special focus, 4.6 (sd = 5.1) for medical/health, 3.7 (sd = 3.6) for master's, 3.1 (sd = 3.1) for associate's, and 2.7 (sd = 2.5) for baccalaureates.[53] (These means exclude CTLs with committee leadership.) CTL age also has an impact, with older centers (30+ years) having a clear advantage over all other age groups.[54] Not surprisingly, CTL personnel size is significantly positively correlated with campus size: both for instructional FTE ($r = 0.4$, $p < .001$) and student FTE ($r = 0.4$, $p < .001$).

The phrase "center of one" arises frequently in discussions among educational developers, suggesting CTLs where a single director wears many hats and can be stretched thin. In this study, 228 CTLs had just one individual listed on their site, which is about a quarter (24%) of all centers with any personnel noted. While they are relatively rare in doctoral CTLs (11%), they are more prevalent in associate's (38%), other special focus (36%), and baccalaureate (33%) institutions. They also occurred regularly in master's (26%) and medical/health (23%) contexts.

In light of all of the other structural changes impacting CTL work, have personnel resources changed as well? Using Sally Kuhlenschmidt's 2010 dataset (see introduction), Jennifer Herman surveyed 782 "teaching and learning development units" (TLDUs) and received responses from 191 institutions.[55] (If institutions had more than one TLDU, only the primary director, as defined by Kuhlenschmidt, was surveyed; programs that focused only on teaching assistants were excluded; and not-for-profits were not surveyed.) Herman's survey elicited staff FTEs at CTLs.

Herman found that among the 191 responding institutions, the mean number of staff was 4.4 FTEs, with a range of 0–25. Although I find a mean of 5.4 individuals in 2020, because Herman measured full-time equivalents and I measured individuals, it is likely that CTL staffing has stayed about the same. (Herman excludes for-profit institutions from her study, and I include them in mine. However, in an analysis that excludes personnel counts from for-profits, the mean size remains the same: 5.4.)

To adjust for size of institution, Herman calculated that the mean ratio was 1 CTL staff member per 2,223 students and 1 CTL individual per 108 faculty (all expressed in FTEs). In a similar calculation using IPEDS data, I find that the mean 2020 ratio for students is larger, or 1 CTL individual per 3,125 FTE students (sd = 5,669) (table 4.1). Because nearly all CTLs identify faculty as a key constituency (chapter 1), the instructional staff ratio is the most indicative of CTL resource strain. For faculty, the ratio is again larger, with a mean of 1 CTL individual per 262 instructional staff (sd = 743).

In 2013, baccalaureate institutions had the smallest faculty ratio and doctoral institutions had the largest, but there were no statistically significant differences by institutional type. In 2020, the trends were similar but with larger proportions all around. Medical/health institutions (not studied in 2013) have a CTL/instructional staff ratio akin to that in doctoral institutions.

By control, in both 2013 and 2020, CTLs at public institutions had higher staff-student and staff-faculty ratios. The ratio at for-profits is much higher but the sample size was very limited, and no comparisons are able to be made with 2013.

Herman's 2013 study did not present data on diverse institutions, but in 2020, CTL staffing ratios suggest differential resourcing, compared to the population at large. For example, CTL personnel-instructor ratios at MSIs (1:288) are above the national mean and women's colleges (1:109) are

TABLE 4.1. CTL staffing ratios in 2013 and 2020, by control and Carnegie type

	Student			Faculty		
	Herman (2013) N=191 Ratio of TLDU FTE to student FTE	Wright (2020) Ratio of CTL individual to student FTE	Number of 2020 institutions with staffing data	Herman (2013) N=191 Ratio of TLDU FTE to instructional FTE	Wright (2020) Ratio of CTL individual to instructional FTE	Number of 2020 institutions with staffing data
All institutions	1:2223	1:3125	869	1:108	1:262	859
Control						
Public	1:2487	1:3923	523	1:125	1:294	515
Private not-for-profit	1:1710	1:1743	330	1:83	1:207	328
Private for-profit	—	1:7362	3	—	1:307	3
Carnegie type						
Associate's	1:1792	1:3364	158	1:106	1:271	158
Baccalaureate	1:1962	1:1487	127	1:62	1:124	124
Master's	1:1985	1:2987	241	1:101	1:266	240
Doctoral	1:2839	1:4142	288	1:175	1:310	287
Special focus (medical/health)	—	1:1280	38	—	1:312	37
Special focus (other)	—	1:1030	13	—	1:142	9

NOTES: Herman's study did not report on the special focus classification nor on for-profits. Number of institutions does not total to 869/859 in control or Carnegie type because of missing information or because percentages are presented for unique institution (control) or Carnegie type. (See appendix 1 for methodology.) Ratios exclude CTLs led by committee. Dashes indicate that information was not collected.

below. However, these differences are not statistically different compared with all other institutions.

CTL Leadership

Key competencies needed for an effective CTL director make for a very long sentence, including budgeting, understanding of institutional politics, hiring and mentoring staff, program evaluation, maintaining visibility, networking, strategic planning, relationship management, internal and external mentorship, knowledge of theories relating to higher education, and expertise as an effective change agent.[56] While individual skills and attributes are certainly helpful for effective CTL leadership, organizational positioning is a structural component that has been less well-examined.

In 2017, educational developers David Green and Deandra Little asked, "Might U.S. universities inadvertently be undermining their own investment in developers by positioning them in such a way that they are less likely to be effective in leading and supporting academic change?" In an international study, Green and Little found that, in comparison to educational developers in 37 other countries, "educational development [in the US] is positioned as an administrative, not an academic, function."[57] For example, only 16% of US educational developers reported that their primary position was academic, compared to 37% globally, even though US educational developers had the highest proportion of doctorates and reported active teaching and research activities. Green and Little argued that faculty status for educational developers is necessary to bridge the faculty-administrative divide and position them to be effective change agents.

If CTLs are serving as organizational change agents, charged with ever-larger mandates, then it is essential to understand how leadership is positioned to do this work. To better understand this dynamic, I examine the titles of CTL leadership, both administrative and academic. First, I study CTL leadership's academic titles to understand how CTL leaders are situated "betwixt and between" in their roles occupying academic and administrative spaces.[58] Next, I examine administrative titles and compare these with Beach, Sorcinelli, Austin, and Rivard's 2012 survey findings (published in 2016) to understand if there are any changes in roles and status. Additionally, I examine highest degree earned and disciplinary background to explore other possible trends in movement of the field.

CTL leadership structures vary widely, including faculty committees, a single leader with an ongoing professional appointment, an individual with a rotating appointment, and teams of faculty with rotating appointments. For this study, CTL leadership titles and structures were obtained for 948 centers with 1,011 leaders. (In the case of CTLs governed by committees—a structure discussed in more detail in the upcoming section on governance—if a chair or co-chairs were listed, these individuals were considered for the analysis of CTL leaders.) If the title or other credentials were not listed on the center's page, I completed a subsequent search on the institution's directory for biographical information. In cases of multiple CTL leaders, the highest faculty rank or degree received is reported.

Faculty Status

Other research suggests that the most common pathway to an educational development position is prior experience as a faculty member; however, this does not work in reverse: educational developers may have more limited opportunities for faculty status.[59] While prior research examines the individual as the unit of analysis, I focus on the organizational unit, or the Center for Teaching and Learning. By center, what proportion have a leader with faculty status and of what rank?

Based on web information, over half of centers (52%) appear to be led by one or more individuals with faculty status. (This proportion was calculated by using the proportion of CTLs listing any leadership.) By Carnegie classification, baccalaureate institutions most frequently list CTL leaders with a faculty appointment, followed by master's and doctoral institutions.[60] The primacy of faculty status in baccalaureates is reflective of models of educational development more common at liberal arts colleges, such as half- and full-time renewable positions that are typically occupied by faculty.[61] There are no statistically significant differences by institutional size, CTL age, control, time of coding, nor MSI or women's college status.

CTL staff size does have a significant negative relationship with the presence of a leader with faculty status.[62] In general, a majority of centers with one to three individuals had a CTL leader with a faculty appointment, as compared to a minority of CTLs with four or more personnel.

By rank, tenured positions are most common, accounting for over half of all academic titles (table 4.2). Although the trends presented in table 4.2 are not statistically significant, full professors do appear to lead larger CTLs at higher proportions.

By Carnegie classification, *full professor* is the most common rank of leadership at baccalaureates, doctoral institutions, master's institutions, medical/health, and other special focus contexts.[63] At associate's institutions, a faculty title with a rank not specified is most common (but when specified, *associate professor* is most frequent). At minority-serving institutions, faculty rank also tends to be a bit lower. *Associate professor* is the most common rank at MSIs (36%), but *full professor* is most frequent at PWIs (41%).[64] There are no other significant differences by institutional feature, CTL characteristic, nor time of coding.

TABLE 4.2. Highest faculty rank of CTL leadership, by CTL size, 2020 (in percentages)

	All (N = 489)	1 individual (n = 111)	2–3 individuals (n = 189)	4–6 individuals (n = 81)	7+ individuals (n = 90)
Assistant	6	6	9	1	0
Associate	30	36	32	31	22
Full	37	35	35	40	43
Emeritus	<1	0	1	0	0
Adjunct	4	4	3	4	7
Non–tenure track, ongoing*	8	5	6	7	17
Faculty (rank unknown)	15	14	15	17	11

NOTES: In the case that leadership was shared by multiple individuals, the highest-ranking title was utilized. Centers are included in "All" that appear to have no dedicated personnel (e.g., a committee structure), and the highest rank of that structure's chair was used.

*Includes professor of practice, research faculty, lecturer, and instructor titles.

Administrative Title

While academic appointments signal a center's positioning with faculty, staff titles convey the administrative status of the CTL leader and, occasionally, suggest reporting lines. As with the faculty analysis, if the CTL page listed multiple leaders, I selected the highest rank.

In 2020, the vast majority of CTL leaders listed on websites hold some type of directorship: 58% as *director*, 6% as *executive director*, and 2% as *faculty director* (table 4.3). *Director* is the most common CTL head title at all Carnegie types, except for medical/health contexts, where *dean* is more common.[65] *Director* is also most common across institutional size quartiles, CTLs of all ages, centers at MSIs and women's colleges, and for units at both publics and private not-for-profits.

Senior leadership positions (deans, vice presidents, provost positions, and CIOs) are held by over one-fifth (21%) of all CTL leaders. These senior leadership titles slightly more frequently signal that the CTL head reports to the provost (e.g., vice provost for teaching and learning) compared to the president (e.g., assistant vice president for faculty affairs).

TABLE 4.3. Highest administrative rank of CTL leadership, by CTL size, 2020 (in percentages)

	All (N = 931)	1 individual (n = 219)	2–3 individuals (n = 305)	4–6 individuals (n = 181)	7+ individuals (n = 205)
Director	58	61	68	59	44
Dean (any rank)	11	7	11	11	14
Provost (any rank)	7	3	4	11	12
Executive director	6	2	3	7	17
Coordinator	6	14	6	3	0
Vice president (any rank)	3	2	1	3	7
Chair	3	3	1	1	1
Faculty director	2	1	2	3	2
Instructional designer/ technologist	1	2	2	1	0
Manager	1	1	0	1	1
Other	2	3	2	1	2

NOTES: In the case that leadership was shared by multiple individuals, only the highest-ranking title was utilized. Centers are included in "All" that appear to have no dedicated personnel (e.g., a committee structure), and generally, the leads of that structure are categorized as "chair" or "other."

Other titles, comprising less than 2% together, include: CIO, facilitator, faculty developer, consultant, facilitator, advisor, counselor, librarian, faculty assistant, faculty fellow, faculty liaison, and instructional support specialist.

The information presented in table 4.3 also suggests that the larger the CTL, the more elevated the leadership role. For example, an *executive director*, assistant/associate *vice president*, or *vice provost* title is most common when a CTL is in the largest quartile of personnel. Looking only at the very largest centers (25+ personnel), the five most common titles are *executive director* (29%), *vice president / assistant vice president* (23%), *director* (19%), *assistant/associate/vice provost* (16%), and *assistant/associate dean* (7%).

To my knowledge, there has not been a comparable prior study of CTL leadership titles. However, if the breakdown of respondents to Beach, Sorcinelli, Austin, and Rivard's study is any indication, there has been an elevation of roles among CTL heads over time. For example, these authors found that only 11% of their respondents were categorized as "Senior-Level Administrators."[66] In contrast, in my 2020 study, this proportion has almost doubled.

Highest Degree and Disciplinary Focus

What are the credentials of today's CTL leaders? Table 4.4 illustrates the distribution of highest degree overall and by staffing category. (In the case of multiple leaders, the highest degree was recorded.) Across CTL size, a doctorate is by far the most common credential. This is also the case across Carnegie types, except for medical/health contexts, where there is a split between the doctorate and medical degrees.[67] A doctorate is also most common across institutional size quartiles, CTLs of all ages, centers at MSI and women's colleges, and for all control types.

The proportion of centers listing leaders with a terminal degree (88%) is higher than levels reported in other research that considers credentialing. For example, Green and Little's 2017 study found that 82% of their US respondents held doctorates, and in Beach, Sorcinelli, Austin, and Rivard's 2016 study, 76% of participants reported a doctorate or other ter-

TABLE 4.4. Highest degree of any CTL leader, overall and by staffing quartile, 2020 (in percentages)

	All (N = 657)	1 individual (n = 130)	2–3 individuals (n = 220)	4–6 individuals (n = 134)	7+ individuals (n = 160)
PhD	73	73	68	78	78
Master's*	11	12	13	12	9
EdD, DA, DeD	10	12	11	5	8
Medical (MD or DO)	4	3	6	4	5
MBA	1	0	1	1	1
Law (JD)	1	0	1	0	0
Bachelor's (BA or BS)	<1	0	0	1	0

NOTES: Centers are included in "All" that appear to have no dedicated personnel (e.g., a committee structure), and the highest degree of that structure's chair was used.

*Includes MA, MBA, MFA, MLS, MM, MPH, MPP, MS, MSW, and MSEd degrees.

minal degree.[68] However, both of these surveys focus on all center staff, and therefore, it follows that CTL leaders may have higher credentials.[69] Although uncommon, it is interesting that in 2020, four CTLs housed leaders with an MBA (as a sole or combined credential), which occurred primarily in digitally infused CTLs.

Next, to examine disciplinary background of CTL leadership, I identify the focus of the primary department of the director's faculty affiliation or, if that was not present, degree area listed on profile pages. Unlike the prior analyses in this section, because of the difficulty of aggregating disciplinary backgrounds, the individual is the unit of analysis. Data are available for 559 individuals at 521 CTLs.

Most frequently, CTL leaders are social scientists in educational fields and other social science disciplines (table 4.5). About a quarter of leaders are in the arts and humanities. Almost a quarter of CTL heads hold STEM disciplinary affiliations, with slightly more in the physical sciences compared to the biological sciences. Professional fields—most frequently, medicine—include another small proportion. ("Other" included interdisciplinary/integrative departments or units like "Liberal Arts and Sciences.")

For comparison with other studies, table 4.5 aligns 2020 CTL directors' disciplinary foci with breakdowns found in other research. The

TABLE 4.5. Disciplinary background of CTL leadership (in percentages)

	2020 CTL heads	2014 Educational developers (Green and Little, 2014)	2011 CTL directors (Beach, Sorcinelli, Austin, and Rivard, 2016)
Social sciences	42	—	64
Other social sciences	24	13	28
Education	18	37	36
Arts and humanities	26	30	22
STEM	22	10	12
Physical sciences	13	—	—
Biological sciences	9	—	—
Professional	10	—	1
Other	1	11	—

NOTES: Disciplinary areas for 576 individuals at 521 CTLs compose the data for this table (i.e., some CTLs have more than one individual in a leadership role). Data for Beach, Sorcinelli, Austin, and Rivard (2016, table 1.9, p. 26) are based on reported field of highest degree for respondents with a director title (N = 184). Data for Green and Little (2014, figure 11, p. 11) are based on reported field of highest degree for all US survey respondents (N = 146) to a survey distributed to the POD discussion list. "Other" in this study includes interdisciplinary/integrative departments or units like "Liberal Arts and Sciences." Dashes indicate that data were not collected.

study presented in *Faculty Development in the Age of Evidence* suggested that of the 184 respondents who were CTL leaders, education was the most frequently reported background, making up 36% of this group.[70] Although not specifically reflecting a leadership role, Green and Little's study of educational developers indicated that of the 146 respondents who were US educational developers, education was also frequently represented, accounting for 37% of the highest degrees.[71] In contrast, my study found a much smaller proportion of education degrees and higher percentages of STEM and professional backgrounds.

What might account for the contrast in these statistics? One possibility may rest with methodology or sampling, with the other studies having fewer data points and eliciting information via survey. For example, healthcare educational development is a relatively new focus of the POD Network's special interest groups, and it may be that directors at medical schools and other health science contexts would not have participated on discussion lists where an invitation to the survey was distributed.

However, the 2020 statistics may also be signaling changes in the field that have been moving through the pipeline for some years, such as the rise in STEM-focused educational grants and disciplinary-based educational research (DBER). For example, Bartholomew's 2015–16 study of educational development job ads indicated that STEM education was one of the most frequent postings, and over time, it is likely that some of these individuals were promoted to leadership positions.[72] Further, the decline of education-specific degrees is an additional indicator of the broadening of CTL leadership roles, which were inclusive of teaching and learning but are widening to other operational and institutional change capacities.

Summary of Staffing and Leadership

In 2018, the American Council on Education and the POD Network developed a rubric called the *ACE-POD Matrix*, designed for CTL strategic planning, self-study, reflection, and development/pivoting. (For full disclosure, I served on the committee that developed this tool.) The *Matrix* is structured by three broad categories: organizational structure (e.g., leadership, staff expertise, and preparation), resource allocation and infrastructure (budget, staffing), and programs and services (scope, reach, impact). I believe that this tool offers an excellent concise overview of operational considerations for centers. I also remember, however, the challenges in discussing the *Matrix* with my collaborators (Mary Deane Sorcinelli, Steven Taylor, Eli-Collins Brown, Catherine Haras, Carol Hurney, Jonathan Iuzzini, and Emily Magruder) in terms of how we would establish context-sensitive benchmarks across a range of CTLs. For example, the rubric indicates that an "accomplished/exemplary" center will have "substantial" staffing. What does "substantial" mean? As an additional example, the *Matrix* suggests that center leadership should be "appropriate for institutional type." How can we better specify what that means as well?

Further, there have been a number of questions from practitioners about CTL organizational dimensions. For example, on the POD Network discussion list, recent inquiries asked about the "average size of faculty centers" or "CTL/CTE comparison data on staff size." A robust discussion asked, "Should a doctorate be required for leaders in our field?"[73]

While not looking at these questions in a prescriptive sense, CTL websites are rich sources of data to describe the types of organizational arrangements that currently exist. In the prior section, I examined staffing and leadership. In summary, 2020 websites suggest that the mean personnel size of CTLs is 5.4 individuals, inclusive of the CTL leader. There is substantial variation when analyzed by number of individuals, with differences by institutional type and CTL age. However, when institution size is controlled, by looking at the data in terms of ratios, most differences disappear. Most striking are historical comparisons of the ratio of the number of CTL personnel to instructors as well as to students. In short, these data suggest that CTLs have been doing more with less.

For CTL leadership, the picture is rosier. Although there are limited comparative data, we can speculatively say that leaders' roles have notched up over time, with a greater proportion now assuming senior positions, particularly in larger centers. In analyses of disciplinary background, this book finds a much smaller proportion of education degrees and higher percentages of STEM and professional backgrounds, which presents an additional indicator of the broadening of these roles. In alignment with the level of position, terminal degrees generally tend to be characteristic of at least one CTL leader in centers. All of these changes in credentials and titles suggest a higher status for the role of CTL leader.

Governance

There are few studies about CTL governance. This gap is interesting in light of the field's extensive focus on center positioning, as well as the credibility and authority felt by educational developers.[74] One exception is Susan Gano-Phillips's 2010 article, "Optimizing Center Staffing and Advisory Boards to Promote Involvement in Institutional Change," which addressed faculty-focused governance structures in CTLs.[75] Gano-

Phillips, a former director of the Thompson Center for Learning and Teaching at the University of Michigan–Flint (now a dean of the College of Arts and Sciences at the same institution) wrote, "The center advisory board, a structure situated between the center, faculty, staff, and administration . . . plays an important role in expanding the work of the center and advocating for its institutional development role."[76]

In addition to mediating positions between the center, administration, and faculty, Gano-Phillips notes three additional objectives for CTL advisory boards. First, they provide avenues for centers to get feedback from faculty. Second, boards support the center's work by assisting with strategic planning and CTL assessment. Finally, board members can serve as allies by advocating for the mission of the center. While these four objectives are evident for faculty-focused boards, in chapter 1 we saw an expansion of the constituencies that CTLs serve. In what ways are undergraduates, graduate students, postdoctoral scholars, and administrators embedded in CTL governance structures?

Sociologists note that in addition to formal structures like advisory boards, organizations contain informal practices. Organizational theorist Richard McDermott termed these structures "double-knit," combining formal practices with informal communities "defined by the opportunities to learn and share they discover and bounded by the sense of collective identity the members form."[77] These informal communities that shape CTL governance include aspects of center work like fellows programs or inclusion of students and instructors as collaborators. As I will discuss, although faculty fellows and student workers are primarily discussed in the CTL literature as staffing, I argue that it is also helpful to consider their role in governance.

What are the general approaches, both formal structures and engagement practices, that CTLs use to guide their work and stay connected with the constituencies they serve? Of CTLs with a web presence, a substantial proportion (44%) list one or more engagement practices or structures.

The most common is a formal structure: **advisory boards** (although sometimes identified by other names such as "steering committees," "faculty development committees," "executive committee," and "leadership council"). Boards are found at over a quarter of centers (29%). For the centers with boards, mean size is 12 individuals with a range of 3 to 48. (If a center had multiple boards, only the largest was included in this analysis.) As an example of the role these bodies play, Colby College's Center for Teaching and Learning in Maine notes that the purpose of its board is:

> to ensure that Center programs and services reflect the values of the Colby academic culture, embrace differences in teaching and learning, invite voluntary participation in non-evaluative experiences, create energy through collaboration and coordination with other academic support offices, and rely on evidence from pedagogical scholarship, learning theories, and the Colby experience.[78]

Interestingly, despite the widening of CTL constituencies, advisory boards are still typically limited to faculty. While about a fifth (21%) involve administrators or campus collaborators, such as librarians or digital learning staff, few (8%) boards include students.

A very small proportion of boards take the shape of a **faculty committee structure**. (*Faculty Development in the Age of Evidence* also found a small proportion (3%) of committee-run centers, most frequently at liberal arts and community colleges.)[79] For example, Central New Mexico Community College's Cooperative for Teaching and Learning included a faculty coordinating committee, described as "a faculty-led team of faculty and instructional administration representing key constituencies across the college." Sub-teams included an "Annual Conference on Teaching and Learning Planning Team" and "Faculty Focus Day Planning Team" as well as those that focused on new faculty support, part-time faculty support, professional development strategies, and communication.

While roles for most committees were not identified on CTL sites, Molloy College Faculty Professional Center in New York did specify its remit. For example, responsibilities of the board's elected members include collaborating with the director to administer the budget, advocate for the center, and assist with the evaluation of the director.[80]

An informal engagement practice, used by 18% of centers, involves the use of **faculty fellows,** or individuals who are engaged by a Center for Teaching and Learning to partner on the work. In their study of 220 faculty fellows programs (also called scholars or ambassadors programs elsewhere), Susan Colby, Laura Cruz, Danielle Cordaro, and Clare Cruz noted these initiatives were typically yearlong and had five core objectives: *honor* (i.e., an honorific appointment with few service expectations), *learning* (includes formal and informal curricula), *advocacy* (focus on a specific discipline or topic), *extension* (grows the personnel of the center), and *capacity* (emphasizes institutional-level strategic change goals).[81]

All of Colby, Cruz, Cordaro, and Cruz's study categories are represented in the data collected for this book. Additionally, it is interesting that faculty fellows frequently serve in roles that align with the five "extended" organizational mandates described at the start of this chapter. For example, North Carolina A&T State University's Center for Teaching Excellence sponsored Digital Learning Faculty Fellows; Stockton University's (NJ) Institute for Faculty Development collaborated with five fellows, including one focused on writing instruction; and North Carolina State University at Raleigh's Office for Faculty Excellence coordinated a large Community Engaged Faculty Fellows Program. In Michigan, Oakland University's Center for Excellence in Teaching and Learning worked with a Chair Fellow to support its Chairs Leadership Institute, and University of Denver's Office of Teaching and Learning hosted Assessment Fellows to support its reaccreditation.

A somewhat similar model, albeit for students, is **employing undergraduate and graduate** students as consultants or staff. A small proportion (4%) of CTL websites indicated that they employ undergraduates in roles such as tutors, writing fellows, teaching consultants, or general office support. Slightly more (5%) do so for graduate students in roles such as teaching consultants, writing associates, research assistants, or general administrative support. Several argue that these programs expand CTL capacity and offer meaningful professional learning for students.[82] I would also add that they offer an engagement structure, allowing students to shape center programs while also contributing to CTLs' aims focused on student learning.

Conclusion

In *Faculty Development in the Age of Evidence*, Beach and others note, "Our current findings suggest that colleges and universities are still grappling with the question of how best to support faculty in all of the roles they are asked to fill."[83] In contrast to the authors' survey findings, my 2020 study suggests instead that CTLs are rapidly moving forward to answer these questions by integrating new areas into their work—while their broader institutional homes may still be grappling with them. In addition to their general teaching and learning mandate, discussed in chapter 3, we see here that the majority of centers have some focus on digital or online teaching and learning, and almost a third have institutionalized this emphasis by including at least one digital learning–focused staff member. Although infrequently involving dedicated staff, holistic professional learning—or leadership and career development, support for research and services, and promotion of well-being—is represented in about half of all centers. About a quarter employ a program to support assessment and evaluation, and a small proportion have staff focused in this area. A similar proportion offers some writing-related program or service, and a few contain an embedded unit or staff that focus on writing, communication, or multilingual learning. Less frequently, CTLs infuse service learning / community engagement, with only a small percentage of centers offering related programs or services or having staff or an embedded unit.

In 2010, educational developer Virginia Lee reflected on emerging CTL organizational trends, such as mergers, consolidation, and reorganization, speculating, "Whether these emerging organizational structures and program types represent the new face of faculty development is hard to say."[84] In light of the fact that the vast majority (83%) of 2020 CTLs offered at least one integrative emphasis (and over half were infused with multiple), these trends appear to be confirmed.

In tandem with these integrations, there are also indications that the backgrounds and roles of CTL leaders have changed. In analyses of disciplinary background, there appear to be a much smaller proportion of education degrees and higher percentages of STEM and professional backgrounds compared to earlier studies. This shift suggests an additional indicator of the broadening of these roles. Leaders' titles have notched up over time, with a greater proportion now assuming senior positions, particularly in larger centers. That is the good news. The bad news associated with growth in the size of centers is that, when institutional size is taken into account, CTL-student and CTL-instructor ratios have increased. In other words, staffing data suggest that CTLs are doing more with less.

Although there is limited historical information about center governance, we observe that centers demonstrate what McDermott termed a "double-knit" structure.[85] Faculty engagement practices include the formal, such as advisory boards or committee-based leadership, as well as more informal practices, such as faculty fellows programs and student employment. Such structures may be responsive to the many pulls faced by a typical CTL. If mandates have expanded but personnel have not, faculty and students—as fellows, consultants, and part-time workers— allow centers to meet the demands of expanding constituencies and mandates. While these structures do not address workload issues, they do allow for more engagement opportunities and diverse specialization in functional areas.

There are three broad implications of these findings. First, the trends documented here are consistent with other threads running throughout this book. In chapter 1, I argued that CTLs are seeing an increase in constituencies served and aims described. In chapter 3, I showed that centers are using a broad array of tactics to support goals related to teaching and learning. In this chapter, I document how CTLs are taking on initiatives outside of the realm of teaching and learning, mandates that were traditionally housed in other spaces of the academy. All of these trends point to a broader role for CTLs on campuses, which supports operational needs, strategic aims, and organizational change.

A second implication is concern for the ongoing sustainability of this increase. As noted in the section on staffing, comparisons with data from less than a decade earlier suggest that CTLs are doing more with fewer resources. As signaled in Kelley, Cruz, and Fire's 2017 article cited at the beginning of this chapter, even with our faculty and student collaborators, this increasing stretch for centers is being felt. Although a broadening mandate brings increased visibility and heightened status for the center, Kelley, Cruz, and Fire's survey emphasized strain, with developers reporting that "the changes did not make for easy adjustments."[86] In the long term, if not attended to carefully, this strain promises to have a detrimental impact on CTL staff's satisfaction, retention, and perhaps even quality of work.

A final implication is how we think about the structure of the field. Responding to Sutherland's question posed at the beginning of this chapter, "Is it time to think more broadly about the academic development project?" Emphatically, my answer is "yes!" to better recognize the work in which CTLs are engaged. These findings also suggest thinking about the foundational unit that is the focus of this book, the Center for Teaching and Learning. Others have critiqued this name, largely focusing on the first word, because *Center* seems to exclude individuals or programs that do educational development work. (An example of this critique is found in Kuhlenschmidt and Herman's work, which used the term *Teaching and Learning Development Units*.)[87] As seen in chapters 2 and 3, however, the predominance of Hub strategies and tactics suggests that in the active sense of this word—or the activity of *centering*—the concern is ill-placed. Instead, we might interrogate the latter half of the name, "Teaching and Learning." If most centers are infusing writing, assessment, digital, community engagement, and/or holistic professional learning, does the "Teaching and Learning" component of CTLs still hold? Individual centers have addressed this question readily with diverse titles that clarify their key functions, but it remains for the educational development field to potentially redefine the nomenclature of its key organizational unit.

In light of significant changes to CTLs documented in this book, the next chapter focuses on evaluation. How can we make our work more visible?

CHAPTER 5

How Do We Make Visible Our Work?

CTL Approaches to Evaluation in Annual Reports

N HIS BOOK about the history of college teaching in the United States, Jonathan Zimmerman wrote that the "perception that college teaching was failing students . . . has been a constant over time."[1] This is both good and bad news for Centers for Teaching and Learning. On the one hand, Kenneth Eble and William McKeachie, founding directors of the first US CTL, wrote over 30 years ago that "it is a fair guess that dissatisfactions with faculty as teachers explain in part the current faculty development movement."[2] In other words, the rise of CTLs, as documented in the introduction, may be partially attributed to this static negative view of higher education. On the other hand, if the role of educational developers is to help "colleges and universities function effectively as teaching and learning communities,"[3] a constant perception that teaching is failing students leaves CTLs vulnerable to criticism.

Indeed, the external and internal disapproval has been extensive. A 2017 American Academy for Arts and Sciences review of "several" center websites noted that "rigorous studies of their effects on faculty members' teaching appear non-existent, or if these do exist, they are not publicly posted."[4] This critique is surprising considering there is strong evidence for the impact of educational development on student learning.

For example, the 2016 volume *Faculty Development and Student Learning* presented a multi-institutional study that carefully connected participation in teaching development workshops to changes in teaching and student learning gains in critical thinking and quantitative reasoning.[5] Similarly, for graduate students, a study of over 3,000 doctoral students at three universities documented long-term teaching outcomes associated with high participation in educational development.[6] Additionally, a recent cross-institutional survey of over 3,500 faculty found that those who report more frequent engagement in formally structured professional development opportunities also indicate more regular interaction with students and use of effective teaching practices.[7] Literature reviews of faculty development in medical education support the claim that well-designed programs are associated with changes in teaching, improved student outcomes and persistence, and organizational impacts, such as more extensive collegial networks.[8] However, like the static message that college teaching is (and always has been) failing students, there is clearly a perceived disconnect between the perception and presence of the existence of high-quality studies of educational development.

This disconnect may result because there is no one more critical about CTL evaluation practices than educational developers themselves. Calls for teaching centers to better demonstrate their impact are not new, beginning with Centra's 1976 study. Over 40 years ago, Judith Levinson-Rose and Robert Menges, in one of the first reviews of educational development research, provided the following critique:

> A well-defined field of inquiry should draw upon coherent theory, subscribe to high standards of research, and build upon previous research in a systematic way. . . . Research on improving college teaching is not a well-defined field. For most studies, the basis in theory is strained and for some it is nonexistent.[9]

Other researchers have since noted similar themes, such as, "The conceptual and methodological underpinning of what little empirical evidence there is . . . leaves a good deal to be desired."[10] In the same year (2010), another article found few examples of rigorous evaluation, an "alarming finding."[11]

Although recent reviews are more favorable,[12] educational developers continue to report struggles with CTL evaluation despite the existence of several established models.[13] Some of the cited difficulties included resources (time and money), the complexity of measuring distal outcomes, poorly conceptualized goals and frameworks, and the organizational identity of many CTLs as service (not research) units.[14] Challenges exogenous to CTLs also include that "outcomes are influenced by individual differences, are difficult to rigorously measure, and their development pathways are unpredictable and sometimes unknown."[15] British academic developer Ranald Macdonald adds:

> Our role is often described as being to improve the quality of teaching and learning in our institutions but we often have little direct contact with students to be able to evaluate the effectiveness of what we are doing. Ours is an indirect effect through staff [i.e., instructors], who will take the credit or blame for the impact of the changes they implement. Similarly, when we are engaged in organizational development activities, we may be unable to measure the impact of our activities separate from the other players with whom we work.[16]

Many of these reasons are similar to those documented almost 50 years ago in Centra's study, which found that key barriers were limited staff, funding, and knowledge about how to conduct assessment.[17]

The 2018 POD Network document *Defining What Matters* presents guidelines for comprehensive center assessment. Echoing others who define research and evaluation as distinct endeavors,[18] *Defining What Matters* denotes "evaluation" as "information used for local decision making, which can also make a CTL's work visible on campus."[19] *Defining What Matters* also adds that the value of evaluation is that it supports reflection and ongoing improvement, which are practices that are constituent of effective teaching. Finally, in line with recommendations from the field of evaluation itself, the guidelines note that, like CTL practice, evaluation is "a contextually bound practice [that] allows for diversity" and is often responsive to intended use by anticipated audiences, such as the questions that senior leaders or faculty advisory boards ask of centers.[20] In line with the Hub-Incubator-Temple-Sieve framework presented in earlier chapters of this book, the guidelines suggest short- and long-term measures that may signal impact with these change strategies.

In the case of CTL annual reports, the primary aim is what some would term a "Level 2" investigation, which is to develop local—as opposed to personal and public—knowledge, informing a group within a shared context—as opposed to informing oneself or a wider audience.[21] To illustrate, educational developers Megan Sanders and Amy Hermundstad Nave found in their 2022 survey of 154 POD Network members that the primary intended audience for most CTL annual reports is the center's direct supervisor (73%) or campus leadership (69%), and the main reasons for authoring such a document are for internal review (67%) or to advocate for continued support for the center (65%).[22] Therefore, as a contextually bound practice designed to share local knowledge, how do CTLs decide to make their impact visible? And how might the field enhance its evaluation practices?

In this chapter, I examine 107 annual reports made public on center websites. First, I analyze the reports using frameworks commonly employed for comprehensive CTL evaluation, which are models developed by Kirkpatrick, Hines, and Kreber and Brook.[23] Combined, these models include the following measures: (1) participation, (2) instructor satisfaction, (3) instructor learning, (4) change in instructors' teaching, (5) change in student learning or experiences of learning environments, and (6) institutional impact. Next, I examine emergent ways that these CTLs make visible their work, which may not be fully captured by extant frameworks. Finally, I make recommendations for CTL evaluation in light of the great value of this activity, yet mindful that the primary mandates of most CTLs are their educational and service missions, not research. Many thanks to Justin Voelker (Brown University recent alumnus), who read through most CTL annual reports in this study, assigning unique participation counts, as well as satisfaction and learning metrics.[24]

Most reports cover the year prior to when I accessed the website (2018–19 or 2019–20, depending on the date of access), but five reports are significantly older, spanning 2010–11 through 2015–16. The majority of reports are from CTLs at doctoral universities (62%) with master's colleges and universities (19%) the next most frequent. Other proportions are baccalaureate (11%), associate's (5%), medical/health (2%), and other special focus (2%). Most (59%) reports are from public institutions, and the remainder are derived from private not-for-profits (41%). In line with the dataset as a whole, smaller proportions are from CTLs at MSIs (11%) or women's institutions (2%). On average, staffing associated with the CTLs that produced these reports is 10.6, with a range of 1 to 68. (Notably, there is only a single "Center of One" report—or an annual report from a center with one staff member—and it is the most dated.) Finally, of CTLs with identifiable founding years (N = 41), slightly more than half have existed for 20 or more years (29% for 20–29 years and 22% for 30+ years), while about one-quarter are relatively new (24% for 0–9 years) or have been in place for 10–19 years (24%).

Participation

In their 1996 article, "Who Uses Faculty Development Services?" Nancy Van Note Chism and Borbála Szabó establish a long history of claims about the extensiveness and nature of those who work with CTLs:

> Faculty developers are accustomed to hearing statements about the characteristics of the users of their services. Some routinely make such generalizations themselves. A commonplace observation is that faculty developers "preach to the converted," that is, they serve mainly those faculty who are already good teachers and have an interest in teaching. In apparent contradiction to this statement, the claim that faculty developers are remediators who concentrate on faculty with significant teaching problems is also frequently made. . . . Observations are also made about how heavily services are used. What seems to characterize most of these observations is that the data sources upon which they are based are not made explicit.[25]

Chism and Szabó's study surveyed 100 centers randomly chosen from a POD Network membership list and found, "On the whole, there is evidence to conclude that most programs, no matter what structure or staff size, take record keeping seriously and have data about their users."[26] When they analyzed the utilization rate (i.e., the proportion of faculty who accessed the CTL compared to the total number of faculty FTEs) by program type, means ranged from 8% (mentoring programs) to 11% (consultations), 47% (events), and 82% (publications like newsletters and handbooks). They also noted that these proportions varied widely by institution and that it would be helpful to have professional associations more regularly survey centers' participation patterns.

Bishop and Keehn's 2015 convenience sample of 171 directors suggested that estimated reach varies widely by control and institution type, ranging from 12% to 49% of full-time faculty, 17% to 34% of part-time faculty, 0% to 25% of graduate students, and 5% to 37% of undergraduates.[27] More systematic studies include a recent Faculty Survey of Student Engagement (FSSE) of over 3,500 faculty, which indicated that across multiple institutions, nearly half (47%) of instructors "visited an office or center that supports faculty (Center for Teaching and Learning, Center for Teaching Excellence, etc.)" in one academic year.[28] FSSE data also suggest that these proportions varied by institutional type in expected ways, from 35% in doctoral universities with the highest research activity to 61% at baccalaureate colleges with an arts and sciences focus.[29] A 2014 administration of the Faculty Survey of Student Engagement for Graduate Student Instructors (FSSE-G) to over 2,500 graduate students at eight research universities found that 20% reported that in the past year that they "visited an office or center that supports graduate student instructors," but higher proportions indicated that they attended a workshop to enhance their teaching (47%) or worked 1:1 with a staff or faculty member to improve their teaching (48%).[30] Other possible guidelines for reach could include those derived from literature on change or the sociology of organizations, such as a threshold of 15–16% to move past "token status" or scale past typical proportions of innovators / early adopters.[31] Despite these studies and possible theoretical frameworks, the field continues to ask questions about appropriate reach.[32]

In the annual reports for this study, most (88%) present participation data in some form. However, only 27 provide unique counts for faculty (i.e., non-duplicated participation in case of attendance at multiple events or services), 13 do so for graduate students, and 9 indicate this number for undergraduates. To get an estimate of "reach," CTLs with unique counts were compared with IPEDS data corresponding to the appropriate annual report year.[33] Out of over 1,200 centers, it is difficult to claim that these are representative statistics. However, in corroboration with other research, they do offer some indication of typical reach.

On average, CTLs report that over half of faculty (51%) engage with their center in any given year, a statistic that is strikingly similar to those found in both the 2019 FSSE study and Chism and Szabó's 1996 figure for events. Although counts are too small to make firm conclusions, the differential proportions are suggestive of carefully accounting for institutional type when considering these benchmarks: baccalaureate (59% of faculty; 4 CTLs), master's (59%, 4 CTLs), associate's (48%, 1 CTL), and doctoral (47%, 18 CTLs) institutions. Again, numbers are small, but age of center does not seem to be heavily associated with reach, with 53% for centers with 0–19 years of existence (4 CTLs) and 49% for those with 20+ years (7 CTLs). Interestingly, reach is also consistent across CTL staffing levels: 1–10 personnel, 51% (17 CTLs); 11–20 individuals, 52% (5 CTLs); and 21–50 staff, 51% (5 CTLs).

For graduate students, comparisons are made to both the total number of graduate and professional students, as well as the total number of graduate teaching assistants, reported by IPEDS in the year associated with the annual report. Not surprisingly, there is a good deal of spread in these numbers: graduate student reach is calculated at 11% (range: 1%–26%) and graduate TAs at 44% (range: 14%–75%), a proportion higher than that found by the FSSE-G. (In four cases, the number of unique graduate students served by the center was higher than the number of graduate TAs listed by IPEDS. If these cases are calculated at 100%, the average rises to 62%.) All CTLs reporting unique graduate student participation are at doctoral institutions.

While it is relatively common for CTLs to cite the number of students indirectly impacted by their work (e.g., number of students in revised courses), very few centers report undergraduates as a direct client. Of the nine that do, mean reach is 32% with a very wide dispersion: 1% to 57% of undergraduates. Proportions for baccalaureate institutions (30%, 2 CTLs) are relatively similar to those from doctoral institutions (33%, 7 CTLs).

Other participation metrics. Beyond counts of individuals, other ways that CTLs with annual reports document their reach are through analytics and by organizational unit. While the former is much more common than the latter, both can be compelling measures.

All of the CTLs in this study had some web presence. Therefore, it is not surprising that in addition to individual participation counts, other indicators of engagement with the center included analytics. About a quarter of CTLs with annual reports (26 centers) listed metrics such as website hits, social media followers, or YouTube followers.

Perhaps because of the time needed to display such an analysis, few centers report participation by specific organizational unit. However, especially because many CTLs express aspirations for organizational change work, information about participation by department offers a helpful lens into organizational development activities. The University of Texas at Austin's Faculty Innovation Center (now the Center for Teaching and Learning) offers an interesting model in its 2016–17 Annual Report. The center counted engaged departments through the following criteria:

(1) Work with the center around curriculum redesign
(2) Home of a grant awardee or Provost's Teaching Fellow (faculty who partner with the center around key events and projects)
(3) Faculty or graduate student instructor participation in at least 10 programs or services, such as events, workshops, or consultations

Through this analysis, the center identified 70 "engaged departments" and was able to map them onto the number of undergraduate degrees offered, allowing it to document that the center "served faculty in departments representing 84% of UT Austin 2016 undergraduate degree recipients across campus."[34] (Due to graphics resolution, the compelling visualization of circles scaled proportionally to undergraduate degrees, and spaced by physical location of department, could not be printed here, but it can be found on the center's website.[35]) This labor-intensive analysis has not been repeated in future reports by the center, but as Leslie

Hall, the staff member (now at the Texas Higher Education Coordinating Board) who created this chart, recollects,

> We were in a challenging time, deep into a series of reorganizations, and so we were really interested in communicating our reach and impact. I was interested in a compelling visual that really spoke to our campus environment and the work that we were doing with faculty and then the follow-on impacts.

Because the number and proportion of participants can also be used to document culture change, and the department is an important locus of teaching innovation, strategic documentation of this kind of organizational impact is valuable.[36] This approach also recognizes that educational development's unit of analysis includes both individuals and communities.[37]

Reasons to measure participation. More fundamentally, why measure participation? It may be, as Chism and Szabó suggested, that it is a helpful statistic to have in one's back pocket to counter claims of working only with "usual suspects" or "preaching only to the choir."[38] As a CTL director, I can verify that participation is the metric I am personally asked about the most. Participation data are often requisite for position requests and program budgets.[39] The Center for Teaching and Learning at the University of North Carolina Asheville's report describes its logic for using this metric as follows: "Because engagement in CTL activities is completely voluntary, the extent to which busy faculty participate in programs is an important indicator of whether our efforts are meeting their needs."[40]

It may also be that CTLs engage in this work because of their theories of change, albeit implicit. For an Incubator strategy (i.e., growth of individuals and ideas), *Defining What Matters* suggested the value of analyzing the breadth of the CTL's reach on campus, such as number of individuals, quantity of departments, and range of disciplines reached. It noted, "As incubators, CTLs prioritize fostering growth and development, cultivating individuals and communities, nurturing relationships, promoting transformation, and creating a sense of belonging."[41]

Jennifer Shinaberger, director of Coastal Carolina University's (SC) Center for Teaching Excellence to Advance Learning, gives an example of this orientation's link to participation: "We have 70% of faculty participating in our programs, and that's not counting new faculty orientation or things that are required. Early career faculty grew up with us and are now chairs, deans, associate provosts and upper-level administrators. See how useful it is!"

Among the 107 annual reports, 14 CTLs did not report participation in any form. It is telling that of those 14, over half (57%) had no Incubator strategies or aims, and none of these centers had "heavy" reliance of this strategy (i.e., six or more Incubator strategies and aims). In contrast, of the 49 annual reports from CTLs with Incubator aims and tactics, nearly all (90%) reported participation.

Satisfaction

Reviews of CTL evaluation practices commonly critique centers for evaluating only participant satisfaction. In one of the first reviews of educational development impact literature, Levinson-Rose and Menges noted, "When studies assess satisfaction and skill at preworkshop, end of workshop, and delayed posttest, the happiness index is known to be seriously misleading."[42] While it is reasonable to expect published research about educational development to engage with longer-term and more distal outcomes, it is also fair to ask if this standard should be extended to a center's annual report.

On the one hand, it is important to have multiple measures of a center's work. However, data about participants' immediate perceptions of a program's effectiveness or usefulness can be particularly helpful for a CTL's formative evaluation practices, which are essential for an effective center.[43] Additionally, understood as "quality of experience of the intervention," this metric "is important as a diagnostic tool for the quality of delivery of an engagement strategy or engagement of awareness."[44] Learning and motivation to change—of both students and instructors—is complex and often involves non-cognitive factors.[45] Finally, framed from a utilization-focused approached to evaluation, many of the stakeholders who hold CTLs accountable—such as deans, vice provosts, provosts, and advisory groups—likely would find participant satisfaction to be a valuable characteristic of a center's work on campus. Therefore, I argue that participant satisfaction is an important metric to report, but I also highlight several CTLs that offer interesting and different approaches to document this outcome.

Of the 107 CTLs with annual reports, almost three-quarters of reports (72%, or 77 CTLs) provide some indication of participant satisfaction. In most of these cases (60 CTLs), feedback is systematically gathered and reported, such as a post-event or an annual center-wide survey. However, in 17 cases, satisfaction data are only selectively presented, such as quotes from enthusiastic attendees. Because peer influence is a helpful motivational tool,[46] such an approach should not be discounted, but it is also the case that because most quotes are anonymously attributed, impact may be muted.

Interesting and efficient approaches to measuring satisfaction included California's Point Loma Nazarene University (PLNU) Center for Teaching and Learning's report, which includes evaluation of its Faculty Development and Scholarship Day. Their follow-up survey suggests that the center's investment in this event contributed to faculty's sense of belonging at the university: "92% Agreed or Strongly Agreed that this event . . . made them feel valued and invested in as a PLNU faculty member."[47] Additionally, CTLs can use satisfaction to simultaneously measure their own goal achievement. For example, the Center for Teaching and Learning at Amherst College's (MA) mission indicates that it seeks to provide a "vibrant, inclusive learning community." Therefore, it is significant that its report notes that participants in a workshop series "indicated that these pedagogical conversations . . . built their sense of Amherst College as a community of teaching practitioners."[48]

A third example highlights the importance of formative evaluation for a center's work. With its workshop evaluation practice, Georgia College's Center for Teaching and Learning offers constructive questions for a CTL to examine and improve its offerings, with opportunities for participants to give feedback in response to statements like, "The goals were clearly stated by the presenter," "The methods used were appropriate to the goals," and "I would recommend this to others."[49] The University of Massachusetts Amherst Center for Teaching and Learning's approach to assessing its Midterm Assessment Process (MAP) was also suggestive of the importance of peer influence for instructor engagement in CTL work: "99% of MAP recipients say they would recommend the MAP to their colleagues."[50] In these four cases, measurement of satisfaction appears to have an additional purpose, whether for formative improvement, assessment of institutional impact, or increasing future scope of the center's work.

Additionally, as suggested by *Defining What Matters*, satisfaction may be an important metric for CTLs with an Incubator theory of change. For example, positive participant feedback offers important information about an Incubator approach, particularly if it suggests "themes of care, collegiality, safety, growth, and connection across difference."[51] Of the 49 CTLs with Incubator strategies and tactics, three-quarters (75%) describe a satisfaction measure, although not usually with the granularity of the nature of the feedback.

Instructor Outcomes

Carolin Kreber and Paula Brook suggest that educational developers can assess impact on participants' teaching and learning beliefs and behaviors through classroom observations, interviews, qualitative analysis of journal entries or teaching philosophy statements, and surveys that ask if beliefs were changed or if changes to teaching were planned.[52] Published CTL examples include an observational study of graduate TAs' abilities to apply evidence-based instructional practices after engagement in a 10-week program, as well as research on the impacts of a one-year instructional development program for new faculty on approaches to teaching.[53]

In 46 cases (43% of annual reports), centers offer some indication of participant learning, impact on teaching, or effect on other aspects of professional practice. For learning, confidence is a relatively frequently used measure perhaps because, as the Reinert Center for Transformative Teaching and Learning (Saint Louis University) explains, "Our logic in asking about degrees of confidence is to consider that instructors are less likely to employ culturally responsive course design and teaching strategies if they are not confident about what those strategies are or when/how they would be useful."[54] As another example, Columbia University's (NY) Center for Teaching and Learning's report describes how it partnered with administrators to redesign the annual orientation for new graduate student instructors in its core curriculum, concluding that "participant survey data has shown immediate impact, including an increase in confidence among new Preceptors."[55]

Other survey-based examples of learning included the Center for Teaching and Learning at the University of North Carolina Asheville, which reported on its faculty learning communities (FLCs) six months post-completion. Responses indicated that the greatest reported impact was on understanding of the specific issue addressed by the FLC, but participants also described impacts for reflection about teaching, teaching practices, scholarship, and sense of belonging at the university.[56] Another interesting FLC evaluation indicates that participants in Santa Clara University's (CA) Faculty Collaborative for Teaching Innovation programs made "an average number of 4 equity-minded changes in their classes during Fall 2019 that ranged from in-class strategies to promote more inclusivity and belonging, modifications to assignments, and changes to the course syllabus to include more diverse voices."[57] As an example of a workshop evaluation, Florida International University's Center for the Advancement of Teaching's report indicates that the vast majority of participants planned to make changes to their teaching as a result of participating in the workshop.[58] Further, a qualitative analysis of these changes conducted by CTL staff suggested that most proposed changes were consistent with learner-centered teaching principles.

For a new faculty orientation, Eastern Illinois University Faculty Development's report notes that CTL staff interviewed participants at the end of their first year, asking questions such as:

- What were you proud of accomplishing this past year?
- What has been your greatest challenge?
- What resources have helped you most?

- As a faculty member, what support would you like in the future?
- Who might you consider a mentor for your work?
- How is your work/life balance?[59]

For CTLs with limited resources, this is a useful example of an evaluation with dual purposes: to gather information and to establish responsive connections with new faculty.

A final group of examples involve use of direct measures to assess impact. These are less frequently reported, possibly because of their resource intensiveness. However, in cases where the CTL was heavily engaged in a course redesign initiative, annual reports describe changes made to assessments or course format as well as the development of new digital learning approaches. Additionally, for centers engaged in SoTL or holistic faculty development work, CTL reports include metrics like writing group outcomes. As one example, the Center for Faculty Excellence at the University of Nebraska Omaha lists an impressive record of outcomes from its 20 communities of practice: 13 grant submissions, 13 redesigned courses, 82 publications, and 98 presentations at conferences.[60] A second illustration is noted in the report for Emory University (GA) School of Medicine's Office of Faculty Advancement, Leadership and Inclusion (now Office of Faculty Academic Affairs and Professional Development). In reference to the Manuscript Mentoring Program, the report indicates, "In just four months, 10 junior faculty have paired with mentors, resulting in one published manuscript, two submitted manuscripts now under peer review, and three manuscripts nearing completion."[61] Although findings were not reported, Sinclair Community College's (OH) Center for Teaching and Learning presents an interesting stage model of faculty professional learning—onboarding, first three years, promotion and tenure, full professor, and beyond—with metrics associated with each.[62]

CTLs also cleverly dual purpose the work products of their initiatives, using them both for assessment and educational development aims. For example, the Fashion Institute of Technology's (NY) Center for Excellence in Teaching included reflective teaching portfolios in its list of assessment approaches, and Vanderbilt University's (TN)

Center for Teaching indicated that its active-learning FLC developed a "cheat sheet" of what they learned at the end of their engagement with the community.

Instructor outcomes might potentially be related to multiple theories of change. For example, *Defining What Matters* suggested that CTLs examine interviews or case studies to determine if instructors attributed the center for helping to inspire pedagogical growth and legitimate time spent on teaching. This approach could be applied to CTLs with either a Temple (i.e., recognition and reward) or Incubator change strategy, while those utilizing a Sieve approach (i.e., evidence and expertise) may wish to examine SoTL, assessment, or research outcomes from faculty collaborations with the center.

Student Learning

As Mary Deane Sorcinelli's excellent history of educational development evaluation documents, interest in measuring student learning outcomes rose in the 1990s; however, it was not until the 2010s that a clear linkage was drawn between professional development and student outcomes.[63] One reason for this delay is that it is no small feat to measure the impact of educational development on student learning, especially because it is a "tertiary effect" that follows a chain of an effective CTL service, fidelity of implementation in the classroom, and student engagement in a complex educational environment.[64] Despite the challenges, there are published examples of a CTL's impact on academic outcomes, which include Wheeler and Bach's 2020 examination of a course design institute and FLC using rates of failure, withdrawal, and low grades ("DFW" rates) by race and gender. Another is the 2016 volume *Faculty Development and Student Learning*, which established a "direct path" between faculty participation in professional development, instructor learning, transfer to teaching, and improvement of students' critical thinking, as measured by writing.[65]

Based on the difficulty of measurement, it is not surprising that a smaller number (22) of CTL annual reports address student learning outcomes, nor that these centers have a relatively high mean staffing level (average = 18 individuals). Not surprisingly, centers that offer direct academic support to students, or an Incubator approach, seem to have a slightly easier time of measuring such impact. To illustrate, Brown University's (RI) Sheridan Center for Teaching and Learning indicates that for one of its pre-orientation programs focused on quantitative skills, undergraduates demonstrated statistically significant gains based on a mathematics pre- and posttest.[66] The report for Northwestern University's (IL) Searle Center for Advancing Learning and Teaching notes multiple examples, including grade boosts for peer-guided study groups and drop-in tutoring, as well as increases in critical thinking and emotional intelligence related to a grant-funded international project.[67]

However, there are also multiple examples for faculty-related programs with Hub or Sieve approaches, particularly for course design initiatives and technology projects at larger centers. The University of Louisville's (KY) Delphi Center for Teaching and Learning reported that students who took a seminar designed by the center (as part of its QEP) had a 20% higher retention rate compared to non–course takers, and its adaptive courseware initiative significantly reduced DFW rates in STEM courses.[68] Although not reporting specific results, both the Center for Research on Learning and Teaching at the University of Michigan–Ann Arbor and Dartmouth's (NH) Center for the Advancement of Learning indicate that they assessed their course redesign initiatives through multiple methods, including student focus groups, analytics, surveys, and analysis of grades. An additional example is Duke University's (NC) Learning Innovation Unit's report, which featured that a digital tool developed by the center increased grades, controlling for prior academic performance and standardized test scores.

Documentation of student learning outcomes, however, should not be limited to larger, well-resourced centers. Like other fields and disciplines, CTLs tap into existing scholarship to guide their practice.[69] An amusing way that one survey respondent described this approach in Chism and Szabó's study was, "We know that Clorox bleaches. We don't have to re-study this before we do every wash."[70] Sinclair Community College's (OH) Center for Teaching and Learning documented its service learning activity by citing articles to demonstrate extant scholarship about the impact on learning, noting, "Research suggests that increasing the use of service and other experiential learning pedagogies increases student retention and completion ... [and also] suggests that first generation and minority students are most helped by service engagement & reflection."[71]

Institutional Impact

Institutional impact studies of CTL work are less frequently published, perhaps because this level was not originally part of the individually focused Kirkpatrick framework, which for decades was influential on many CTL evaluations.[72] However, published examples of research include Amundsen and d'Amico's 2019 study of the alignment between an institutional strategic plan and center grant projects, as well as Meizlish, Wright, Howard, and Kaplan's 2017 examination of the impact of a new faculty teaching academy on continued engagement with the CTL.[73]

In contrast, institutional impact is one of the more frequently measured outcomes in CTL reports, which may be suggestive of increasing organizational development roles or attention to an audience attuned to this metric. Half of the reports analyzed here (54 centers) list one or more institutional-level or societal-level outcome. Most frequently (and not surprisingly, based on the timing of these documents), centers discuss their significant contributions to academic continuity during COVID. For example, Centre College's (KY) Center for Teaching and Learning reported detailed statistics on this work: "During the spring 2020 semester we supported a total of 25,070 Zoom meetings, which included 3,084,756 meeting minutes with 113,458 participants."[74] Although less frequently noted, other common measures of institutional impact noted by multiple centers are contributions to reaccreditation and revision of teaching evaluation processes. The University of Rhode Island's Office for the Advancement of Teaching and Learning documented changes to the culture of assessment, which is an activity in its mandate: "Most notable is the steady increase in respondents' positive perceptions about URI's infrastructure to support program assessment and level of university-wide achievement on assessment reporting efforts."[75]

In the age of attention to return on investment, it is also notable that two centers at state universities reported on savings to students as a result of their open educational resources initiatives. SUNY at Fredonia's Professional Development Center estimated almost $200,000 in savings, and CUNY John Jay College of Criminal Justice's Teaching and Learning Center documented over $400,000 in saved books and materials costs. Although not explicitly termed as such, other revenue generation strategies that are highlighted by multiple centers include engagement with grants and development of new online programs and degrees. (Several centers detail their budget and allocations, and it is both interesting and telling that these reports included a broad range of institutional contexts, including the University of Cincinnati's [OH] Center for the Enhancement of Teaching and Learning, Point Loma Nazarene University's [CA] Center for Teaching and Learning, the University of Wisconsin–Stevens Point Center for Inclusive Teaching and Learning, and Yale University's [CT] Poorvu Center for Teaching and Learning.)

Centers also document the intersection of their work with their university's strategic initiatives. For example, the University of Tennessee at Chattanooga's Walker Center for Teaching and Learning wrote, "Much of our work is aligned with goals of UTC's Strategic Plan including support of experiential learning—a high impact practice—and assisting faculty with accessible course content."[76] Similarly, the Center for Teaching Excellence at Indiana University–Purdue University Indianapolis mapped its work onto 10 university strategic goals, such as the promotion of an inclusive campus climate and the increase in capacity for graduate education. One center that includes service learning in its charge, Kentucky Wesleyan College's Center for Engaged Teaching and Learning, also documented its impact on the community. For example, it noted that in 2019, student volunteers for its income tax preparation program saved taxpayers an estimated $28,250 in tax preparation fees.

Committee service, collaboration, and community building were listed in multiple reports as evidence of institutional impact. If a CTL aspires to organizational change goals, these networks are an important metric and, indeed, measures of extent of collaboration can be found in the general evaluation literature.[77]

Committee service is noted in over a quarter (26%) of annual reports. Campus collaborations, particularly around key institutional initiatives, may also be an important signal of Hub-related impact.[78] Of the 28 CTLs who list committee service in their annual reports, most (64%) are aligned with a Hub approach. To illustrate, Saint Louis University's Reinert Center for Transformative Teaching and Learning referenced all four Hub components in its statement of purpose and included both committee service and key campus collaborators in its report.

Relatedly, key collaborators are also frequently listed, occurring in approximately one in five (21%) reports. Of the 22 CTLs that list on-campus collaborators in their annual reports, the majority (68%) are also aligned with a Hub approach. The University of California, Los Angeles Center for the Advancement of Teaching effectively visualized these and also notes on its website that "connections keep us apprised of the teaching needs of our campus, make us aware of global educational trends, and enable synergies with other groups in order to better serve our constituents."[79] Additionally, Seattle University's (WA) Center for Faculty Development described the value of this activity in its 2020 report: "Acting as boundary-spanners across campus is also a key function of our center, not only through co-sponsorships, but also by connecting faculty to one another across disciplinary and organizational silos."[80] Although noted much less frequently, five reports described community-building activities, and most (80%) of these centers are also associated with a Hub strategy.

Kreber and Brook suggest that other possible ways to evaluate a CTL's impact on the institution include surveying students about their perceptions of learning environments, measuring the extent to which instructors value and allocate time to teaching, asking chairs and deans if/how they encourage participation in professional learning, and examining how frequently educational development is referred to in university publications or leaders' speeches.[81] Institutional-level indicators can also include many of those already listed above, such as the proportion of faculty engaging with the center, the percentage of participants who go on to receive grants or awards, participant satisfaction, and the presence of an annual report.[82] Indeed, based on the variety of possible approaches,

Defining What Matters suggested that centers choose those that best align with their aims and change strategies. Possibilities include:

- Hub: "What networks were created when there was CTL involvement in projects that bring people together from different disciplines to work toward a common goal? How many cross-disciplinary teams or projects were developed in response to CTL programs?"
- Incubator: "Is there an increased sense of institutional belonging for those who use CTLs, as measured by campus climate data?"
- Temple: "Do institutional messages (e.g., leadership talks, institutional incentives) encourage instructors or university staff to participate in CTL activities?"
- Sieve: "Is there evidence of raised institutional awareness of evidence-based practices in teaching and learning (e.g., new policies or practices that have an explicit research basis)?"[83]

As Carolin Kreber and Paula Brook note in their widely cited article about impact evaluation of educational development programs, the theory of change (which they call the "intervention strategy") needs to drive decisions about the evaluation strategy.[84]

Making CTL Work Visible

Previous chapters of this book introduced the Hub-Incubator-Temple-Sieve framework to characterize CTL work according to four possible theories of change. In a Hub role, centers promote connection, sponsor collaborative initiatives, bring people together in learning communities, and coordinate centralized programs and resources. As an Incubator, CTLs support individual growth and development through orientations and mentoring, and they foster innovative initiatives through programs like grants. The key approach for a Temple strategy is to elevate the value of teaching, learning, and educational development, largely through recognition and reward. Finally, a Sieve strategy ensures that actions are carefully aligned with evidence-based practice, supporting assessment, evaluation, quality standards, scholarly teaching, and the scholarship of teaching and learning.

While the evaluation levels presented—participation, satisfaction, instructor outcomes, student learning, and institutional impact—are commonly used for educational development research, it may be the case that they do not fully depict the impact of CTL work. For example, others suggest that the Kirkpatrick model does not capture the complexity of educational development, as well as the multiple goals, approaches, and length of programs, because it is largely derived from corporate training.[85] Other educational developers argue that for CTLs with faculty as their primary constituents, a focus on student learning outcomes "overmuch often risks distracting centers from their primary audience: the faculty."[86] Are there other emergent aspects of CTL work that are presented in annual reports, which may not be captured by the six commonly used metrics for educational development research? And how do these emergent themes align with CTLs' change strategies, as expressed in their statements of purpose?

Publications and presentations by CTL staff are one additional metric found in multiple annual reports. In 1997, Chism and Szabó observed that results of evaluation efforts were "seldom" published or presented.[87] However, 1 in 5 (20%) reports analyzed here include citations for CTL work made public. Most clearly aligned with a Sieve approach, these sections make visible the contributions that centers offer to evidence-based practice and generalizable knowledge. Of the 21 reports that identify center research, it is not surprising that most (71%) originate from centers that are aligned with a Sieve strategy. While externally focused sharing is not a typical metric in existing CTL evaluation models, this approach is present in the general evaluation literature. For example, one evaluation of a complex change initiative in the English healthcare sector examines department or team outcomes, noting that "preparing and supporting others to change by sharing information" and "informing wider practice improvement" are important indicators of success in organizational change.[88]

Multiple reports (16%) also documented goals, progress to goal achievement, or needs assessments. Because these are specific to particular goals, the metrics used are customized. Assessment and evaluation are associated with a Sieve change strategy, and of the 17 CTLs that used this approach in their reports, most (71%) have Sieve elements in their statements of purpose.

There are other activities frequently noted in annual reports that do not align as well with theories of change suggested by purpose statements. Grant awardees and projects were a common inclusion, noted in 29% of CTL reports. Such detail demonstrates fiscal responsibility. In this book, grants are aligned with an Incubator approach; however, of the 31 reports that noted grant activity, less than half (48%) are associated with CTLs that referenced an Incubator strategy elsewhere. Similarly, CTL staff's teaching and advising responsibilities are described in five reports, an activity that might also align best with an Incubator approach. However, only two of the five centers (40%) name an Incubator strategy elsewhere. In both of these cases, it may be that other social structures, such as financial resources or position classifications, play a greater role than strategic orientation in guiding these activities.

Conclusion

Evaluation scholar Murray Saunders describes evaluation as a "social practice . . . undertaken by people, within structures of power and resource allocation, bounded by the purpose, intention or function of attributing value or worth to individual, group, institutional or sectoral activity."[89] In other words, as a socially constructed activity, what CTLs evaluate suggests what they value—or what they perceive those who allocate resources to value. In their annual reports, a majority of centers include participation, and for those that include unique counts, CTL data consistently suggest that over half of faculty, approximately two-fifths of graduate student teaching assistants, and about a third of undergraduates engage with their center in any given year. Participant satisfaction and institutional-level outcomes are also commonly included in annual reports. In smaller proportions, CTLs feature instructor and student learning outcomes, but inclusion may also be a function of staffing resources or constituencies that the CTL serves.

Beyond these commonly used measures, other emergent metrics that centers define as important to making their work visible include committee work, collaborations, publications, grants, goals and needs assessments, and teaching and advising responsibilities. By excluding these types of activities from our evaluation frameworks, we may unintentionally be undermining our own efforts to make visible our own centers' strengths. In most cases, these metrics align with center theories of change as described in their purpose statements.

Commonly used models of CTL evaluation, which I apply here, examine six levels of impact: (1) participation, (2) instructor satisfaction, (3) instructor learning, (4) change in instructor's teaching, (5) student learning or experiences of learning environments, and (6) institutional impact. However, in light of CTLs' annual reports and change ambitions, it would be useful to add an additional level: (7) external influence or sharing. Examples might include publications, presentations, or engagement in educational development consortia. This additional level borrows from both CTL work on leading change, as well as evaluation literature, and it better captures that CTL impact might span from the micro (individual or course) to the mega (educational development field).[90] Impact beyond the campus is also an especially important metric for CTLs engaged in service learning or community engagement work.

Centra's 1976 report indicated that only 14% of faculty development programs in the United States evaluated their programs in any way. Published research and center annual reports indicate that the field has come a long way since that time. Both genres offer a wide-ranging and compelling use of research and evaluation that, in many cases, aligns with theories of change. The landscape is certainly not as bleak as critics both internal and external to the field would have us believe, and there has been a particular maturation of CTL evaluation starting in the last decade.[91]

On the other hand, there is room to grow. Fewer than 1 in 10 CTLs (9%) offered an annual report, or similar artifact, publicly on their websites, and of the examples that are available, some are dated. Here, I am not suggesting that only 9% of CTLs evaluate their work. It is likely the case

TABLE 5.1. CTL annual report recommendations

	Metrics for all annual reports
Theory of change and purpose	☐ Describe the center's theory of change and purpose statement (i.e., one or more of the following: mission, vision, goals, and values/guidelines).
Participation	☐ Provide unique counts (i.e., non-duplicated participation) of key constituencies.
	☐ Consider constituency: Offer benchmarks by constituency and institutional type (see pages 179–81).
	☐ Consider strategic orientation by documenting participation by sub-unit (e.g., department, division) every year if center has a strong Hub focus or, if not, periodically to assess reach.
Satisfaction	☐ Offer some systematic indicator of participant satisfaction or engagement, such as a post-event or an annual center-wide survey. This also helps to document good formative practice.

	These annual report metrics should vary depending on factors such as constituency, aim, resources, integrative focus, and strategic orientation (e.g., Hub, Incubator, Temple, Sieve)
Instructor outcomes	☐ Consider constituency: Documentation of instructor outcomes—such as confidence, self-reported changes in teaching, and future plans to make changes—is particularly important for faculty-focused centers.
	☐ Consider tactic: For course design institutes, SoTL programs, and holistic faculty development work (e.g., writing), consider reporting direct measures such as redesigned syllabi and manuscript submissions.
	☐ For centers with limited resources, consider dual-purposing the annual report with relationship-building, e.g., interview new faculty at the end of their first year of engagement with the center.
Student learning	☐ Consider orientation: Documentation of student learning or experience outcomes is more important for Incubator-oriented, or integrated, centers that directly serve students.
	☐ For centers with limited resources, consider referencing existing scholarship on expected outcomes for educational development initiatives.
Institutional impact	☐ Consider aim: For centers seeking to align with the strategic mission or with larger institutional change aims, document key contributions and outcomes, e.g., academic continuity, saved costs, mapping activity onto university/college strategic plan.
	☐ Consider orientation: For Hub-oriented CTLs, committee service, collaboration, and community-building efforts can serve as key indicators. For other orientations, see page 194.
External impact	☐ Consider orientation: For Sieve-oriented CTLs, list publications, presentations, and engagement in educational development consortia.
	☐ Consider integrative units: Impact beyond the campus may also be an especially important metric for CTLs engaged in service learning or community engagement work.

that evaluation takes other forms, that reports are shared locally, or that information is behind institutional firewalls. Over 25 years ago, Chism and Szabó noted a similar trend among CTLs: "Observations in the literature that charge that faculty development programs do not evaluate their services contradict our findings. What appears to be the case is that evaluations are done routinely, but not shared publicly."[92] It may also be the case that by not making public their evaluation practices, CTL directors are expressing another value, pushing back against "an increasing preoccupation with quality assurance" in higher education broadly and CTL literature specifically.[93] Regardless of the reason, CTL evaluation as a private affair leaves the field open to critiques, such as the ones presented at the beginning of this chapter.

An additional growth area rests with a theme running throughout this book: theories of change. Although CTL evaluation approaches appear to implicitly align with CTL theories of change, as suggested by alignment of report data with statements of purpose, there is limited indication of intentionality. Some CTL annual reports (named above) referenced their logic in metric selection, but there was a much more limited description of the logic of program design in relation to key aims. There are no reports that explicitly listed a theory of change—and here, I admittedly include the 2019–20 report from the center that I currently direct. (One CTL used the specific language of "theory of change" in its report—but did not state what it is.) Theories of change are essential to comprehensive CTL evaluation.[94] In annual reports, these might take the shape of simply noting the purpose of the CTL overall (i.e., mission) or intended outcomes for a specific program, indicating why a specific initiative can help achieve these aims, and selecting appropriate evidence to illustrate connections between aim, activity, and outcomes. By adding theories of change to our evaluation repertoire, Centers for Teaching and Learning will more effectively be able to make visible the strengths of our centers and field. Table 5.1 offers other recommendations for CTL annual reports, which should vary in format depending on themes discussed in this book: constituency, aim, and theory of change.

Re-Centering Teaching and Learning in US Higher Education

N THIS BOOK, I have spotlighted the role that Centers for Teaching and Learning are playing in US higher education. These organizational units are growing in both number and scope. Even over just the past decade, we see that CTLs are now playing a broader role on their campuses to support operational needs, strategic aims, and organizational change.

This book documents changes in the number and permeation of CTLs in US higher education compared to a decade earlier. Contexts that saw an increase in the proportion of institutions that house at least one CTL include doctoral universities, master's institutions, baccalaureates, private non-profits, private for-profits, minority-serving institutions, and women's colleges. The very small decline of CTLs in two-year colleges stands in contrast to the increases in other institutions, although consortia-based or networked approaches to educational development may be an emerging alternative system in this context. Coverage grew in every US region over the decade except for US service schools, which showed a very small decrease in CTLs. However, this and a prior study found no CTL presence at tribal colleges and universities, and attention to this sector's educational development needs—whether through centers or other structures—should be an ongoing concern for higher education.[1]

In parallel to an increase in the number of centers, I also confirm that there has been an increase in the mean number of constituencies CTLs report that they directly serve or collaborate with in their work. According to CTL statements of purpose—or combined missions, visions, goals, and values—CTLs invite faculty, staff, and administrators at similar rates, compared to prior missions collected 15 years ago. However, there has been a concomitant expansion into serving student learners, academic units, and external communities. In spite of these changes, faculty continue to be the number one constituency named by CTLs.

Along with broadening of CTLs' constituency base, we have seen a change in CTL goals as expressed in statements of purpose. In 2020, the majority of centers named student learning as a key aim. Because faculty are the key constituency for most CTLs, it is not surprising that instructor-oriented outcomes (such as lifelong learning or reflective teaching) accounted for the second most frequent goal. Change and innovation goals, the third most cited aim, were also common across centers. All three of these ambitions show a substantial increase from prior research on CTL missions. Two emergent aims, not captured in prior scholarship, were also documented in about one in five statements of purpose: (1) promoting scholarly and creative work and (2) diversity, equity, and inclusion (DEI).

This study of CTL statements of purpose also witnessed declines in some key goals, most significantly, those that express support for their campus's institutional mission, strategic plan, or goals. This decline is surprising in light of prior research that suggests the importance of responsiveness to institutional missions, and it is possible that this orientation could prove problematic to CTLs. However, viewed in the context of the rise of change/innovation, DEI, and even instructor outcome goals, there may be another interpretation. In chapter 1, I argued that the constellation of these trends in CTL objectives represents a conversation among educational developers about ways to be situated within their academic institutions while also pushing for change. With their statements of purpose, CTLs are positioning themselves as organizational change agents, working on multiple scales of engagement. I also noted in chapter 1 that an additional challenge for CTLs is increasing frequency of administrative leadership changes and visions in higher education. In fact, we see in this book that even in the span of two years, some of these have resulted in new names or new organizational structures. An alignment too tightly coupled to a senior leader's aims can also make a center more vulnerable to transition when new priorities are established.

Center strategies, or theories of change, were featured in chapter 2 of this study. Once CTLs have established their goals, what can we learn from statements of purpose regarding how they propose to meet these aims? It is here that I established the central theoretical framework used for the remainder of the book, Hub-Incubator-Temple-Sieve (HITS), which is adopted from a review of the scholarship of the sociology of higher education.[2] In a Hub role, centers promote connection, sponsor collaborative initiatives, bring people together in learning communities, and coordinate centralized programs and resources. As an Incubator, CTLs support individual growth and development, as well as innovative initiatives, through programs like grants, orientations, and mentoring. A Temple strategy works to elevate the value of teaching, learning, and educational development largely through recognition and reward. Finally, a Sieve orientation takes a curational approach to highlight the expertise of CTL staff and ensure that actions are carefully aligned with evidence-based practice, doing research and supporting assessment, evaluation, quality standards, scholarly teaching, and the scholarship of teaching and learning (SoTL).

As theories of change, Hub approaches are articulated most frequently across all CTLs, followed by Sieve, Incubator, and Temple. More specifically, signature change approaches for achieving key CTL aims include promoting dialogue and collaboration, as well as designing and offering programs and services. However, there are some variations by Carnegie classification (baccalaureate and master's institutions are ordered Hub-Incubator-Sieve-Temple), and certain strategies more frequently appear in tandem with key aims (e.g., half of the purpose statements with a goal related to change and innovation also noted a Hub: dialogue and collaboration strategy). We do not have precise comparative data to suggest the growth or decline of change strategies over time. However, comparison with a prior analysis of verbs used in CTL mission statements suggests that Hub and Sieve change strategies are growing while Incubator and Temple are relatively stable.[3]

Chapter 3 examined tactics, or the specific programs and services that CTLs listed on their websites in 2020 to carry out their strategies. This chapter challenged the claim that CTLs' approach consists of a small repertoire of programs and services by presenting a wide range of Center for Teaching and Learning tactics, also organized by the HITS strategic framework. By describing some commonalities in most CTLs' approaches, it also combats some perceptions of the field as fractured.

As in previous studies of educational development work, the most utilized tactic was interactive workshops (a Hub approach), listed on over two-thirds of center websites. However, of those centers listing workshops, over a third indicated a program type with an expectation that the participant would have longer-term engagement (e.g., series, certificate, or course). Most frequently, these programs addressed topics related to teaching and learning, including digital approaches and DEI. Because purpose statements that lay out aims of student and faculty learning also frequently tend to list "programs and services" as a strategy and "workshops" as a tactic, the topics of these programs suggest strong alignment between change strategies and practice in this area.

Another frequently used tactic was a community to promote dialogue and collaboration (also a Hub approach), such as a book group, journal club, professional learning community, community of practice, teaching circle, affinity group, or change team. Over two-fifths of centers listed such an initiative. Most frequent topics for these initiatives were teaching enhancement, DEI, and cultivating student learning. Because purpose statements that lay out aims of DEI and quality of teaching also frequently tend to list "learning communities" as a tactic, the topics of these groups suggest some alignment between goals and practice. (Although not the most frequently listed Hub tactic for student learning aims, learning communities is a close second.) Although widely employed, dialogue and collaboration communities could strategically be used even more in alignment with theories of change to foster other common CTL aims, namely change and innovation, culture, and community building.

In comparison to prior survey findings, longer-term tactical initiatives appear with more frequency compared to reports by educational developers only a decade ago. Many CTLs are also highlighting initiatives that shift the unit of analysis of CTL work, focusing on the course and institution, to promote change more effectively. Emergent program types include course transformation initiatives, university-wide events, feedback models that center students, and alternative approaches to recognize teaching, such as open classroom weeks.

Just as Hub theories of change are articulated most frequently across all CTLs, Hub is the most frequently adopted tactical approach. This is followed closely by Incubator. The very high application of Hub and Incubator approaches signals a high level of coherence in approach to practice. Sieve and Temple tactics are less frequently applied. By Carnegie type, emphases change a little (e.g., baccalaureate, Incubator-Hub-Sieve-Temple; medical/health, Hub and Incubator-Temple-Sieve; other special focus, Incubator-Hub-Temple-Sieve).

Aligning the findings of chapters 1, 2, and 3, table C.1 presents the top nine center aims, alongside the theories of change that appear most frequently in these statements of purpose, and the tactics that most frequently appear among CTL websites with the same goals. This table is a blunt instrument—it co-locates ideas found on various spaces on CTL websites (i.e., statements of purpose and listings of programs and services), rather than analyzing the full logic of a center's strategic plan. It does, however, point to more coherence for some CTL aims compared to others. For example, for community-building aims, the most frequently associated theory of change (Hub: dialogue and collaboration) is also matched with a related tactic (Hub: learning communities). There are also some striking dissonances, namely for DEI aims. Among centers expressing goals around diversity, equity, and inclusion, a Sieve theory of change is most frequently articulated in purpose statements, but Incubator and Hub tactics most commonly appear on websites. It may be that the more recent emergence of DEI aims in center missions means

TABLE C.1. Alignment of CTL aims, theories of change, and tactics

CTL aim	Frequently paired theory of change	Frequently paired tactics
Student learning	Hub: Dialogue and collaboration Hub: Programs and services	**Incubator: Reflective consultation** Hub: Workshop (brief)
Instructor outcome	Hub: Programs and services	**Incubator: Orientation** Hub: Workshop (brief)
Change and innovation	Hub: Dialogue and collaboration	**Hub: Workshop (brief)** Incubator: Reflective consultation
Culture, climate, and environment	Hub: Dialogue and collaboration	**Incubator: Orientation** Hub: Learning communities
Scholarly and creative work	Hub: Programs and services	**Incubator: Orientation** Hub: Workshop (brief) and Learning communities
Diversity, equity, and inclusion	Sieve: SoTL and EBT	**Incubator: Orientation** and Reflective consultation Hub: Learning communities
Institutional mission	Hub: Programs and services	**Hub: Learning communities** Incubator: Reflective consultation and Orientation
Teaching effectiveness and excellence	Hub: Programs and services	**Incubator: Reflective consultation and Orientation** Hub: Learning communities
Community building	Hub: Dialogue and collaboration	**Hub: Learning communities** Incubator: Reflective consultation

NOTE: Bold indicates the most frequently named tactic in statements of purpose that also reference a given aim.

that strategies and approaches are still in experimental mode, but more alignment would be helpful for achieving these critical goals.

While chapter 3 centered on tactics focused primarily on teaching and learning, chapter 4 examined new mandates that have historically been organizationally located elsewhere in the academy. These include instructional technology and online learning, assessment, writing, service learning and community engagement, and career and leadership development. The vast majority of CTL websites showed program types that encompass at least one of these five integrative emphases. Most frequently, over half of centers offer some programmatic focus on digital or online teaching and learning, and over a quarter have institutionalized this emphasis by including at least one digital learning–focused staff member. Assessment and evaluation, career and leadership development, and writing also have programmatic presence and, to a smaller degree, staff specifically assigned to these areas. Least frequently, CTLs infused service learning / community engagement, with only a small proportion of centers offering related programs or services or having staff or an embedded unit.

As observed in prior research on CTL integrative trends,[4] these synergies bring roses and thorns. On the one hand, there are indications that the faculty and administrative titles of CTL leaders have been elevated, with a greater proportion now assuming senior positions, particularly in larger centers. On the other, there does not appear to be a concomitant increase in CTL personnel that would help to take on these new functions. In light of increased constituency size and expanding missions and tactics, these data suggest that CTLs are doing more with less. This chapter cautions that if not attended to carefully, this strain promises to have a detrimental impact on centers.

One organizational response has been the emergence of new engagement and governance structures. While over a quarter of CTLs have formal advisory boards, informal structures such as programs for faculty fellows and student employment (e.g., graduate and undergraduate teaching consultants) are common among CTLs and allow centers to meet the demands of expanding constituencies and mandates. While these structures do not lessen CTL personnel workload, they do allow for more diverse specialization, and they can afford a higher degree of faculty and student buy-in and engagement.

While chapters 1–4 suggested that CTLs are now playing a broader role on their campuses to support operational needs, strategic aims, and organizational change, chapter 5 examined how educational developers can best make this work visible. CTLs have long been subjects of critique for their evaluation practice. This may be related to a static negative perception of US college teaching, as documented by historians of the academy.[5] It is also the case that we can understand centers' evaluation practice better if we shift our understandings of evaluation from standards needed to produce generalizable research. Instead, a more reasonable framing is metrics consistent with the change orientations of our centers and the purposes of evaluation in CTL work.

Chapter 5 analyzed over 100 annual reports that are publicly available on CTL websites. I applied commonly used CTL evaluation metrics to document the degree to which centers employ them in their annual reports and spotlight some innovative models for their presentation. A majority of CTLs report on participation, instructor satisfaction, and institutional impact. Close to half offer some indication of instructor learning, impact on teaching, or effect on other aspects of professional practice. A smaller number, most frequently at larger centers or those offering direct academic support, report student learning outcomes.

I then applied the HITS framework to understand other ways that CTLs make their work visible, which may be more compatible with their own orientations. Hub-related impacts are frequently noted, such as committee service and key collaborators. About one in five CTLs document their scholarly activity aligned with a Sieve strategy, and over a quarter list grant projects, which could be an Incubator approach. A small number report teaching and advising activity, which could be aligned with an Incubator orientation. Here, I proposed that commonly used models of CTL evaluation—now at six levels, from participation to institutional impact[6]—should be extended by an additional level: external influence, sharing, and impact on the field. This can be documented by publications, presentations, or engagement in educational development consortia.

While chapter 5 identified great strengths in the annual reports that are found on CTL sites, it also calls attention to their relative infrequency. It also notes the absence of any reports that explicitly list a theory of change. I argued that through both of these absences, we limit opportunities for CTLs to make their work visible.

Alignment and Intentionality

A key thesis running throughout this book is that Centers for Teaching and Learning are important change agents on campus with strategies that are important and impactful—but sometimes unarticulated or unaligned. Information found on statements of purpose (theories of change, or strategy) and programs and services listed on websites (tactics), for each of the four HITS orientations is compared in table C.2.

Although Hub is the most frequently used orientation, from both strategic and tactical standpoints, there is curiously not a statistically significant correlation between the number of Hub strategies named in CTL purpose statements and the number of Hub-related programs or services. However, most (64%) centers' sites suggest some alignment by naming a strategy and tactics—or by not doing both. For Sieve, there is similar alignment (61%).

Interestingly, although Temple is the least used change strategy and tactic, if alignment is an indicator, there may be the greatest intentionality with this orientation. Over two-thirds (68%) of CTLs align their change strategy with use of the approach.

There is least coherence for an Incubator theory of change, one of oldest approaches in educational development. Although there is a small positive association between the number of Incubator strategies and tactics, a majority (55%) of centers showed some misalignment. Most frequently, this happened when a CTL offered an Incubator program (mentoring, orientation, consultations and observations, and grants)

TABLE C.2. Alignment of CTL strategy and tactics (in percentages)

	Name strategy and list tactics	Name neither strategy nor tactics	Name strategy but not tactics	Name tactics but not strategy	Correlation between number of strategies and tactics
Hub	58	6	12	24	$r = .04$
Incubator	31	14	6	49	$r = .10*$
Sieve	21	41	19	19	$r = .28*$
Temple	7	61	12	20	$r = .14*$

*Significant at $p < .001$

but did not articulate a related theory of change. Because many Incubator strategies are among the most traditional in the educational development portfolio, this gap may reflect longstanding assumptions held about the work that educational developers do not feel the need to articulate. More simply, it also could reflect a lag in how frequently CTLs update programs compared to missions.

In all four cases of the HITS framework, there was a small association between the presence of the change strategy in a center's statement of purpose and reported utilization of that approach on its website. This may explain Gibbs's observation from across the Atlantic in 2013 that strategic change and improvement "is still relatively rare in the USA, where teaching development often remains largely peripheral and focuses on change tactics."[7] If we are to use a change strategy, it is important to be explicit about it in order to maximize its impact.[8]

Further, in the age of scarce resources allocated to higher education, it is doubly important to consider how tactics align with aim and theory of change. Programs listed on websites of over three-quarters (77%) of CTLs suggest use of more than one tactical orientation, and over 1 in 10 (16%) apply all four. Just as CTL constituencies and aims have expanded, CTL tactical approaches were also quite broad. In light of all of strains on CTL resources presented in chapter 4, a critical project for CTLs becomes alignment of aim, theory of change, and tactics.

Advice for CTL Leaders Engaged in Strategic Planning

Appendix 2 offers several models for fostering discussion within CTLs, or campuses more broadly, about CTL strategic planning. These models were developed by directors at three centers and shared at a November 2018 POD Network conference session.[9] Additionally, I add a fourth model that I used with the Sheridan Center Advisory Groups in fall 2020 to remotely initiate our five-year strategic planning process. My hope is that others will find these to be useful tools for prompting reflection and discussion about CTL ambitions, theories of change, and aligned tactics.[10] These models also suggest a modification to how centers typically engage in strategic planning, particularly for new centers.

Most advice holds that the creation of a clearly defined mission and goals should be the very first step that a new or re-envisioning center should take.[11] However, missions and goals are difficult genres to author. Instead, I hope that this book offers a useful contribution to the strategic planning process: begin with identifying key aims and a strategic orientation. Based on key desired aims and campus needs, in which orientation(s) does a center primarily seek to guide its work: Hub, Incubator, Temple, or Sieve? Once the aims and primary orientations are identified, they can shape statements of purpose and help a center develop priorities.

It can be tempting for a CTL, especially one that is newly formed, to have ambitious plans and try to meet many campus needs. Interestingly, well-established centers tend to have fewer aims and strategies, compared to those that have been in existence for under 10 years (table C.3). While most centers have more than one aim and strategic orientation, it is useful for a new center to start more conservatively to avoid resource strain.

In contrast, the relationship between CTL age and number of tactical orientations is better aligned. Most (65%) mature centers employ all four, but new CTLs most commonly employ between two (33%) and three (36%) tactical orientations.

Center size is related to number of aims, strategies, and tactics in expected ways. For example, "centers of one" express a mean of 2.6 aims,

TABLE C.3. Mean number of aims, strategies, and tactics, by CTL age

	0–9 years (n = 72)	10–19 years (n = 49)	20–29 years (n = 42)	30+ years (n = 20)
Aims (out of 9 possible)	3.0	2.8	2.8	2.5
Strategies (out of 4 possible)	2.0	1.8	1.6	1.8
Tactics* (out of 4 possible)	2.6	2.8	2.9	3.3

*N = 183, F = 2.9, df = 3 & 179, p < .05. Bonferroni post-hoc test shows significant differences for 30+ years and 0–9 years (p < .05).

1.6 strategies, and 1.9 tactics, while the largest CTLs report 2.7, 1.6, and 3.0, respectively.[12]

Notes for Senior Leaders

My own perspective as a frequent participant in discussions with CTL colleagues is that center leaders often feel overlooked and misunderstood by senior administrators, believing that campus leadership does not fully understand the depth of the relationship between centers and their campus constituencies (e.g., links to faculty) or the strategic roles that centers can play. However, I believe that the findings of this book suggest otherwise. In many ways, CTLs have been asked to take on—and have been responsive to—adding new constituencies, missions, and mandates. While centers of the past may have been in the process of "coming in from the margins,"[13] CTLs today are embodying the "Center" in their titles by working at the center of their campuses and centering much of their activity. This is exemplified in the Hub orientation that takes such prominence in CTL work.

This dynamic is due to a recognition that the work of Centers for Teaching and Learning is foundational to the success of the academy. As corroborated by previous research and in this study, on aggregate, CTLs engage a majority of faculty and substantial proportions of graduate students and undergraduates in any given year.[14] Because of these networks, the work of CTLs positively impacts the experiences and outcomes of these constituencies.

For students, there is strong evidence supporting the impact of educational development on student learning, student success, and equitable outcomes.[15] Similarly, for graduate students, high participation in educational development is related to success in the academic job market and use of evidence-based practices in subsequent faculty positions.[16] Faculty professional learning around teaching is connected to retention, satisfaction, and productivity.[17] Additionally, faculty teaching networks play an important role in creating a culture of teaching and are associated with positive student feedback.[18] In medical education, well-designed programs are associated with similar outcomes in teaching behaviors, improved student outcomes and persistence, and organizational impacts such as more extensive collegial networks.[19] Finally, the social networks or learning communities that many CTLs create can be used as powerful change strategies to move forward institutional initiatives.[20]

To fully realize this promise, it is important for senior leaders to position and resource CTLs appropriately. While well-resourced centers can have transformative impacts on their campuses, CTLs are particularly vulnerable to leadership transition, and too much change can erode their capacity.

Supportive senior leaders can partner with CTLs to assess resource needs. Earlier sections of this book suggest that although centers have taken on new mandates, staffing has not increased proportionately over time. At minimum, it is important to reference the mean staffing level of 1 CTL staff per 262 instructional FTE when hiring for a center—although additional functions, constituencies, and aims may certainly call for additional personnel. While people are the resource that is most centrally analyzed here, other critical resources to help a CTL be successful include budget, access to information and influence (e.g., positioning on key standing and ad hoc committees), and visibility (e.g., highlighting the center's work in speeches or college/university communications).[21]

Second, it is important to be mindful of the strain of these mandates on CTLs. In addition to the five key expansionary areas named in chapter 4, I found a range of other functions in center missions, including global learning, dual enrollment and early college, clerical professional development, disability services, testing and scanning services, outreach, robot loans, honors programs, photographic services, academic integrity reporting, and poster printing—to name a few. The operative point is not that any of these is a bad idea; indeed, there may be strategic reasons to integrate these tasks with the work of a CTL. However, additional mandates to a Center for Teaching and Learning result in accompanying challenges, including communication with campus stakeholders and integration of staff who bring with them different work cultures and values. These integrations should be carefully considered in partnership with CTL staff.

Third, when selecting CTL leadership, supportive senior leaders should consider how best to position that individual or team. Senior leadership positions for CTL directors are becoming more common, such as assistant and associate provost positions. Although there are debates in the field about requiring a terminal degree for all center staff positions, it is clear that most directors have this credential. However, flexibility in some job criteria may result in a better pool for CTL leadership searches: directors have a variety of disciplinary backgrounds, and faculty status is also variable, being less common for larger centers.

Finally, supportive leaders can be mindful of the extensive resources needed to carry out CTL evaluation, particularly on outcomes related to student learning. While CTLs should certainly be accountable to their home institutions and key constituencies, it is also important to understand that the key function of most centers is as an administrative or service unit, not as an academic department or a research center. Therefore, expectations should be consistent. Senior leaders can review table 5.1 with their CTL head to define what benchmarks make sense to report publicly, in line with a center's staffing, orientation, and constituency base.

CTLs in a Time of COVID

At the time of this writing, US higher education is still grappling with the impact of the COVID-19 pandemic. Some case studies of CTL work during this time, particularly in 2020, point to new prominence for the work of CTLs, as well as expanded workloads.[22] While these narratives also resonate with my experience as a CTL director, it is interesting that there was only one instance in which the time of coding variable showed statistically significant differences in the group of websites visited in the early months of 2020 as compared to the later part of the year. (CTLs coded in the latter part of 2020 have lower presence of Incubator strategies compared to those in the early months of the year.) One interpretation of this finding (or lack thereof) is that the full impact of the pandemic on US Centers for Teaching and Learning, at least as evidenced on center websites, will take time to manifest. However, it may also be that these trends were already in motion, as suggested by Kim and Maloney's research (published on the cusp of the pandemic) that found "responsibilities and impact of CTLs are growing and . . . learning innovation is at the heart of this shift."[23]

Indeed, while the COVID pandemic certainly made Center for Teaching and Learning work more visible, it is also clear that their work as organizational change agents was already becoming more prominent. Looking back over the decades, the field I entered is no longer the field in which I work. With the growth of Hub and Sieve strategies, educational development has moved from a craft focused on the individual instructor to an evidence-based endeavor, focused on bridging multiple levels (individual and organizational) and constituencies. Yet these have been positive changes. I hope that the next few decades are as fruitful for the field and that across the landscape of higher education there will be a more consistent focus in research and practice regarding the significant roles that Centers for Teaching and Learning play in organizational change.

This appendix offers definitions of key variables used, as well as explanation of approaches to statistical tests. The web methodology for identification of Centers for Teaching and Learning (CTLs) is described in the introduction. Readers interested in the list of 2020 CTLs can contact the author, although the POD Network Center Directory (https://podnetwork.org/centers-programs/) will likely have more updated records.

Key variables that are used throughout this book are as follows:

Carnegie classification. This variable relies on, but modifies, institutional type as defined by the Carnegie Foundation and recorded in the Carnegie Foundation 2018 datafile.[1] The Carnegie classification reports out 32 different institutional types, but for this analysis I have reduced these to 6 broad types, including associate's, baccalaureate, doctoral, and master's. Medical schools and health science units, as well as other disciplinary-specific units are recoded as "Special focus: medical/ health" and "Special focus: other" (even if their larger institutional home is a different Carnegie classification). The introduction presents the breakdown by modified Carnegie classification in this dataset.

Control is analyzed in three categories: private for-profit, private not-for-profit, or public, as defined by the Carnegie Foundation 2018 datafile. The introduction presents the breakdown by control in this dataset.

Institutional mission is analyzed for minority-serving institutions (MSIs) or women's colleges, also as recorded by the Carnegie Foundation 2018 datafile. The introduction presents the breakdown by diverse missions and foci.

Presence of digital learning staff. Job titles that were coded as "digital learning staff" include those that include the following key terms: Instructional Designer, LMS, Computer Support, Digital, Technology/Technologist, Media/Multimedia, Distance/Online Learning, Instructional Support for Technology, Learning Experience Designer, Course Production, Software Applications, Video, Digital/Web Accessibility, e-Learning, and Web.

Carnegie Community Engagement Elective Classification is used in some analyses. This variable is also pulled from the 2018 Carnegie datafile, and it records the elective classification as of 2015. Using unique institutions, a quarter (25%) of centers in this dataset are associated with institutions that had Carnegie engaged status at this time.

Full-time equivalent student enrollment (full-time plus one-third part-time) is also recorded in the Carnegie datafile and 2020 IPEDS data.[2] I use two years: 2017 (introduction) and 2020 (all other chapters). Using unique institutions, median student enrollment data for 2020 is 4,618 FTE. Student FTE data for 2020 are often transformed into quartiles: Quartile 1: 29–2,218 (25%), Quartile 2: 2,219–4,618 (25%), Quartile 3: 4,619–10,136 (25%), Quartile 4: 10,137–87,002 (25%). This variable is applied only to centers serving the full campus or with a unique IPEDS designation.

Full-time equivalent instructional staff is based on 2020 IPEDS data.[3] Using unique institutions, median instructional staff for 2020 is 319 FTE. Instructional FTE data for 2020 are often transformed into quartiles: Quartile 1: 16–181 (25%), Quartile 2: 182–319 (25%), Quartile 3: 320–648 (25%), Quartile 4: 649–7,444 (25%). This variable is applied only to centers serving the full campus or with a unique IPEDS designation.

CTL age is calculated for 183 centers that have the year of founding available on their websites, based on a calculation in 2020 (2020 minus year of founding). The groups used are 0–9 years old (39%), 10–19 years (27%), 20–29 years (23%), and 30+ years (11%). In cases where the center underwent reorganization, the original year of founding was still applied as the age.

CTL personnel is calculated by identifying the number of individuals listed on center web pages, such as on their "About Us" pages. I omit any student employees (identified as such) as well as individuals with titles that suggest that they are part of faculty service (e.g., "Faculty Development Committee Chair") rather than engaged in a fully or partially compensated role at the center. More on this calculation can be found in chapter 4.

Time of coding is recorded in a binary: (1) before or during March 2020 and (2) post–March 2020. The intention of this variable is to analyze possible shifts in CTL approach during the early months of COVID-19.

Tests of Significance

With my web methodology, I attempted to determine the population of CTLs in 2020. Although I went to great lengths to include as many centers as possible, I acknowledge that it is likely that my process did not capture every CTL in the United States in 2020, resulting in a sample.

In most cases in this book, I present frequencies. However, in some cases, I do also present tests of significance. I encourage readers to interpret my statistical analyses with recognition that my sampling methodology (as outlined in the introduction) is not random sampling. While random sampling is a preferred method for promoting representative samples, I was not able to utilize true random sampling. (A list of the whole population of all CTLs from which to randomly sample does not exist.) Statistical inferences about a population are only meaningful to the extent that the sample represents the target population. Having outlined my methodology here and in the introduction, readers can determine whether my sample should be understood as sufficiently representative for making meaningful inferences.

Because some institutions have multiple CTLs, when I compute tests of statistical significance for some institutional-level analyses, I use unique institutions to maintain assumptions of independent measures. These tests take place in two forms. First, for analyses by Carnegie classification type, I consider all centers at an IPEDS institution that have a different Carnegie type (as defined above). For example, if a university has two centers, one located in the main campus and the other in its veterinary school, these are considered different Carnegie types, and both centers are included in the analysis. If the two CTLs are associated with similar classifications, I select the one that has larger staffing (see above for methodology for identifying staffing). If staffing levels are identical, I randomly select one. In analyses of statements of purpose, which form the bulk of this book, an analysis of unique institutions by Carnegie classifications reduces 1,105 statements of purpose to 1,080 statements of purpose. These represent 309 CTLs at doctoral institutions, 289 master's institutions, 199 associate's institutions, 167 baccalaureates, 88 medical / health-related contexts, 27 other special focus institutions, and 1 missing.

Second, for all other institutional characteristics (e.g., control, mission, size), I also use unique institutions. In this case, I choose the center with the largest staffing (regardless of Carnegie classification). In analyses of statements of purpose, which form the bulk of this book, an analysis of unique institutions reduces 1,105 statements of purpose to 1,025 statements of purpose. These represent 302 CTLs at doctoral institutions, 288 master's institutions, 198 associate's institutions, 165 baccalaureates, 55 medical / health-related contexts, 16 other special focus institutions, and 1 missing.

Finally, for any CTL-level tests of significance (CTL personnel, CTL age, presence of digital learning staff), all CTLs with websites are included. In this case, the 1,105 statements of purpose are distributed among 324 CTLs at doctoral institutions, 290 master's institutions, 206 associate's institutions, 167 baccalaureates, 90 medical / health-related contexts, 27 other special focus institutions, and 1 missing.

NOTES

1. Indiana University Center for Postsecondary Research, Carnegie Classifications, 2018 public data file, http://carnegieclassifications.iu.edu/downloads/CCIHE2018 -PublicDataFile.xlsx.

2. US Department of Education, National Center for Education Statistics, Integrated Postsecondary Education Data System (IPEDS), 2020.

3. US Department of Education, 2020.

Yale Center for Teaching and Learning Impact Retreat (July 2018)
(Developed by Jennifer Frederick, Poorvu Center for Teaching and Learning
Executive Director and Associate Provost for Academic Initiatives)

Time: 3 hours, 15 min
Retreat Goals:
1. Deeply consider how and why we measure the impact of our CTL work.
2. Expand our understanding of the Yale CTL impact by considering the reach of several of our teams.
3. Identify several high-priority ways we can improve articulation of our impact in the year ahead:
    a. As discrete teams focused on a particular population
    b. As integrated units committed to advancing teaching and learning excellence at Yale

Participants: a subset of CTL teams, including Faculty Teaching Initiatives, Graduate and Postdoctoral Teaching Development, and Undergraduate Writing and Tutoring

Pre-work
1. Read *Defining What Matters*[1] and Mary Wright's chapter.[2]
2. (optional) Read Stevens et al.[3] that provides the theoretical basis for the categories of impact in the guidelines.
3. Each team will fill out relevant sections on a Google spreadsheet to document (a) current evaluation efforts and (b) programs/services by department/school.

After the retreat, new sub-groups refine and further analyze data collected. We met again for 1.5 hours to continue our collaborative work.

Group 1: Categorize the data to see what else can be learned (by type of data collected, by POD document categories, by size/outreach of initiative, etc.).
   October retreat activity: We reviewed newly tabulated information about the types of evaluation activities conducted and data collected (e.g., observation, reflection, survey, interview). Teams used this information to consider what additional evaluation effort would be feasible and effective for demonstrating our impact. This reflection activity translated into a concrete action plan for each team participating.

Time	Activity	Facilitation/Format
30 min	**Overview and big ideas** Why are we doing this? Goals and alignment Our context—institutional realities shaping our work	Facilitator leads with input from all
60 min	**Reflections on our current evaluation efforts, and outreach as a center** What did we learn from completing the "Programs by level" tab (listing evaluation efforts)? What did we learn from completing and reviewing the "Programs by dept/school" tab? Going deeper: How do our efforts map to POD evaluation guidelines (incubator, sieve, hub, temple)? Is this a useful way to think about impact indicators?	Each team comments, raises questions
45 min	**Where are the gaps? What opportunities should we prioritize?** Are there research-based practices we promote, where data may strengthen our case about influence on teaching and learning? How might we demonstrate our influence on diversity, equity, inclusivity?	Group discussion
45 min	**Action planning** Time for teams, or mixed groups, to prioritize a specific type of impact to evaluate	Small groups
15 min	**Wrap up** Revisit goals and respond to some reflective prompts What did you gain from this retreat? What next steps will you/your team take after this retreat? Next retreat: when shall we return to this effort as a group?	Spokesperson from small groups Facilitator concludes and collects input on index cards

Group 2: Add nuance to the department/school data (which ones are strongest partners and might we leverage that information?).

October retreat activity: We reviewed newly sorted data about level of engagement by department and school (none, low, medium, high). We considered directionality of these engagements (did they come to us, or did we reach out to them?). We used this information as the basis for a conversation about strategy. Should we focus on moving departments from none to low engagement, double down on the high engagement departments, and so on. We did not resolve this question, though it will be expanded to include more of the CTL staff and eventually our advisory board.

Group 3: Develop a new prompt (such as what surprised me most about our current efforts) and gather input. As a second step, look for themes in the responses and attempt to add a layer of ratings (e.g., from listening for input to pushing an agenda). This exercise could supply new insights for the next retreat.

October retreat activity: We examined six themes that emerged from individual responses using a gallery walk to collect additional comments on each theme. Example themes that emerged included "respecting department cultures" and "building trust that the CTL is not a repair shop and we offer value to all."

University of Denver Office of Teaching and Learning Directors' Retreat
(Submitted by Bridget Arend, now at Center for Teaching, Learning and Design, Metropolitan State University of Denver. Ideas developed collectively by University of Denver OTL Directors)

Collective Theory of Change
We each brought an article or reading that informs our own theory of transformative change and began to create an emerging collective theory of change for our office. We found ourselves especially focusing on change that happens at the:

- o   micro (individual),
- o   meso (community/microculture), and
- o   macro (university) levels,

and what/how our work should touch many of those levels or at least strongly influence one or two. We returned to some of the same ideas/themes such as culture change at every level, a sense of belonging, how rituals and structures support change, a focus on communities, going from participation to reflection to change, developing habits of reflection, inclusion and continual learning, and the idea of thriving.

Metaphors for Our Office
We worked through a framework proposed by a POD Network sub-group envisioning new ways to see our impact on campus (see *Defining What Matters*). We

found ourselves reframing this framework from a place-based concept to a role-based concept, such as:

- Incubator → Gardener (incubate ideas)
- Sieve → Curator (best practices)
- Hub → Weaver (connecting)
- Temple → Guide (sanctuary and legitimizer)

Prioritizing Work

We also found ourselves heavily using a metaphor about creating a healthy fire, based on the poem "Fire" by Judy Sorum Brown. A fire needs good strong logs, but also space and air to keep the fire burning. If there are too many logs, the fire burns out. At the end of the last day, we worked through specific initiatives and priorities, sorting them into fire-themed categories:

- Big Logs (those things we need to prioritize)
- Kindling (things we still need to do but may need to set boundaries around), and
- The Woodpile (things we need to set aside for now so that we can have time to focus on priorities)
- Compost [?] (things we need to stop doing)

Retreat to Develop Evaluation Strategic Plans
(Developed by Mary Wright, Associate Provost for Teaching and Learning and Executive Director, Sheridan Center for Teaching and Learning, Brown University)

Time: 3 hours
Motivating Big Question: What are feasible ways to document the work of your center to key people who most need to know?

Objectives:
- Discuss how to target assessment.
- Identify key questions CTLs often ask about their work and how to tailor them to our own contexts.
- Develop a preliminary, feasible evaluation plan.
- Identify strategies for communicating your impact.

Key work products:
- Comprehensive evaluation plan
- Evaluation communication plan

Time	Activity
10 min	Introductions and framing
5 min	"Theory minute": Summative and formative evaluation; utilization-focused evaluation
15 min	Think-pair-share: Imagine that you are standing next to your university president at a reception. What is one thing your president most wants to know about your CTL's work? Ending activity: Record a key question on your evaluation plan.
15 min	Mini presentation: Three frameworks for organizing questions CTLs often ask about their work 1. What are the outcomes of faculty who use my CTL (faculty outcomes framework)? 2. What are the outcomes of the CTL (e.g., application and transfer; Kirkpatrick-based frameworks)? 3. What are the outcomes of the CTL by the key function(s) on your campus (see *Defining What Matters*)?
15 min	Working break: Skim the 9 principles of the *Defining What Matters* document.
15 min	Think-Pair-Share: What is one principle that resonates with you? One that raises questions for you?
5 min	Mini-presentation on Hub-Incubator-Temple-Sieve heuristic.
30 min	Application activity: Apply one of the evaluation models to outline additional questions you want to ask about their center. Add other key questions you want to be asking about your CTL's work to your evaluation plan.
10 min	Mini Presentation on Data Sources: - Two perspectives on participation metrics - Two perspectives on post-workshop evaluations - Other data sources
25 min	Carousel brainstorm at table: Ideas for data sources that would answer a key question. Ending activity: Add possible data sources to your evaluation matrix.
5 min	Communicating Your Impact Theory Minute on reporting standards.
25 min	Annual report show and tell: In pairs, take a tour through an annual report. What questions is the CTL asking about its work? What "story" is it telling key stakeholders? What is effective? Report out of 1–2 useful approaches.
5 min	Session evaluation

Advisory Board Activity to Initiate Strategic Planning Through HITS Orientations

(Developed by Mary Wright, Associate Provost for Teaching and Learning and Executive Director, Sheridan Center for Teaching and Learning, Brown University)

Objectives: Identify key goals and activities associated with the HITS Orientations
Time needed: 60 minutes
Modality: Can be completed online or in person

Time	Activity
10 min	Explain the four HITS orientations using definitions in *Defining What Matters* (POD Network, 2018).
20–25 min	Break up into 4 small groups for a carousel brainstorm. In rotations, groups brainstorm needed CTL goals or activities associated with each orientation. (The prompt might be phrased, "Based on the needs of our college/university, which goals should we have in these areas?") If meeting online, idea generation can happen with a tool such as Jamboard. If meeting in person, participants can document their ideas on index cards. Groups rotate after 5 minutes, each adding ideas onto those previously generated.
10 min	In the last rotation, each group should arrive at its starting topic. The task of the group is to summarize the key themes documented on index cards or Jamboard posts.
15–20 min	Each group reports out 1–2 key ideas.

NOTES

1. POD Network, *Defining What Matters: Guidelines for Comprehensive Center for Teaching and Learning (CTL) Evaluation* (Nederland, CO: POD Network, 2018), https://podnetwork.org/content/uploads/POD_CTL_Evaluation_Guidelines__2018_.pdf.

2. Mary C. Wright, "Measuring a Teaching Center's Effectiveness," in *Advancing the Culture of Teaching on Campus: How a Teaching Center Can Make a Difference*, edited by Constance Cook and Matt Kaplan (Sterling, VA: Stylus Publishing, 2011), 38–49.

3. Mitchell L. Stevens, Elizabeth A. Armstrong, and Richard Arum, "Sieve, Incubator, Temple, Hub: Empirical and Theoretical Advances in the Sociology of Higher Education," *Annual Review of Sociology* 34 (2008): 127.

Introduction. How Many Centers for Teaching and Learning Are There?

1. Sally Kuhlenschmidt, "Distribution and Penetration of Teaching-Learning Development Units in Higher Education: Implications for Strategic Planning and Research," *To Improve the Academy* 29, no. 1 (2011): 274–87.

2. Joshua Kim and Edward Maloney, *Learning Innovation and the Future of Higher Education* (Baltimore, MD: Johns Hopkins University Press, 2020), 46.

3. C. Wright Mills, *The Sociological Imagination* (Oxford: Oxford University Press, 1959).

4. Peter Felten, Alan Kalish, Allison Pingree, and Kathryn Plank, "Toward a Scholarship of Teaching and Learning in Educational Development," *To Improve the Academy* 25 (2007): 93. Also see Ranald Macdonald's definition of academic development in "Developing a Scholarship of Academic Development: Setting the Context," in *The Scholarship of Academic Development*, edited by Heather Eggins and Ranald Macdonald (New York: McGraw Hill, 2003), 1–10.

5. Adrianna Kezar, Sean Gehrke, and Susan Elrod, "Implicit Theories of Change as a Barrier to Change on College Campuses: An Examination of STEM Reform," *Review of Higher Education* 38, no. 4 (2015): 479–506.

6. Mitchell L. Stevens, Elizabeth A. Armstrong, and Richard Arum, "Sieve, Incubator, Temple, Hub: Empirical and Theoretical Advances in the Sociology of Higher Education," *Annual Review of Sociology* 34 (2008): 127.

7. Mary Deane Sorcinelli, Ann E. Austin, Pamela L. Eddy, and Andrea L. Beach, *Creating the Future of Faculty Development: Learning from the Past, Understanding the Present* (Bolton, MA: Anker, 2006), 12.

8. Andrea Beach, Mary Deane Sorcinelli, Anne E. Austin, and Jaclyn Rivard, *Faculty Development in the Age of Evidence: Current Practices, Future Imperatives* (Sterling, VA: Stylus Publishing, 2016).

9. Connie Schroeder, Phyllis Blumberg, and Nancy Van Note Chism, eds., *Coming in from the Margins: Faculty Development's Emerging Organizational Development Role in Institutional Change* (Sterling, VA: Stylus Publishing, 2010).

10. Diane Ebert-May, Terry L. Derting, Janet Hodder, Jennifer L. Momsen, Tammy M. Long, and Sara E. Jardeleza, "What We Say Is Not What We Do: Effective Evaluation of Faculty Professional Development Programs," *BioScience* 61, no. 7 (2011): 550.

11. POD Network, "Membership," accessed January 28, 2022, https://podnetwork.org/members/.

12. Brown University's Institutional Review Board declared this study not regulated.

13. Macdonald, "Developing a Scholarship of Academic Development," 3.

14. Houston H. Harte Center for Teaching and Learning, Washington and Lee University, Virginia, https://my.wlu.edu/carpe-(harte-center)/frequently-asked -questions.

15. Tracy Bartholomew, "Analysis of Educational Development Position Advertise-ments," POD Network News, fall 2016, https://sites.google.com/a/podnetwork.org /wikipodia/pod-network-news-page/pod-network-news-archives/fall-2016-archive /special-column-job-ads-fall-2016.

16. John A. Centra, *Faculty Development Practices in U.S. Colleges and Universities* (Princeton, NJ: Educational Testing Service, 1976), 13.

17. Glenn Erickson, "A Survey of Faculty Development Practices," *To Improve the Academy* 100 (1986), 182, https://digitalcommons.unl.edu/podimproveacad/100.

18. Erickson, "A Survey of Faculty Development Practices," 182.

19. Erickson, "A Survey of Faculty Development Practices," 183.

20. Kuhlenschmidt, "Distribution and Penetration," 278.

21. Kuhlenschmidt, "Distribution and Penetration," 285.

22. See Beach et al., *Faculty Development in the Age of Evidence*; Sorcinelli et al., *Creating the Future of Faculty Development*; Schroeder, Blumberg, and Chism, *Coming in from the Margins*.

23. Mary C. Wright, "How Many Centers for Teaching and Learning Are There?" *POD Network News*, 2019, https://podnetwork.org/content/uploads/Wright_PNN _NoCTLs_Jan2019_update2pdf.pdf.

24. Mark Lieberman, "New Database of Teaching and Learning Centers Nation-wide," *Inside Higher Ed*, May 1, 2019, https://www.insidehighered.com/digital-learning /insights/2019/05/01/new-database-offers-contact-information-teaching-and-learning.

25. The POD Network discussion list is currently available at https://podnetwork .org/centers-programs/.

26. Kuhlenschmidt, "Distribution and Penetration."

27. Felten et al., "Toward a Scholarship," 93.

28. Kuhlenschmidt, "Distribution and Penetration."

29. These include the Great Lakes Colleges Association; the University System of Georgia; Kansas City Professional Development Council; Center for the Integration of Research, Teaching, and Learning (CIRTL); University of Wisconsin system; Connecti-cut community college system; CUNY City Council; Alamo Colleges District; California State University System; and Maricopa Community Colleges.

30. This figure was computed using fall 2017 FTE equivalent (full-time equivalent enrollment, or full-time plus one-third part-time) from IPEDS data.

31. Kuhlenschmidt, "Distribution and Penetration."

32. See Constance E. Cook, "Introduction: CRLT and Its Role at the University of Michigan," in *Advancing the Culture of Teaching on Campus: How a Teaching Center can Make a Difference*, edited by Constance Cook and Mathew Kaplan (Sterling, VA: Stylus Publishing, 2011), 1–12; and Leslie Ortquist-Ahrens, "Beyond Survival: Educa-tional Development and the Maturing of the POD Network," *To Improve the Academy* 35, no. 1.

33. Kuhlenschmidt, "Distribution and Penetration."

34. Kuhlenschmidt, "Distribution and Penetration."

35. Kuhlenschmidt, "Distribution and Penetration."

36. A fourth small group has data that were not reported or were missing.

37. Catherine Haras, Steven C. Taylor, Mary Deane Sorcinelli, and Linda von Hoene, *Institutional Commitment to Teaching Excellence: Assessing the Impacts and Outcomes of Faculty Development* (Washington, DC: American Council on Education, 2017), https://www.acenet.edu/Documents/Institutional-Commitment-to-Teaching -Excellence.pdf.

Chapter 1. What Are We Trying to Do?

Epigraph. Benjamin Mays, "What a Man Lives By," in *Best Black Sermons*, edited by William M. Philpot (King of Prussia, PA: Judson Press, 1972).

1. Güven Ozdem, "An Analysis of the Vision and Mission Statements on the Strategic Plans of Higher Education Institutions," *Educational Sciences: Theory and Practice* 11, no. 4 (2011): 1888–89.

2. Laura Cruz, Michelle Parker, Brian Smentkowski, and Marina Smitherman, *Taking Flight: Making Your Center for Teaching and Learning Soar* (Sterling, VA: Stylus Publishing, 2020), 63.

3. Tara Gray and Susan Shadle, "Launching or Revitalizing a Teaching Center: Principles and Portraits of Practice," *Journal of Faculty Development* 23, no. 2 (2009): 5–12.

4. Christopher Morphew and Matthew Hartley, "Mission Statements: A Thematic Analysis of Rhetoric across Institutional Type," *Journal of Higher Education* 77, no. 3 (2006): 456–71.

5. Connie Schroeder, "Investigating Institutional Involvement and Change Agency," in *Coming in from the Margins: Faculty Development's Emerging Organizational Development Role in Institutional Change*, edited by Connie Schroeder, Phyllis Blumberg, and Nancy Van Note Chism (Sterling, VA: Stylus Publishing, 2010), 77–110.

6. Cruz et al., *Taking Flight*, 63.

7. Schroeder, "Aligning and Revising Center Mission Statements," in Schroeder, Blumberg, and Chism, *Coming in from the Margins*, 239.

8. Schroeder, "Aligning and Revising," 239.

9. Schroeder, "Aligning and Revising," 241.

10. To examine this possibility, I repeated Schroeder's analysis, with one key difference. I coded each constituency separately rather than grouping them in clusters. For example, the current purpose statement of the Sheridan Center for Teaching and Learning indicates that we serve "all members of the Brown teaching and learning community, including full-time and part-time faculty, postdoctoral fellows, teaching fellows and teaching assistants, undergraduates, staff and administrators." In my analysis, this statement would be coded multiple times, noting the constituencies of faculty, administrators, community, part-time faculty, TAs and postdocs, and students, while Schroeder counts "faculty, staff, and students" as a cluster. Fortunately, her helpful book includes all of the data she received, making it possible to disaggregate and compare across the decade.

11. Standard deviations for these means are 0.83 (associate's), 1.08 (doctoral), 1.01 (medical/health), 0.85 (baccalaureate), 0.89 (master's), and 0.97 (other special focus).

12. In analyses of unique institutions (N = 1025), there are statistically significant differences in mean number of constituencies by women's college status: t = 3.34, df = 9.5, p < .01. Additionally, in analyses of particular constituency type, only *students* have a statistically significant difference (N = 1025, x^2 = 4.06, df = 1, p < .05). Of CTLs at women's institutions, 30% name *students*, compared to 10% of those at coeducational institutions.

13. Schroeder, "Aligning and Revising," 241.

14. Calculation based on Schroeder, "Aligning and Revising," 241.

15. In analyses of unique Carnegie type (N = 1079) for faculty, there were statistically significant differences (x^2 = 20.3, df = 5, p < .01). In this case, percentages were medical/health (86%), master's (83%), baccalaureate (81%), associate's (77%), doctoral (70%), and other special focus (70%).

16. In analyses of unique Carnegie type (N = 1079) for educators/instructors, there were statistically significant differences (x^2 = 18.9, df = 5, p < .01). In this case, percentages were other special focus (22%), doctoral (13%), medical/health (11%), associate's (10%), baccalaureate (7%), and master's (5%).

17. K. C. Culver and Adrianna Kezar, *Designing Accessible and Inclusive Professional Development for NTTF* (Los Angeles, CA: Pullias Center for Higher Education, University of Southern California, 2021).

18. In analyses of unique Carnegie type (N = 1079) for part-time/adjunct faculty, there were statistically significant differences (x^2 = 12.3, df = 5, p < .05). In this case, percentages were associate's (10%), master's (7%), medical/health (5%), doctoral (4%), baccalaureate (3%), and other special focus (0%).

19. POD Network, "What Is Educational Development?" POD Network, last modified June 2016, https://podnetwork.org/about/what-is-educational-development/.

20. Calculation based on Schroeder, "Aligning and Revising," 241.

21. In analyses of unique Carnegie type (N = 1079) for staff/administrators, there were statistically significant differences (x^2 = 40.1, df = 5, p < .001). Percentages were associate's (35%), baccalaureate (20%), master's (16%), doctoral (15%), other special focus (15%), and medical/health (11%).

22. Mary Prentice and Rene O. Guillaume, "Job Perceptions of Community College and University Department Chairs," *Community College Journal of Research and Practice* 45, no. 5 (2021): 351–65.

23. San Diego Mesa College, "Professional Learning," https://www.sdmesa.edu/about-mesa/professional-learning/.

24. John A. Logan College, "Teaching and Learning Center (TLC)," https://www.jalc.edu/tlc/.

25. Schroeder, "Aligning and Revising," 240.

26. In analyses of unique Carnegie type (N = 1079) for community / all employees, there were statistically significant differences (x^2 = 17.1, df = 5, p < .01). Percentages were associate's (16%), doctoral (15%), master's (13%), medical/health (6%), baccalaureate (5%), and other special focus (4%).

27. In analyses of unique Carnegie type (N = 1079) for academic units, there were statistically significant differences (x^2 = 17.6, df = 5, p < .01). Percentages were doctoral (11%), master's (8%), baccalaureate (7%), medical/health (5%), other special focus (4%), and associate's (2%).

28. Alison Cook-Sather, Catherine Bovill, and Peter Felten, *Engaging Students as Partners in Learning and Teaching: A Guide for Faculty* (San Francisco: Jossey-Bass, 2014).

29. In analyses of unique Carnegie type (N = 1079) for students, there were statistically significant differences (x^2 = 13.9, df = 5, p < .05). Percentages were baccalaureate (17%), medical/health (15%), other special focus (15%), doctoral (10%), master's (9%), and associate's (7%).

30. In analyses of unique Carnegie type (N = 1079) for TAs, graduate students, or postdocs, there were statistically significant differences (x^2 = 68.3, df = 5, p < .001). Percentages were doctoral (14%), master's (2%), baccalaureate (2%), medical/health (1%), associate's (1%), and other special focus (0%).

31. Milwaukee Area Technical College, "Center for Teaching Excellence," https:// guides.matc.edu/offerings.

32. California Baptist University, "The Teaching and Learning Center," https:// calbaptist.edu/teaching-learning-center/.

33. In 2022, this CTL was on temporary hiatus pending a new director (email correspondence with Dean Mary Walsh Fitzpatrick, August 2022). The mission is located at https://iaals.du.edu/profile/albany-law-school.

34. Calculation based on Schroeder, "Aligning and Revising," 241.

35. In October 2021, CETL changed its mission to reflect the breadth of the unit. It continues to reference faculty, teaching assistants, students, and departments—and now also adds high school students (email correspondence with Associate Vice Provost Peter Diplock, August 2022). The 2020 mission can be found at https://web.archive.org /web/20200803212332/https://cetl.uconn.edu/about-us/.

36. University of Tennessee Health Science Center, "Support," https://www.uthsc .edu/tlc/support.php.

37. Schroeder, "Aligning and Revising," 241.

38. Themes from Schroeder not used as aims were (1) resources/expertise/information, (2) programs, (3) conversation/dialogue, (4) initiatives, (5) support, (6) technology, and (7) professional development. In subsequent chapters, I apply some of these as theories of change (chapter 2), some as tactics (chapter 3), and one as a CTL organizational type (chapter 4).

39. Mary Deane Sorcinelli, Ann E. Austin, Pamela L. Eddy, and Andrea L. Beach, *Creating the Future of Faculty Development: Learning from the Past, Understanding the Present* (Bolton, MA: Anker, 2006), 1–5; Robert B. Barr and John Tagg, "From Teaching to Learning: A New Paradigm for Undergraduate Education," *Change* 27, no. 6 (1995): 13–25.

40. Schroeder, "Aligning and Revising," 235–59.

41. Andrea Beach, Mary Deane Sorcinelli, Anne E. Austin, and Jaclyn Rivard, *Faculty Development in the Age of Evidence: Current Practices, Future Imperatives* (Sterling, VA: Stylus Publishing, 2016), 31.

42. In analyses of unique Carnegie type (N = 1079) for student learning, there were statistically significant differences (x^2 = 40.1, df = 5, p < .001). Percentages were master's (72%), doctoral (71%), baccalaureate (64%), associate's (62%), other special focus (52%), and medical/health (39%).

43. In analyses of unique institutions (N = 996), there were statistically significant differences by instructional FTE in quartiles (x^2 = 9.8, df = 3, p < .05). Percentages were Quartile 4: 649+ (73%), Quartile 3: 320–648 (68%), Quartile 1: 16–181 (67%), Quartile 2: 183–319 (60%).

44. Aims Community College, "Faculty Teaching and Learning Center," https://catalog.aims.edu/content.php?catoid=22&navoid=2142.

45. Scottsdale Community College, "Center for Teaching and Learning," https://sites.google.com/scottsdalecc.edu/scc-ctl.

46. Stanislaus State, "Faculty Center for Excellence in Teaching and Learning," https://www.csustan.edu/faculty-center.

47. In 2022, Mills College merged with Northeastern University. The Mills Center for Faculty Excellence no longer has a web presence, but the 2020 mission can be found at https://web.archive.org/web/20210323235927/https://www.mills.edu/center-for-faculty-excellence/.

48. Lewis University, https://lewisu.edu/facultycenter/index.htm.

49. In spring 2021, this mission was updated to reflect new programming to "prepare college instructors to be critically reflective about their academic and professional knowledge and experiences as they work towards implementing concrete changes that contribute to an interdisciplinary, experiential, and equitable learning environment for students" (email correspondence with Director Joshua Abreu, August 2022). The 2020 mission can be found at https://web.archive.org/web/20200426220927/https://www.albertus.edu/academicservices/.

50. Monmouth University, "The Center for Excellence in Teaching and Learning," https://www.monmouth.edu/cetl/.

51. Winston-Salem State University, "The Center for Innovative and Transformative Instruction," https://www.wssu.edu/administration/faculty-and-staff/citi/index.html.

52. The center has since changed this line in its mission, from "Rooted in Ignatian pedagogy and the scholarship of teaching and learning, we advocate innovative teaching and the use of student-centered technology while partnering with faculty as they prepare Marquette students to be agents of change for a global community," to "Rooted in Ignatian pedagogy and the scholarship of teaching and learning, the CTL is committed to the professional development of the campus teaching community. We work with faculty to support sound pedagogical practice while respecting individual learning differences, and help all instructors create a learning environment where all teachers and learners can succeed and flourish" (email correspondence with Director Jennifer Maney, August 2022).

53. This statement has been updated to focus more on "respecting individual learning differences." The 2020 statement can be found at https://web.archive.org/web/20200619063643/https://www.marquette.edu/center-for-teaching-and-learning/.

54. Lenoir-Rhyne University, "Centers and Institutes," https://www.lr.edu/academics/centers-institutes.

55. Schroeder, "Aligning and Revising," 245.

56. POD Network, "What Is Educational Development?" last modified June 2016, https://podnetwork.org/about/what-is-educational-development/.

57. Schroeder, "Aligning and Revising," 239–59; Sorcinelli et al., *Creating the Future of Faculty Development*, 1–5.

58. In analyses of unique Carnegie type (N = 1079) for instructor outcome, there were statistically significant differences (x^2 = 27.1, df = 5, p < .001). Percentages were medical/health (69%), master's (54%), baccalaureate (50%), doctoral (49%), associate's (42%), and other special focus (26%). There were also statistically significant differences by instructional FTE quartile for unique institutions (N = 996, x^2 = 14.7, df = 3, p < .01). Percentages were Quartile 3: 320–648 FTEs (56%), Quartile 2: 183–319 FTEs (51%), Quartile 4: 649–7,444 FTEs (51%), and Quartile 1: 16–181 FTEs (40%).

59. University of Illinois Urbana-Champaign, "The Center for Innovation in Teaching and Learning (CITL)," https://citl.illinois.edu/about-citl/about-us.

60. The ITL mission has changed, but full- and part-time faculty, as well as staff, continue to be referenced in its "Welcome" message (https://ysu.edu/institute-teaching -and-learning). According to Assistant Provost for Teaching and Learning Hillary Fuhrman, the office continues to address faculty-focused holistic services (such as well-being and tenure and promotion preparation) although it also now includes assess- ment and institutional research services, and has shifted its focus more toward a student success and support focus (email correspondence with Hillary Fuhrman, August 2022).

61. Marine Corps University, "About Faculty Development," https://www.usmcu .edu/About-MCU/Faculty/Faculty-Development/.

62. Morehouse School of Medicine, "Faculty Development," https://www.msm.edu /Education/FacultyAffairs/FacultyDevelopment.php.

63. In August 2022, this line of the mission was updated slightly to read: "The mission of the Center for Teaching Excellence is to inspire and enable faculty to enhance teaching potential and effectiveness" (email correspondence with Director Megan Lin, August 2022). The 2020 mission can be found at https://web.archive.org /web/20201024142958/https://www.lcc.edu/cte/about/.

64. Angelo State University, "Faculty Learning Commons," https://www.angelo.edu /faculty-and-staff/faculty-learning-commons/.

65. Medical College of Wisconsin, "Faculty Development Program," https://www .mcw.edu/departments/medicine/faculty-development-program.

66. KerryAnn O'Meara, Mark Rivera, Alexandra Kuvaeva, and Kristen Corrigan, "Faculty Learning Matters: Organizational Conditions and Contexts That Shape Faculty Learning," *Innovative Higher Education* 42 (2017): 355–76.

67. Randy Bass, Bret Eynon, and Laura M. Gambino, *The New Learning Compact: A Framework for Professional Learning and Educational Change* (Boulder, CO: Every Learner Everywhere, 2019), https://www.everylearnereverywhere.org/resources/the-new -learning-compact/.

68. In analyses of unique institutions by Carnegie type (N = 1079) for change or innovation, there were statistically significant differences (x^2 = 14.1, df = 5, p < .05). Percentages were doctoral (43%), associate's (39%), baccalaureate (37%), master's (35%), other special focus (26%), and medical/health (23%). In analyses of unique institutions (N = 996), there are statistically significant differences by instructional FTE quartile

($x^2 = 9.5$, df $= 3$, p $< .05$). Percentages were Quartile 4: 649–7,444 FTEs (42%), Quartile 3: 320–648 FTEs (40%), Quartile 2: 183–319 FTEs (39%), Quartile 1: 16–181 FTEs (30%).

69. Josh Kim and Edward Maloney, *Learning Innovation and the Future of Higher Education* (Baltimore, MD: Johns Hopkins University Press, 2020).

70. Beach et al., *Faculty Development in the Age of Evidence*, 31.

71. University of the Virgin Islands, "Center for Excellence in Teaching and Learning," https://www.uvi.edu/administration/its/its-info_for_faculty.html.

72. King's College, "Center for Excellence," https://www.kings.edu/academics/resources/center_for_excellence.

73. Iowa, "Office of Teaching, Learning, and Technology," https://teach.its.uiowa.edu/organizations/about-us.

74. Sandhills Community College Center for Teaching and Learning, https://web.archive.org/web/20201008104121/https://sites.google.com/site/sandhillstlc/home.

75. This vision statement has been replaced by an updated CEE mission and values, a process that took place in summer 2020 (email correspondence with Director Lisa Nunn, August 2022). The 2020 statement can be found at https://web.archive.org/web/20200926003306/https://www.sandiego.edu/cee/about/.

76. Kim and Maloney, *Learning Innovation*, 44.

77. William G. Ouchi and Alan L. Wilkins, "Organizational Culture," *Annual Review of Sociology* 11 (1985): 457–83.

78. William G. Tierney, "Organizational Culture in Higher Education: Defining the Essentials," *Journal of Higher Education* 59 (1988): 2–21.

79. Beach et al., *Faculty Development in the Age of Evidence*, 31; Sorcinelli et al., *Creating the Future of Faculty Development*, 1–5.

80. Schroeder, "Aligning and Revising," 239–59.

81. Washtenaw Community College, "Teaching and Learning Center," https://www.wccnet.edu/mywcc/faculty-staff/training/tlc/.

82. Middlesex College, "Center for the Enrichment of Learning and Teaching (CELT)," https://www.middlesexcc.edu/celt/about-us/.

83. Kenneth E. Eble and William J. McKeachie, *Improving Undergraduate Education through Faculty Development* (San Francisco: Jossey Bass, 1985), 5.

84. Constance E. Cook, "Introduction: CRLT and Its Role at the University of Michigan," in *Advancing the Culture of Teaching on Campus: How a Teaching Center Can Make a Difference*, edited by Constance Cook and Mathew Kaplan (Sterling, VA: Stylus Publishing, 2011).

85. In analyses of unique institutions (N $= 1079$) for scholarly and creative work, there were statistically significant differences by Carnegie type ($x^2 = 41.6$, df $= 5$, p $< .001$). Percentages were medical/health (31%), master's (29%), baccalaureate (19%), doctoral (19%), associate's (8%), and other special focus (7%).

86. Mary C. Wright, Nandini Assar, Edward L. Kain, Laura Kramer, Carla B. Howery, Kathleen McKinney, Becky Glass, and Maxine Atkinson, "Greedy Institutions: The Importance of Institutional Context for Teaching in Higher Education," *Teaching Sociology* 32 (2004): 144–59.

87. In analyses of unique institutions (N = 996), there were statistically significant differences by instructional FTE (x^2 = 12.6, df = 3, p < .01). Percentages are Quartile 4: 649–7,444 FTEs (27%), Quartile 3: 320–648 FTEs (19%), Quartile 2: 183–319 FTEs (17%), and Quartile 1: 16–181 FTEs (15%).

88. Rachel Franklin, "The Roles of Population, Place, and Institution in Student Diversity in American Higher Education," *Growth Change* 44, no. 1 (2013): 30–53, https://doi.org/10.1111/grow.12001.

89. In analyses of CTLs with an identified year of founding (N = 179), there were statistically significant differences by CTL age (x^2 = 9.6, df = 3, p < .05). Percentages are 30+ years (40%), 0–9 years (34%), 10–19 years (17%), and 20–29 years (14%).

90. Tia Brown McNair, Estela M. Bensimon, and Lindsey Malcom-Piqueux, *From Equity Talk to Equity Walk: Expanding Practitioner Knowledge for Racial Justice in Higher Education* (Hoboken, NJ: Jossey-Bass, 2010), 6–7.

91. The center's vision is no longer found on its website, but the 2020 information can be found at https://web.archive.org/web/20200802184421mp_/https://www.wm.edu/offices/stli/our-mission/index.php.

92. Cal Poly Pomona, "Center for the Advancement of Faculty Excellence (CAFE)," https://www.cpp.edu/cafe/about-us/who-we-are.shtml.

93. This text no longer appears on the De La Salle Institute website because of a refocusing of its mission to evidence-based practice, the scholarship of teaching and learning, and community-engaged learning (email correspondence with Director Frank Mosca, August 2022). The 2020 statement can be found at https://web.archive.org/web/20200812214441/https://www.lasalle.edu/dlsi/about-us/.

94. Pratt, "Teaching, Learning, and Assessment," https://www.pratt.edu/about/offices/office-of-the-provost/teaching-learning-and-assessment/.

95. In July 2020, the University of Washington Bothell's Teaching and Learning Center reorganized, with global studies, community-based learning and research, and undergraduate research now in the Office of Connected Learning, while the student academic support units moved to the Office for Student Academic Success (email correspondence with Assistant Vice Chancellor Carolyn Brennan, August 8, 2022). The 2020 statement can be found at https://web.archive.org/web/20200120210533/https://www.uwb.edu/tlc.

96. California State University, Long Beach, "Vision, Mission, & Goals of the Faculty Center," https://www.csulb.edu/faculty-center/vision-mission-goals-of-the-faculty-center.

97. University of California, Riverside, School of Medicine, "Mission, Philosophy and Strategic Planning," https://facdev.ucr.edu/mission-philosophy-and-strategic-planning.

98. Schroeder, "Aligning and Revising," 239–59.

99. University of Cincinnati, "Welcome to the Center for the Enhancement of Teaching and Learning," https://www.uc.edu/about/cetl.html.

100. Valparaiso University, "Mission and Vision," https://www.valpo.edu/vital/about-vital/mission-and-vision/.

101. Indiana University Southeast, "Institute for Learning and Teaching Excellence," https://www.ius.edu/ilte/about-us/our-mission.php.

102. American River College, "Center for Teaching and Learning," https://inside.arc.losrios.edu/collegewide/center-for-teaching-and-learning.

103. Ray Land, "Agency, Context, and Change in Academic Development," *Journal for Academic Development* 6, no. 1 (2001): 4–20.

104. John A. Logan College, "Teaching and Learning Center (TLC)," https://www.jalc.edu/tlc/.

105. Anna Maria College, "Center for Teaching Excellence (CTE): Home," https://libguides.annamaria.edu/CenterForTeachingExcellence.

106. In January 2021, the Center for Teaching Excellence became the Empirical Educator Center, and the mission changed to "provide professional development for all members of the college community and encourage the exploration of different approaches of engagement to support the ideal student experience" (email correspondence with Director Laura Lane-Worley, August 2022). The 2020 mission can be found at https://web.archive.org/web/20200214160013/https://www.lee.edu/groups/cte/.

107. Schroeder, "Aligning and Revising," 239–59.

108. In analyses of unique institutions by Carnegie type (N = 1079) for community building, there were statistically significant differences (x^2 = 22.5, df = 5, p < .001). Percentages are master's (17%), baccalaureate (11%), doctoral (10%), associate's (7%), medical/health (6%), and other special focus (0%).

109. American Public University System, "Mission and Vision," https://web.archive.org/web/20190513000158/https://www.apus.edu/about/mission/.

110. Recently, the Centers for Teaching and Learning at Miami University Middletown (OH) and Miami University Hamilton (OH) were combined to serve both campuses (email correspondence with Co-Coordinator Leah Henson, August 2022). Although the specific text has changed, the mission has similar emphases, now to "foster a sense of community and collaboration among all campus educators: full- and part-time faculty, staff, and administrators."

111. SUNY Cortland, "Faculty Development Committee," https://www2.cortland.edu/offices/fdc/.

112. O'Meara et al., "Faculty Learning Matters," 355–76.

113. Peter Felten and Nancy Chick, "Is SoTL a Signature Pedagogy of Educational Development?" *To Improve the Academy* 37, no. 1 (2018), http://dx.doi.org/10.3998/tia.17063888.0037.114.

114. Focusing on the "end state" goals analyzed here, there was a mean of 1.99 aims per mission in 2006, compared to 2.60 per CTL purpose statement in 2020. Schroeder, "Aligning and Revising," 244.

115. Virginia Commonwealth University, "Center for Teaching and Learning Excellence and Faculty Success," https://ctle.vcu.edu/.

116. Schroeder, "Aligning and Revising," 239–59.

117. Cook, "Introduction: CRLT and Its Role"; Mary C. Wright Debra Lohe, Tershia Pinder-Grover, and Leslie Ortquist-Ahrens, "The Four Rs: Guiding CTLs with

Responsiveness, Relationships, Resources, and Research," *To Improve the Academy* 37, no. 2 (2018): 271–86.

118. William Bergquist, "Unconscious Values within Four Academic Cultures: An Address Given at the 1994 POD Annual Conference," *To Improve the Academy* (1994): 349–72.

119. Torgny Roxå and Katarina Mårtensson, "Agency and Structure in Academic Development Practices: Are We Liberating Academic Teachers or Are We Part of a Machinery Suppressing Them?" *International Journal for Academic Development* 22, no. 2 (2017): 95–105.

120. Angela Brew and Joyde Cahir, "Achieving Sustainability in Teaching and Learning Initiatives," *International Journal for Academic Development* 19, no. 4 (2013): 341–52.

121. Julie Hall and David A. Green, "Leading an Academic Development Unit," in *Advancing Practice in Educational Development*, edited by David Baume and Celia Popovic (Oxfordshire, England: Taylor and Francis, 2016), 245–57.

122. Bass, Eynon, and Gambino, *The New Learning Compact*.

123. Graham Gibbs, "Reflections on the Changing Nature of Educational Development," *International Journal for Academic Development* 18, no. 1 (2013): 4–14; Schroeder, "Aligning and Revising," 239–59.

124. Bass, Eynon, and Gambino, *The New Learning Compact*.

125. Cynthia Weston, Jennie Ferris, and Adam Finkelstein, "Leading Change: An Organizational Development Role for Educational Developers," *International Journal of Teaching and Learning in Higher Education* 29, no. 2 (2017): 270–80.

126. Land, "Agency, Context, and Change," 4–20.

Chapter 2. How Do We Get There?

1. Peter D. Ashworth, "Qualitative Research Methods in Higher Education Development," in *The Scholarship of Educational Development*, edited by Heather Eggins and Ranald Macdonald (London: Open University Press, 2003), 94–103.

2. Josh Kim and Edward Maloney, *Learning Innovation and the Future of Higher Education* (Baltimore, MD: Johns Hopkins University Press, 2020).

3. Daniel L. Reinholz and Tessa C. Andrews, "Change Theory and Theory of Change: What's the Difference Anyway?" *International Journal of STEM Education* 7, no. 2 (2020): 3.

4. Mark R. Connolly and Elaine Seymour, *Why Theories of Change Matter* (WCER working paper no. 2015-2) (Madison: Wisconsin Center for Education Research, University of Wisconsin, 2015), https://files.eric.ed.gov/fulltext/ED577054.pdf.

5. Adrianna Kezar, Sean Gehrke, and Susan Elrod, "Implicit Theories of Change as a Barrier to Change on College Campuses: An Examination of STEM—Reform," *Review of Higher Education* 38, no. 4 (2015): 479–506.

6. Mitchell L. Stevens, Elizabeth A. Armstrong, and Richard Arum, "Sieve, Incubator, Temple, Hub: Empirical and Theoretical Advances in the Sociology of Higher Education," *Annual Review of Sociology* 34 (2008): 127.

7. POD Network, *Defining What Matters: Guidelines for Comprehensive Center for Teaching and Learning (CTL) Evaluation* (Nederland, CO: POD Network, 2018), https://podnetwork.org/content/uploads/POD_CTL_Evaluation_Guidelines__2018_.pdf.

8. Andrea Beach, Mary Deane Sorcinelli, Ann E. Austin, and Jaclyn Rivard, *Faculty Development in the Age of Evidence: Current Practices, Future Imperatives* (Sterling, VA: Stylus Publishing, 2016), 76–77.

9. Beach et al., *Faculty Development in the Age of Evidence*, 53.

10. Here, our educational development collaborative (2018) departs from Stevens, Armstrong, and Arum's (2008) understanding of the Temple role in understanding higher education scholarship, which describes the legitimization of official knowledge in institutions like libraries. POD Network, *Defining What Matters*, 8, https://podnetwork.org/content/uploads/POD_DWM_R3-singlepage-v2.pdf.

11. Beach et al., *Faculty Development in the Age of Evidence*, 29.

12. This definition is also a departure from Stevens, Armstrong, and Arum's (2008) conception of the metaphor, which is primarily used to describe the social stratification dimensions of higher education.

13. POD Network, *Defining What Matters*, 9.

14. Beach et al., *Faculty Development in the Age of Evidence*, 93.

15. Ray Land, "Agency, Context, and Change in Academic Development," *Journal for Academic Development* 6, no. 1 (2001): 4–20.

16. St. Edward's University, "Center for Teaching Excellence," https://www.stedwards.edu/academics/centers-institutes/center-teaching-excellence.

17. Laura Cruz, Michelle Parker, Brian Smentkowski, and Marina Smitherman, *Taking Flight: Making Your Center for Teaching and Learning Soar* (Sterling, VA: Stylus Publishing, 2020).

18. Connie Schroeder, "Aligning and Revising Center Mission Statements," in *Coming in from the Margins: Faculty Development's Emerging Organizational Development Role in Institutional Change*, edited by Connie Schroeder, Phyllis Blumberg, and Nancy Van Note Chism (Sterling, VA: Stylus Publishing, 2010).

19. Anna L. Carew, Geraldine Lefoe, Maureen Bell, and Lenore Armour, "Elastic Practice in Academic Developers," *International Journal for Academic Development* 13, no. 1 (2008): 51–66.

20. POD Network, "Vision, Mission, and Values," https://podnetwork.org/about/vision-mission-and-values/.

21. Camden County College, "Teaching and Learning Center," https://www.camdencc.edu/faculty-and-staff/tlc/.

22. The center's welcome statement has since been changed but still emphasizes hub elements. The 2020 text can be found at https://web.archive.org/web/20200715135845/https://wp.stolaf.edu/cila/.

23. Cornell University, "Center for Teaching Innovation," https://teaching.cornell.edu/about-us/mission-vision-values.

24. University of Hawai'i–West O'ahu, "Office of Professional Development and Academic Support," https://westoahu.hawaii.edu/academics/office-of-professional-development-and-academic-support/.

25. The center's purpose statement has changed, but the 2020 "What We Do" statement can be found at https://web.archive.org/web/20200226001836/http://sites.austincc.edu/fctl/about/.

26. Mary C. Wright, Deborah R. Lohe, and Deandra Little, "The Role of a Center for Teaching and Learning in a De-Centered Educational World," *Change: The Magazine of Higher Learning* 50, no. 3 (2018): 41.

27. Medgar Evers College, "Center for Teaching and Learning Excellence," https://www.mec.cuny.edu/academic-affairs/center-for-teaching-and-learning-excellence/.

28. Cincinnati State, "Center for Teaching and Learning," https://www.cincinnatistate.edu/about-cincinnati-state/center-for-teaching-and-learning/.

29. George Mason University, "Stearns Center for Teaching and Learning," https://stearnscenter.gmu.edu/.

30. This text has since been changed. The 2020 version is available at https://web.archive.org/web/20200815044917/https://lib.stpetersburg.usf.edu/innovative.

31. Milton D. Cox, "Introduction to Faculty Learning Communities," *New Directions for Teaching and Learning* 97 (2004): 5–23; Etienne Wenger, Richard McDermott, and William Snyder, *Cultivating Communities of Practice* (Boston, MA: Harvard Business School Press, 2002).

32. Adrianna Kezar, "What Is the Best Way to Achieve Broader Reach of Improved Practices in Higher Education?" *Innovative Higher Education* 36 (2011): 235–47; Everett M. Rogers, *Diffusion of Innovations* (New York: Free Press, 1962); Nancy Van Note Chism, Matthew Holley, and Cameron J. Harris, "Researching the Impact of Educational Development: Basis for Informed Practice," *To Improve the Academy* 31 (2012): 129–45.

33. Robert H. Stupnisky, Nathan C. Hall, Lia M. Daniels, and Emmanuel Mensah, "Testing a Model of Pre-Tenure Faculty Members' Teaching and Research Success: Motivation as a Mediator of Balance, Expectations, and Collegiality," *Journal of Higher Education* 88, no. 3 (2017): 376–400.

34. Mary C. Wright, *Always at Odds? Creating Alignment between Faculty and Administrative Values* (Albany: SUNY Press, 2008).

35. Wright et al., "The Role of a Center for Teaching and Learning." See also K. Lynn Taylor, Natasha A. Kenny, Ellen Perrault, and Robin A. Mueller, "Building Integrated Networks to Develop Teaching and Learning: The Critical Role of Hubs," *International Journal of Academic Development* 27, no. 3 (2022): 279–291.

36. Ronald S. Burt, "Structural Holes and Good Ideas," *American Journal of Sociology* 110, no. 2 (2004): 351.

37. David Parsons, Inge Hill, Jane Holland, and Dick Wills, *Impact of Teaching Development Programmes in Higher Education* (Heslington, England: Higher Education Academy, 2012); Yvonne Steinert, Karen Mann, Brownell Anderson, Bonnie Maureen Barnett, Angel Centeno, Laura Naismith, David Prideaux, John Spencer, Ellen Tullo, Thomas Viggiano, Helena Ward, and Diana Dolmans, "A Systematic Review of Faculty Development Initiatives Designed to Improve Teaching Effectiveness: A 10-Year Update: BEME Guide" (No. 40), *Medical Teacher* 38, no. 8 (2016): 1–18, http://dx.doi.org/10.1080/0142159X.2016.1181851; Ann Stes, Mariska Min-Leliveld, David Gijbels, and Peter Van

Pategem, "The Impact of Instructional Development in Higher Education: The State-of-the-Art of the Research," *Educational Research Review* 5 (2010): 25–49; Chism, Holley, and Harris, "Researching the Impact of Educational Development."

38. Maura Borrego and Charles Henderson, "Increasing the Use of Evidence-Based Teaching in STEM Higher Education: A Comparison of Eight Change Strategies," *Journal of Engineering Education* 103, no. 2 (2014): 220–52; Charles Henderson, Andrea Beach, and Norman Finkelstein, "Facilitating Change in Undergraduate STEM Instructional Practices: An Analytic Review of the Literature," *Journal of Research in Science Teaching* 48, no. 8 (2011): 952–84, https://doi.org/10.1002/tea.20439.

39. Steinert et al., "A Systematic Review"; Stes et al., "The Impact of Instructional Development"; Chism, Holley, and Harris, "Researching the Impact of Educational Development"; Borrego and Henderson, "Increasing the Use of Evidence-Based Teaching."

40. Daniel T. Reinholz, Isabel White, and Tessa Andrews, "Change Theory in STEM Higher Education: A Systematic Review," *International Journal of STEM Education* 8, no. 27 (2021), https://doi.org/10.1186/s40594-021-00291-2.

41. Matthew T. Hora and Bailey B. Smolarek, "Examining Faculty Reflective Practice: A Call for Critical Awareness and Institutional Support," *Journal of Higher Education* 89, no. 4 (2018): 555.

42. Diana Bilimoria and Xiangfen Liang, *Gender Equity in Science and Engineering: Advancing Change in Higher Education* (New York: Routledge, 2012); Daniel L. Reinholz, Alanna Pawlak, Courtney Ngai, and Mary Pilgrim, "Departmental Action Teams: Empowering Students as Change Agents in Academic Departments," *International Journal for Students as Partners* 4, no. 1 (2020): 128–37.

43. Adrianna Kezar, Sean Gehrke, and Samantha Bernstein-Sierra, "Communities of Transformation: Creating Changes to Deeply Entrenched Issues," *Journal of Higher Education*, 89, no. 6 (2018): 832–64.

44. Stephen Brookfield, *Becoming a Critically Reflective Teacher* (San Francisco: Jossey Bass, 1995); Donald Schön, *The Reflective Practitioner: How Professionals Think in Action* (London: Basic Books, 1983).

45. St. Petersburg College, "About CETL," https://facultysupport.spcollege.edu/about-cetl/.

46. Cornerstone University, "Center for Excellence in Learning and Teaching," https://www.cornerstone.edu/university-offices/center-for-excellence-in-learning-and-teaching/.

47. John A. Centra, *Faculty Development Practices in U.S. Colleges and Universities* (Princeton, NJ: Educational Testing Service, 1976), 18.

48. Mary Deane Sorcinelli, Ann E. Austin, Pamela L. Eddy, and Andrea L. Beach, *Creating the Future of Faculty Development: Learning From the Past, Understanding the Present* (Bolton, MA: Anker, 2006), 1–5.

49. IUPUI, "Center for Teaching and Learning," https://ctl.iupui.edu/About.

50. Saint Louis University, "About the Reinert Center," https://www.slu.edu/cttl/about/index.php.

51. In analyses of unique Carnegie types (N = 1080), there are statistically significant differences for presence of an Incubator theory of change ($x^2 = 20.2$, df = 5, p < .01).

Percentages are master's (44%), baccalaureate (43%), other special focus (41%), doctoral (34%), medical/health (34%), and associate's (26%).

52. In analyses of unique institutions (N = 1023), there are statistically significant differences by control ($x^2 = 10.1$, df = 2, p < .01). Percentages are private not-for-profits (43%), private for-profits (38%), and publics (33%).

53. There are statistically significant differences by time of coding ($x^2 = 4.5$, df = 1, p < .05). Percentages are pre-COVID (41%), post-COVID (34%).

54. Percentages are CTLs with digitally focused staff (32%), CTLs without (39%) (N = 1105, $x^2 = 4.6$, p < .05).

55. Beach et al., *Faculty Development in the Age of Evidence*, 54, 76.

56. Borrego and Henderson, "Increasing the Use of Evidence-Based Teaching," 226; Keith Trigwell, Michael Prosser, and Fiona Waterhouse, "Relations between Teachers' Approaches to Teaching and Students' Approaches to Learning," *Higher Education* 37 (1999): 57–70.

57. Brookfield, *Becoming a Critically Reflective Teacher*, 1995; Schön, *The Reflective Practitioner*, 1983.

58. Carol A. Hurney, Christine, A. Rener, and Jordan D. Troisi, *Midcourse Correction for the College Classroom: Putting Small Group Diagnosis to Work* (Sterling, VA: Stylus Publishing, 2022); Mark V. Redmond and D. Joseph Clark, "Small Group Instructional Diagnosis: A Practical Approach to Improving Teaching," *AAHE Bulletin* 810 (February 1982).

59. William G. Tierney and Robert A. Rhoads, *Enhancing Promotion, Tenure, and Beyond: Faculty Socialization as a Cultural Process* (ASHE-ERIC Higher Education Report, No. 6) (New York: Jossey Bass, 1993).

60. Deborah Meizlish, Mary C. Wright, Jay Howard, and Matthew Kaplan, "Measuring the Impact of a New Faculty Program Using Institutional Data," *International Journal for Academic Development* 23, no. 2 (2017): 72–85; Michael S. Palmer, Adriana Streifer, and Stacy Williams-Duncan, "Systematic Assessment of a High-Impact Course Design Institute," *To Improve the Academy* 35, no. 2 (2016): 339–61; Lindsay Wheeler and Dorothe Bach, "Understanding the Impact of Educational Development Interventions on Classroom Instruction and Student Success," *International Journal for Academic Development* 26, no. 1 (2020): 24–40.

61. Chism, Holley, and Harris, "Researching the Impact of Educational Development"; Jung H. Yun, Brian Baldi, and Mary Deane Sorcinelli, "Mutual Mentoring for Early-Career and Underrepresented Faculty: Model, Research, and Practice," *Innovative Higher Education* 41, no. 5 (2016): 441–51; Abigail J. Stewart and Virginia Valian, *An Inclusive Academy: Achieving Diversity and Excellence* (Cambridge, MA: MIT Press, 2018).

62. Kenneth Zahorski, "Honoring Exemplary Teaching in the Liberal Arts Institutions," in *Honoring Exemplary Teaching*, edited by Marilla D. Svinicki and Robert J. Menges (San Francisco: Jossey-Bass, 1999), 89.

63. Chism, Holley, and Harris, "Researching the Impact of Educational Development"; Mary C. Wright, Constance E. Cook, and Elizabeth Brady, *Using Grants to Enhance Student Learning* (CRLT Occasional Paper No. 13) (Ann Arbor: University of

Michigan, 2000), http://www.crlt.umich.edu/sites/default/files/resource_files/CRLT
_n013.pdf.

64. Alison Cook-Sather, Catherine Bovill, and Peter Felten, *Engaging Students as Partners in Learning and Teaching: A Guide for Faculty* (San Francisco: Jossey-Bass, 2014); Mary Wright, Cynthia J. Finelli, and Deborah Meizlish, "Facilitating the Scholarship of Teaching and Learning at a Research University," *Change: The Magazine of Higher Learning* 42, no. 2 (2011): 50–56.

65. Kalamazoo College, "Teaching Commons," https://teachingcommons.kzoo.edu /about/mission-and-vision/.

66. Curry College, "Faculty Center for Professional Development and Curriculum Innovation," https://my.curry.edu/web/faculty/faculty-center.

67. Cruz et al., *Taking Flight*, 51. See also Anne Schoening and Sarah Oliver, "Connect, Change, and Conserve: Building a Virtual Center for Teaching Excellence," *To Improve the Academy* 35, no. 2 (2016): 362–76 and Nancy Van Note Chism, "The Role of Educational Developers in Institutional Change: From the Basement Office to the Front Office," *To Improve the Academy* 17 (1997): 141–54.

68. University of the Virgin Islands, "Center for Excellence in Teaching and Learning," https://www.uvi.edu/administration/its/its-info_for_faculty.html.

69. Indiana University Southeast, "Institute for Learning and Teaching Excellence," https://www.ius.edu/ilte/about-us/our-mission.php.

70. Central Connecticut State University, "Center for Teaching and Faculty Development," https://www.ccsu.edu/ctfd/advisors.html.

71. The center recently expanded its mission to include staff professional development and sought a more inclusive name (email correspondence with Director Keri Dutkiewicz, August 2022). The center's mission and vision are the same as in 2020 and be found at https://davenport.libguides.com/cetl/about-us.

72. Evergreen State College, "Washington Center for Improving Undergraduate Education," https://wacenter.evergreen.edu/about-the-commons.

73. This line no longer appears in the center mission. The mission was updated in 2021 after the unit was moved out of the provost's office and into the college, with the intention of highlighting the center's role in fostering community around teaching and learning (email correspondence with Interim Director Joseph Lambert, August 2022). The 2020 mission can be found at https://web.archive.org/web/20210413200023 /https://teaching.uchicago.edu/about/.

74. Ohio State University, "Michael V. Drake Institute for Teaching and Learning," https://drakeinstitute.osu.edu/about/mission-vision-values-and-goals.

75. In analyses of unique institutions (N = 1080), there are statistically significant differences by Carnegie type for presence of a Temple theory of change (x^2 = 15.1, df = 5, p < .05). Percentages are master's (24%), doctoral (22%), other special focus (19%), associate's (16%), medical/health (13%), and baccalaureate (12%).

76. Mary C. Wright, Nandini Assar, Edward L. Kain, Laura Kramer, Carla B. Howery, Kathleen McKinney, Becky Glass, and Maxine Atkinson, "Greedy Institutions: The Importance of Institutional Context for Teaching in Higher Education," *Teaching Sociology* 32 (2004): 144–59.

77. Beach et al., *Faculty Development in the Age of Evidence-Based Teaching*, 34.

78. Jonathan Zimmerman, *The Amateur Hour: A History of College Teaching in America* (Baltimore, MD: Johns Hopkins University Press, 2021).

79. Chism, "The Role of Educational Developers"; Chism, Holley, and Harris, "Researching the Impact of Educational Development"; Emily M. Walter, Andrea L. Beach, Charles Henderson, Cody Williams, and Ivan Ceballos-Madrigal, "Understanding Conditions for Teaching Innovation in Postsecondary Education: Development and Validation of the Survey of Climate for Instructional Improvement (SCII)," *International Journal of Technology in Education* 4, no. 2 (2021): 166–99; Wright, Cook, and Brady, *Using Grants to Enhance Student Learning*.

80. Jon F. Wergin, "Beyond Carrots and Sticks," *Liberal Education* 87, no. 1 (2001): 50.

81. David Cooperrider and Diana D. Whitney. *Appreciative Inquiry: A Positive Revolution in Change* (San Francisco: Berrett-Koehler Publishers, 2005).

82. Walter et al., "Understanding Conditions," 2021.

83. Laura Cruz, "The Idea of Educational Development: An Historical Perspective," *To Improve the Academy* 37, no. 1 (2018), http://dx.doi.org/10.3998/tia.17063888.0037.106.

84. Peter Felten, "Institutionalizing Inclusion in the In-Between," *Liberal Education* 103, no. 3–4 (2017); Melanie Walker, "Pedagogy for Rich Human Being-ness in Global Times," in *Global Inequalities and Higher Education*, edited by Elaine Unterhalter and Vincent Carpentier (New York: Palgrave MacMillan, 2009), 219–40.

85. Chism, "The Role of Educational Developers."

86. In 2022, the goals became even more Sieve-like, as the student academic support services previously provided by the center moved to student affairs. The TLC goals now read: (1) Equity and inclusion. (2) Collaborate with faculty and staff to develop, improve, and implement best practices in teaching and course design. (3) Provide educational assessment and evaluation expertise to support programmatic improvement and institutional initiatives. (4) Advise programs on curricular development for continuous program improvement. (email correspondence with Director Lisa Hatfield, August 2022). The 2020 version can be found at https://web.archive.org/web/20200427150712/https://www.ohsu.edu/education/teaching-and-learning-center.

87. Patricia Hutchings and Lee Shulman, "The Scholarship of Teaching: New Elaborations, New Developments," *Change* 31, no. 5 (1999): 11–15.

88. Meghan E. Bathgate, "Perceived Supports and Evidence-Based Teaching in College STEM," *International Journal of STEM Education* 6, no. 11 (2019), https://doi.org/10.1186/s40594-019-0166-3.

89. Georgia Southwestern State University, "Office of Teaching and Learning," https://www.gsw.edu/faculty-resources/teaching-learning/.

90. Yale, "Poorvu Center for Teaching and Learning," https://poorvucenter.yale.edu/about#Guiding%20Principles.

91. Thomas A. Angelo, "Reassessing (and Defining) Assessment," *AAHE Bulletin* 48, no. 3 (1995): 149; Ross Miller and Andrea Leskes, *Levels of Assessment: From the Student to the Institution* (Washington, DC: Association of American Colleges and Universities, 2005).

92. Peggy L. Maki, *Assessing for Learning: Building a Sustainable Commitment across the Institution* (Herndon, VA: Stylus Publishing, 2004), 2; POD Network, *Defining What Matters*, 3.

93. Beach et al., *Faculty Development in the Age of Evidence*, 2016.

94. Anna Maria College, "Center for Teaching Excellence (CTE): Home," https://libguides.annamaria.edu/CenterForTeachingExcellence.

95. Mary C. Wright, Molly Goldwasser, Wayne Jacobson, and Christopher Dakes, "Assessment from an Educational Development Perspective," *To Improve the Academy* 36, no. 1 (2017): 39–49, http://dx.doi.org/10.3998/tia.17063888.0036.101.

96. Iowa, "Office of Teaching, Learning, and Technology," https://teach.its.uiowa.edu/organizations/about-us.

97. This text no longer appears on the CNDLS website, but there is a separate page about "Inquiry and Scholarship," including recent publications by center staff and areas of inquiry. It continues to appear on Georgetown's Office of the Provost site: https://provost.georgetown.edu/academicaffairs/teaching-and-learning-innovations/.

98. St. Augustine College, "Office of Academic Effectiveness," https://www.staugustine.edu/office-of-academic-effectiveness/.

99. This specific text is no longer on the Teaching and Learning Center's website, as of August 2022. (The 2020 text can be found at https://web.archive.org/web/20200928230225/https://warrington.ufl.edu/teaching-and-learning-center/). However, the page does currently indicate that the center supports assessment, and "assurance of learning" is a separate page on the Teaching and Learning Center's website.

100. The full 2020 statement is, "University of Pennsylvania's Center for Teaching and Learning (CTL) works to help instructors at Penn excel in their teaching, to enhance the culture of teaching at the university, and, in turn, to increase the quality of education at Penn." (The 2020 statement can be found at https://web.archive.org/web/20200123231206/https://www.ctl.upenn.edu/.) As of 2022, this statement has been updated to a longer mission-like statement that ends with the line, "Through this effort, CTL enhances the learning and learning experiences of all our students, and, ultimately, the quality of education at Penn."

101. In fall 2021, CETL revised its mission to read that it "promotes quality and innovation in teaching, striving to engage all faculty in effective and equitable teaching practices, and cultivating a community of educators at College of the Canyons. The Center is designed to develop educators to their fullest potential through pathways that focus on best teaching practices, increasing student learning, and providing career enhancement strategies" (email correspondence with Robert Wonser and Julie Johnson, faculty coordinators, August 2022).

102. Grand Canyon University, "Center for Innovation in Research and Teaching," https://web.archive.org/web/20201020003412/https://cirt.gcu.edu/home/mission.

103. University of Wisconsin–Whitewater, "LEARN Center," https://www.uww.edu/learn.

104. University of Louisville, "Delphi Center for Teaching and Learning," https://louisville.edu/delphi/about/annual-report.

105. In analyses of unique institutions (N = 1080), there are statistically significant differences by Carnegie type for a Sieve theory of change ($x^2 = 18.6$, df = 5, p < .01). Percentages are doctoral (47%), medical/health (39%), master's (41%), other special focus (41%), baccalaureate (37%), and associate's (29%).

106. In analyses of unique institutions (N = 997), there are statistically significant differences by instructional FTE quartile ($x^2 = 21.4$, df = 3, p < .001). Percentages are Quartile 4: 649–7,444 FTEs (52%), Quartile 3: 320–648 FTEs (37%), Quartile 2: 183–319 FTEs (36%), and Quartile 1: 16–181 FTEs (35%).

107. CTLs with digital learning staff (48%) vs. those without (37%) ($x^2 = 12.4$, df = 1, p < .001).

108. These values are Support (r = 0.15, p. < 001), Promote (r = .19, p < .001), Foster (r = .17, p < .001), Collaborate or Partner (r = .16, p < .001), Advance, Drive, or Catalyze (r = .16, p < .001), Engage (r = .13, p < .001), Lead, Instigate, or Initiate (r = .13, p < .001), Disseminate or Distribute (r = .11, p < .001), Evaluate (r = .11, p < .001), Integrate (r = .09, p < .01), Conduct (r = .15, p < .001), Serves (r = .09, p < .01), and Use, Apply, or Implement, 5% (r = .12, p < .001).

109. Lindsay Bernhagen and Emily Gravett, "Educational Development as Pink-Collar Labor: Implications and Recommendations," *To Improve the Academy* 36, no. 1 (2017): 16.

110. Bernhagen and Gravett, "Educational Development," 10, 18.

111. Jeffrey E. Froyd, Charles Henderson, Renée S. Cole, Debra Friedrichsen, Raina Khatri, and Courtney Stanford, "From Dissemination to Propagation: A New Paradigm for Education Developers," *Change* 49, no. 4 (2017): 38.

112. Carl C. Wieman, *Improving How Universities Teach Science: Lessons from the Science Education Initiative* (Cambridge, MA: Harvard University Press, 2017), 25–26.

113. Henderson, Beach, and Finkelstein, "Facilitating Change."

114. Borrego and Henderson, "Increasing the Use of Evidence-Based Teaching," 240.

115. Henderson, Beach, and Finkelstein, "Facilitating Change"; Constance E. Cook, Mary C. Wright, and Chris O'Neal, "Action Research for Instructional Improvement: Using Data to Enhance Student Learning at Your Own Institution," *To Improve the Academy* 25 (2007): 123–38; Kurt Lewin, *Resolving Social Conflicts* (Washington, DC: American Psychological Association, 1997).

116. Hora and Smolarek, "Examining Faculty Reflective Practice," 572.

117. Connolly and Seymour, *Why Theories of Change Matter*, 2.

118. Adrianna Kezar, *How Colleges Change: Understanding, Leading, and Enacting Change*, 2nd ed. (New York: Routledge, 2018), 31.

119. All strategies are significantly correlated at the p < .001 level: Hub with Incubator (r = 0.2), Temple (r = 0.1), and Sieve (r = 0.1); Incubator with Temple (r = 0.2) and Sieve (r = .2); and Temple with Sieve (r = 0.2).

Chapter 3. What Tactics Do We Employ?

1. Virginia Lee, "Program Types and Prototypes," in *A Guide to Faculty Development*, edited by Kay J. Gillespie and Douglas L. Robertson (San Francisco: Jossey-Bass, 2010), 22.

2. Steven Mintz, "Why We Need Centers for Educational Innovation, Evaluation and Research," *Inside Higher Education*, November 30, 2020, https://www.insidehighered.com/blogs/higher-ed-gamma/why-we-need-centers-educational-innovation-evaluation-and-research.

3. Charles Henderson, Andrea Beach, and Norman Finkelstein, "Facilitating Change in Undergraduate STEM Instructional Practices," *Journal of Research in Science Teaching* 48, no. 8 (2011): 952–84, https://doi.org/10.1002/tea.20439.

4. Deandra Little, "Reflections on the State of the Scholarship of Educational Development," *To Improve the Academy* 33, no. 1 (2014), http://dx.doi.org/10.3998/tia.17063888.0033.104.

5. Peter Felten, Alan Kalish, Allison Pingree, and Kathryn Plank, "Toward a Scholarship of Teaching and Learning in Educational Development," *To Improve the Academy* 25 (2007), 93.

6. Graham Gibbs, "Reflections on the Changing Nature of Educational Development," *International Journal for Academic Development* 18, no. 1 (2013): 4–14.

7. Andrea Beach, Mary Deane Sorcinelli, Ann E. Austin, and Jaclyn Rivard, *Faculty Development in the Age of Evidence: Current Practices, Future Imperatives* (Sterling, VA: Stylus Publishing, 2016); John D. Emerson and Frederick Mosteller, "Development Programs for College Faculty," in *Educational Media and Technology Yearbook*, vol. 25, edited by Robert M. Branch and Mary A. Fitzgerald (New York: Springer, 2000), 26–42; Gibbs, "Reflections on the Changing Nature," 4–14; Lee, "Program Types and Prototypes."

8. John A. Centra, *Faculty Development Practices in U.S. Colleges and Universities* (Princeton, NJ: Educational Testing Service, 1976), 13.

9. Michael S. Palmer, "Graduate Student Professional Development: A Decade after Calls for National Reform," in *Studies in Graduate and Professional Student Development*, edited by L. L. B. Border (Stillwater, OK: New Forums Press, 2011), 1–17.

10. Beach et al., *Faculty Development*, 75–78, 87.

11. Maura Borrego and Charles Henderson, "Increasing the Use of Evidence-Based Teaching in STEM Higher Education: A Comparison of Eight Change Strategies," *Journal of Engineering Education* 103, no. 2 (2014): 220–52; Henderson, Beach, and Finkelstein, "Facilitating Change"; Nancy Van Note Chism, Matthew Holley, and Cameron J. Harris, "Researching the Impact of Educational Development: Basis for Informed Practice," *To Improve the Academy* 31 (2012): 129–45.

12. Beach et al., *Faculty Development*, 75–78.

13. Emerson and Mosteller, "Development Programs"; Emily O. Gravett and Andreas Broscheid, "Models and Genres of Faculty Development," in *Reconceptualizing Faculty Development in Service Learning / Community Engagement: Exploring Intersections, Frameworks, and Models of Practice*, edited by Becca Berkey (Sterling, VA: Stylus Publishing, 2018), 85–106; Yvonne Steinert, Karen Mann, Brownell Anderson, Bonnie Maureen Barnett, Angel Centeno, Laura Naismith, David Prideaux, John Spencer, Ellen Tullo, Thomas Viggiano, Helena Ward, and Diana Dolmans, "A Systematic Review of Faculty Development Initiatives Designed to Improve Teaching Effectiveness: A 10-Year Update: BEME Guide No. 40," *Medical Teacher* 38, no. 8 (2016): 1–18, http://dx.doi.org/10.1080/0142159X.2016.1181851.

14. Workshops were documented by looking for website postings or newsletter listings, ideally capturing offerings within the full academic year. In some cases, a center indicated that it offered workshops but (a) did not list the title or (b) listed titles that were more than a year out of date. These were counted as "non-specified" workshops. Only noncommercial workshops are included in this analysis. Programs listed as institutes, or longer-term programs described as having a specific focus on course design/redesign, are described separately.

15. In analyses of unique institutions (N = 1162), there are statistically significant differences by Carnegie type (x^2 = 18.0, df = 5, p < .01). Percentages are doctoral (80%), medical/health (73%), master's (70%), other special focus (66%), associate's (67%), and baccalaureate (66%).

16. There are statistically significant differences by CTL staffing quartile (N = 948, x^2 = 27.1, df = 3, p < .001). Percentages are 1 individual (66%), 2–3 individuals (76%), 4–6 individuals (80%), and 7+ individuals (86%). In analyses of unique institutions, there are statistically significant differences by instructional FTE (N = 1068, x^2 = 36.4, df = 3, p < .001). Percentages are Quartile 1: 16–181 (60%), Quartile 2: 183–319 (70%), Quartile 3: 320–648 (75%), and Quartile 4: 649+ (83%).

17. Emmajane Rhodenhiser worked with me to code 28 topics for over 4,000 programs. I used her work for the second phase of coding, where I made some adjustments and added two new topics. Topics are categorized on the center level; in other words, if a CTL offered multiple programs on diversity, equity, and inclusion, this was counted only once. Because Brown University's policy states that the university owns intellectual property of staff utilizing university resources, I would like to state that Emmajane's work was personally financed.

18. Palmer, "Graduate Student Professional Development," 1–17; Linda Von Hoene, "Graduate Student Teaching Certificates," in *Studies in Graduate and Professional Student Development*, edited by L. L. B. Border (Stillwater, OK: New Forums Press, 2011), 101–23.

19. Dieter J. Schönwetter, Donna Ellis, K. Lynn Taylor, and Valery Koop, "An Exploration of the Landscape of Graduate Courses on College and University Teaching in Canada and the USA," *Studies in Graduate and Professional Student Development* 11 (2008): 22–44.

20. Centra, *Faculty Development Practices*.

21. Centra, *Faculty Development Practices*.

22. Mary C. Wright and Emmajane Rhodenhiser, "How Did Center for Teaching and Learning (CTL) Programs Shift during the COVID-19 Pandemic?" Pandemic Pedagogy Research Symposium, Duke University, 2021, YouTube video, https://www .youtube.com/watch?v=2TeANok6bLo.

23. Devshikha Bose, Lisa Berry, Rob Nyland, Anthony Saba, and Teresa Focarile, "Flexible Teaching for Student Success: A Three-Tiered Initiative to Prepare Faculty for Flexible Teaching," *Journal on Centers for Teaching and Learning* 12 (2020): 87–135; Kristine Larsen, Christina Robinson, Jason A. Melnyk, Jennifer Nicoletti, Amy Gagnon, Kelly McLaughlin, and Mina Hussaini, "Finding Our Voice: Highly Flexible ED for the Hyflex World," *To Improve the Academy* 40, no. 2 (2021), https://doi.org/10.3998/tia.467.

24. Gravett and Broscheid, "Models and Genres," 100.

25. Chantal Levesque-Bristol, *Student-Centered Pedagogy and Course Transformation at Scale: Facilitating Faculty Agency to IMPACT Institutional Change* (Sterling, VA: Stylus Publishing, 2021); Edward L. Deci and Richard M. Ryan, "Self-Determination Theory: A Macrotheory of Human Motivation, Development, and Health," *Canadian Psychology* 49, no. 3 (2008): 182–85.

26. Michael S. Palmer, Adriana Streifer, and Stacy Williams-Duncan, "Systematic Assessment of a High-Impact Course Design Institute," *To Improve the Academy* 35, no. 2 (2016): 339–61; Lindsay Wheeler and Dorothe Bach, "Understanding the Impact of Educational Development Interventions on Classroom Instruction and Student Success," *International Journal for Academic Development* 26, no. 1 (2020): 24–40, https://doi.org/10.1080/1360144X.2020.1777555.

27. Beach et al., *Faculty Development*, 78.

28. Cara Meixner, Melissa Altman, Megan Good, and Elizabeth Ben Ward, "Longitudinal Impact of Faculty Participation in a Course Design Institute (CDI): Faculty Motivation and Perception of Expectancy, Value, and Cost," *To Improve the Academy* 40, no. 1 (2021): 49–74, https://doi.org/10.3998/tia.959.

29. In analyses of unique institutions (N = 1162), there are statistically significant differences by Carnegie type (x^2 = 108.9, df = 5, p < .001). Percentages are doctoral (36%), master's (19%), baccalaureate (12%), associate's (7%), other special focus (3%), and medical/health (3%).

30. There are statistically significant differences by CTL staffing quartile (N = 948, x^2 = 84.9, df = 3, p < .001). Percentages are 1 individual (8%), 2–3 individuals (17%), 4–6 individuals (22%), and 7+ individuals (43%). In analyses of unique institutions, there are statistically significant differences by instructional FTE (N = 1068, x^2 = 130.4, df = 3, p < .001). Percentages are Quartile 1: 16–181 (6%), Quartile 2: 183–319 (12%), Quartile 3: 320–648 (17%), and Quartile 4: 649+ (42%). In analyses of unique institutions (N = 1099), there are also statistically significant differences by MSI status (x^2 = 8.5, df = 1, p < .01). Percentages are MSI (12%), PWI (21%).

31. Michael S. Palmer, Carol Hurney, Lori Leaman, Jordan Troisi, and Mary Wright, "What's the Special Sauce? Evolution Toward High-Impact Course Design Institutes," workshop presented at the virtual POD Network Annual Conference, November 2021.

32. In analyses of unique institutions (N = 1162), there are statistically significant differences by Carnegie type (x^2 = 36.1, df = 5, p < .001). Percentages are doctoral (46%), associate's (32%), master's (32%), medical/health (25%), baccalaureate (25%), and other special focus (17%).

33. There are statistically significant differences by CTL staffing quartile (N = 948, x^2 = 8.7, df = 3, p < .05). Percentages are 1 individual (31%), 2–3 individuals (34%), 4–6 individuals (39%), and 7+ individuals (44%). In analyses of unique institutions, there are statistically significant differences by instructional FTE (N = 1068, x^2 = 53.9, df = 3, p < .001). Percentages are Quartile 1: 16–181 (21%), Quartile 2: 183–319 (30%), Quartile 3: 320–648 (39%), and Quartile 4: 649+ (50%).

34. In analyses of unique institutions (N = 1100), there are statistically significant differences by control (x^2 = 13.9, df = 2, p < .001). Percentages are private not-for-profit (27%), private for-profit (38%), public (38%).

35. Beach et al., *Faculty Development*, 2016.

36. In analyses of unique institutions (N = 1162), there are statistically significant differences by Carnegie type (x^2 = 56.4, df = 5, p < .001). Percentages are doctoral (56%), master's (44%), baccalaureate (40%), medical/health (30%), associate's (28%), and other special focus (17%).

37. There are statistically significant differences by CTL staffing quartile (N = 948, x^2 = 18.2, df = 3, p < .001). Percentages are 1 individual (35%), 2–3 individuals (47%), 4–6 individuals (48%), and 7+ individuals (55%). In analyses of unique institutions, there are statistically significant differences by instructional FTE (N = 1068, x^2 = 56.8, df = 3, p < .001). Percentages are Quartile 1: 16–181 (27%), Quartile 2: 183–319 (38%), Quartile 3: 320–648 (44%), and Quartile 4: 649+ (59%).

38. Sean Gehrke and Adrianna Kezar, "The Roles of STEM Communities of Practice in Institutional and Departmental Reform in Higher Education," *American Education Research Journal* 54, no. 5 (2017): 4; see also Etienne Wenger, Richard McDermott, and William M. Snyder, *Cultivating Communities of Practice* (Boston: Harvard Business Review Press, 2002).

39. Milton D. Cox, "Introduction to Faculty Learning Communities," *New Directions for Teaching and Learning* 97 (2004): 5–23.

40. Kerri Heffernan and Mary C. Wright, "Collective Muscle: How Partnerships between Faculty Members and Athletic Coaches Can Serve Our Academic Missions," *Liberal Education* 105, no. 3–4 (2019).

41. Lee, "Program Types and Prototypes," 21–33; Patricia Hutchins and Lee Shulman, "The Scholarship of Teaching: New Elaborations, New Developments," *Change* 31, no. 5 (1999): 11–15.

42. Inken Gast, Kim Schildkamp, and Jan T. van de Veen, "Team-Based Professional Development Interventions in Higher Education: A Systematic Review," *Review of Educational Research* 87, no. 4 (2017): 736–67.

43. Cox, "Introduction to Faculty Learning Communities."

44. Leslie Ortquist-Ahrens and Roben Torosyan, "The Role of the Facilitator in Faculty Learning Communities: Paving the Way for Growth, Productivity, and Collegiality," *Learning Communities Journal* 1, no. 1 (June 2009): 31.

45. Beach et al., *Faculty Development*, 2016.

46. See "USC Definition of Excellence in Teaching," Center for Excellence in Teaching, https://cet.usc.edu/about/usc-definition-of-excellence-in-teaching/.

47. See "Fearless Teaching Framework," Teaching and Learning Transformation Center, https://tltc.umd.edu/researchers/fearless-teaching-framework.

48. See "Contemplative Practice Examples," Office for Faculty Excellence, https://www.montclair.edu/faculty-advancement/current-development-programs/contemplative-pedagogy-program/contemplative-practice-examples/.

49. In analyses of unique institutions (N = 1162), there are statistically significant differences by Carnegie type (x^2 = 37.5, df = 5, p < .001). Percentages are doctoral (91%), master's (82%), medical/health (81%), associate's (77%), baccalaureate (74%), and other special focus (66%).

50. There are statistically significant differences by CTL staffing quartile (N = 948, x^2 = 27.6, df = 3, p < .001). Percentages are 1 individual (76%), 2–3 individuals (87%), 4–6

individuals (87%), and 7+ individuals (94%). In analyses of unique institutions, there are statistically significant differences by instructional FTE (N = 1068, x^2 = 43.1, df = 3, p < .001). Percentages are Quartile 1: 16–181 (70%), Quartile 2: 183–319 (80%), Quartile 3: 320–648 (85%), and Quartile 4: 649+ (92%).

51. Emerson and Mosteller, "Development Programs for College Faculty," 26–42; David Parsons, Inge Hill, Jane Holland, and Dick Wills, *Impact of Teaching Development Programmes in Higher Education* (Heslington, England: Higher Education Academy, 2012); Steinert et al., "A Systematic Review"; Ann Stes, Mariska Min-Leliveld, David Gijbels, and Peter Van Pategem, "The Impact of Instructional Development in Higher Education: The State-of-the-Art of the Research," *Educational Research Review* 5 (2010): 25–49; Chism, Holley, and Harris "Researching the Impact."

52. Adrianna Kezar, "What Is the Best Way to Achieve Broader Reach of Improved Practices in Higher Education?" *Innovative Higher Education* 36 (2011): 235–47; Adrianna Kezar, *Scaling and Sustaining Change and Innovation: Lessons Learned from the Teagle Foundation's 'Faculty Work and Student Learning' Initiative* (New York: Teagle Foundation, 2015); Everett M. Rogers, *Diffusion of Innovations* (New York: Free Press, 1962); Chism, Holley, and Harris, "Researching the Impact," 129–45.

53. Kathleen T. Brinko, "The Interactions of Teaching Improvement," in *Practically Speaking: A Sourcebook for Instructional Consultants in Higher Education*, edited by Kathleen T. Brinko and Robert J. Menges (Stillwater, OK: New Forums Press, 1997), 3–8.

54. Centra, *Faculty Development Practices*, 216; Angela R. Penny and Robert Coe, "Effectiveness of Consultation on Student Ratings Feedback: A Meta-Analysis," *Review of Educational Research* 74, no. 2 (2004): 235.

55. Penny and Coe, "Effectiveness of Consultation," 235.

56. Beach et al., *Faculty Development*, 78.

57. Beach et al., *Faculty Development*, 78.

58. In analyses of unique institutions (N = 1162), there are statistically significant differences by Carnegie type (x^2 = 72.1, df = 5, p < .001). Percentages are doctoral (62%), master's (42%), other special focus (41%), baccalaureate (40%), medical/health (34%), and associate's (28%).

59. Lee, "Program Types and Prototypes."

60. In analyses of unique institutions (N = 1099), there are statistically significant differences by MSI status (x^2 = 12.9, df = 1, p < .001). Percentages are MSI (34%), PWI (47%). By CTL staffing quartile (N = 948, x^2 = 61.9, df = 3, p < .001), percentages are 1 individual (31%), 2–3 individuals (44%), 4–6 individuals (53%), and 7+ individuals (68%). In analyses of unique institutions, there are statistically significant differences by instructional FTE (N = 1068, x^2 = 68.6, df = 3, p < .001). Percentages are Quartile 1: 16–181 (30%), Quartile 2: 183–319 (37%), Quartile 3: 320–648 (45%), and Quartile 4: 649+ (64%).

61. There are statistically significant differences by presence of digital learning staff in the CTL (N = 1196, x^2 = 34.1, df = 1, p < .001). Percentages are has digital staff (57%), does not have (39%).

62. Lee, "Program Types and Prototypes," 21–33; Peter A. Cohen, "Effectiveness of Student-Rating Feedback for Improving College Teaching: A Meta-Analysis of Findings," *Research in Higher Education* 13 (1980): 321–41; Penny and Coe, "Effectiveness

of Consultation," 235; Cynthia J. Finelli, Tershia Pinder-Grover, and Mary C. Wright, "Consultations on Teaching: Using Student Feedback for Instructional Improvement," in *Advancing the Culture of Teaching on Campus: How a Teaching Center Can Make a Difference*, edited by Constance Cook and Mathew Kaplan (Sterling, VA: Stylus Publishing, 2011), 65–79.

63. Lee, "Program Types and Prototypes," 21–33.

64. Penny and Coe, "Effectiveness of Consultation," 237.

65. Michelle K. Smith, Francis H. M. Jones, Sarah L. Gilbert, and Carl E. Wieman, "The Classroom Observation Protocol for Undergraduate STEM (COPUS): A New Instrument to Characterize University STEM Classroom Practices," *CBE-Life Sciences Education* 12, no. 4 (2013), https://www.physport.org/assessments/assessment.cfm?A=COPUS.

66. See "Grants Programs," Sewanee, accessed November 25, 2021, https://new.sewanee.edu/offices/the-college-of-arts-sciences-offices/dean-of-the-college/center-for-teaching/grants-programs/.

67. Mark V. Redmond and D. Joseph Clark, "Small Group Instructional Diagnosis: A Practical Approach to Improving Teaching," *AAHE Bulletin* 810 (February 1982); Barbara J. Millis and Jose Vazquez, "Down with the SGID! Long Live the QCD!" *Essays on Teaching Excellence*, 22, no. 4 (2010–2011), https://podnetwork.org/content/uploads/V22_N4_Millis_Vasquez.pdf.

68. Finelli, Pinder-Grover, and Wright, "Consultations on Teaching."

69. Carol A. Hurney, Nancy L. Harris, Samantha C. Bates Prins, and S. E. Kruck, "The Impact of a Learner-Centered, Mid-Semester Course Evaluation on Students," *Journal of Faculty Development* 28, no. 3 (2014): 55–62; Carol A. Hurney, Christine A. Rener, and Jordan D. Troisi, *Midcourse Correction for the College Classroom: Putting Small Group Instructional Diagnosis to Work* (Sterling, VA: Stylus Publishing, 2022).

70. Arthur W. Chickering and Zelda F. Gamson, "Seven Principles for Good Practice in Undergraduate Education," *American Association of Higher Education* (March 1987): 3–7; Rebecca L. Taylor, Kris Knorr, Michelle Ogrodnik, and Peter Sinclair, "Seven Principles for Good Practice in Midterm Student Feedback," *International Journal for Academic Development* 25, no. 4 (2020): 350–62.

71. Alison Cook-Sather, Catherine Bovill, and Peter Felten, *Engaging Students as Partners in Learning and Teaching: A Guide for Faculty* (San Francisco: Jossey-Bass, 2014), 73–74.

72. D. Lynn Sorenson, "College Teachers and Student Consultants: Collaborating about Teaching and Learning," in *Student-Assisted Teaching: A Guide to Faculty-Student Teamwork*, edited by Judith E. Miller, James E. Groccia, and Marylyn S. Miller (Bolton, MA: Anker, 2001), 200–201.

73. Beach et al., *Faculty Development*, 2016; Mary Deane Sorcinelli, Ann E. Austin, Pamela L. Eddy, and Andrea L. Beach, *Creating the Future of Faculty Development: Learning from the Past, Understanding the Present* (Bolton, MA: Anker, 2006), table 4.1.

74. In analyses of unique institutions (N = 1162), there are statistically significant differences by Carnegie type (x^2 = 57.9, df = 5, p < .001). Percentages are doctoral (61%), master's (39%), associate's (36%), baccalaureate (35%), other special focus (35%), and

medical/health (33%). By CTL staffing quartile (N = 948, x^2 = 24.8, df = 3, p < .001), percentages are 1 individual (35%), 2–3 individuals (49%), 4–6 individuals (53%), and 7+ individuals (57%). In analyses of unique institutions (N = 1100), there are also statistically significant differences by control (x^2 = 9.8, df = 2, p < .01). Percentages are public (47%), private not-for-profit (38%), and private for-profit (38%). In analyses of unique institutions, there are statistically significant differences by instructional FTE (N = 1068, x^2 = 70.0, df = 3, p < .001). Percentages are Quartile 1: 16–181 (26%), Quartile 2: 183–319 (40%), Quartile 3: 320–648 (50%), and Quartile 4: 649+ (61%).

75. Ann Stes, Liesje Coertjens, and Peter Van Petegem, "Instructional Development for Teachers in Higher Education: Impact on Teaching Approach," *Higher Education* 60 (2010): 187–204; Deborah Meizlish, Mary C. Wright, Jay Howard, and Matthew Kaplan, "Measuring the Impact of a New Faculty Program Using Institutional Data," *International Journal for Academic Development* 23, no. 2 (2017): 72–85.

76. Deborah Meizlish et al., "Measuring the Impact of a New Faculty Program."

77. "About," BYU Hawaii, accessed November 26, 2021, https://clt.byuh.edu/about.

78. Beach et al., *Faculty Development*, table 4.1.

79. This is 22% of doctoral universities, which is a lower proportion than seen in earlier studies. The "Mapping the Range of Graduate Professional Development" study found that 57% of doctoral institutions had TA preparation programs (Palmer, "Graduate Student Professional Development"). However, the 2011 study asked institutions to report the location no matter the institutional location (e.g., Graduate School), while my study focuses on CTLs only.

80. Nadia Dimitrov, Ken Meadows, Erika Kustra, Tim Ackerson, Laura Prada, Nick Baker, Pierre Boulos, Gayle McIntyre, and Michael K. Potter, *Assessing Graduate Teaching Development Programs for Impact on Future Faculty* (Toronto: Higher Education Quality Council of Ontario, 2013); S. Spencer Robinson, "An Introductory Classification of Graduate Teaching Assistant Orientations," in *Studies in Graduate and Professional Student Development*, edited by L. L. B. Border (Stillwater, OK: New Forums Press, 2011), 19–33.

81. Dimitrov et al., *Assessing Graduate Teaching Development Programs.*

82. Laura Lunsford, Gloria Crisp, Erin L. Dolan, and Brad Wuetherick, "Mentoring in Higher Education," in *The SAGE Handbook of Mentoring*, edited by David A. Clutterbuck, Frances K. Kochan, Laura Lunsford, Nora Dominguez, and Julie Haddock-Millar (London: Sage Publications, 2017), 316–34.

83. In analyses of unique institutions (N = 1162), there are statistically significant differences by Carnegie type (x^2 = 23.3, df = 5, p < .001). Percentages are medical/health (35%), doctoral (27%), master's (24%), baccalaureate (17%), associate's (16%), and other special focus (10%).

84. By CTL staffing quartile (N = 948, x^2 = 18.1, df = 3, p < .001), percentages are: 1 individual (17%), 2–3 individuals (31%), 4–6 individuals (19%), and 7+ individuals (27%). In analyses of unique institutions, there are statistically significant differences by instructional FTE (N = 1068, x^2 = 18.1, df = 3, p < .001). Percentages are Quartile 1: 16–181 (16%), Quartile 2: 183–319 (18%), Quartile 3: 320–648 (26%), and Quartile 4: 649+ (29%).

85. Lunsford et al., "Mentoring in Higher Education," 316–64; Mary Deane Sorcinelli and Jung Yun, "From Mentor to Mentoring Networks: Mentoring in the New Academy," *Change: The Magazine of Higher Learning* 39, no. 6 (2007): 58–61; Abigail J. Stewart and Virginia Valian, *An Inclusive Academy: Achieving Diversity and Excellence* (Cambridge, MA: MIT Press, 2018); Jung H. Yun, Brian Baldi, and Mary Deane Sorcinelli, "Mutual Mentoring for Early-Career and Underrepresented Faculty: Model, Research, and Practice," *Innovative Higher Education* 41, no. 5 (2016): 441–51.

86. Laura L. Paglis, Stephen G. Green, and Talya N Bauer, "Does Adviser Mentoring Add Value? A Longitudinal Study of Mentoring and Doctoral Student Outcomes," *Research in Higher Education* 47, no. 4 (2006): 451–76; Chris M. Golde, "Should I Stay or Should I Go? Student Descriptions of the Doctoral Attrition Process," *Review of Higher Education* 23, no. 2 (2000): 199–227, https://doi.org/10.1353/rhe.2000.0004; Barbara E. Lovitts, *Leaving the Ivory Tower: The Causes and Consequences of Departure from Doctoral Study* (Lanham, MD: Rowman and Littlefield, 2001).

87. Laura N. Schram and Mary C. Wright, "Teaching Mentorship Programs for Graduate Student Development," *Studies in Graduate and Professional Student Development* 14 (2011): 53–68.

88. Chism, Holley, and Harris, "Researching the Impact," 129–45; Mary C. Wright, Constance E. Cook, and Elizabeth Brady, *Using Grants to Enhance Student Learning* (CRLT Occasional Paper No. 13) (East Lansing: University of Michigan, 2000), http://www.crlt.umich.edu/sites/default/files/resource_files/CRLT_no13.pdf; Kenneth E. Eble and William J. McKeachie, *Improving Undergraduate Education through Faculty Development* (San Francisco: Jossey Bass, 1985); Cheryl Amundsen and Laura D'Amico, "Using Theory of Change to Evaluate Socially-Situated, Inquiry-Based Academic Professional Development," *Studies in Educational Evaluation* 61 (2019): 196–208.

89. In analyses of unique institutions (N = 1162), there are statistically significant differences by Carnegie type (x^2 = 48.2, df = 5, p < .001). Percentages are doctoral (41%), master's (32%), baccalaureate (29%), other special focus (21%), associate's (18%), and medical/health (14%).

90. There are statistically significant differences by CTL age (x^2 = 18.2, df = 3, p < .001). By CTL age quartile, percentages are 0–9 years old (21%), 10–19 years (39%), 20–29 years (55%), and 30+ years (60%). By CTL staffing quartile (N = 948, x^2 = 21.7, df = 3, p < .001), percentages are: 1 individual (21%), 2–3 individuals (29%), 4–6 individuals (37%), and 7+ individuals (39%). In analyses of unique institutions, there are statistically significant differences by instructional FTE (N = 1068, x^2 = 22.4, df = 3, p < .001). Percentages are Quartile 1: 16–181 (21%), Quartile 2: 183–319 (30%), Quartile 3: 320–648 (33%), and Quartile 4: 649+(40%).

91. Beckman Humor Project, accessed on November 27, 2021, https://www.up.edu/beckmanhumor/.

92. "A. T. Still University Presents SparkTank: Igniting Innovative Ideas," accessed on November 27, 2021. https://www.atsu.edu/sparktank.

93. William Condon, Ellen R. Iverson, Cathryn A. Manduca, Carol Rutz, and Gudrun Willet, *Faculty Development and Student Learning: Assessing the Connections*

(Bloomington: Indiana University Press, 2016); Mary C. Wright, "Faculty Development Improves Teaching and Learning," *POD Speaks* 2 (2018): 1–5.

94. In analyses of unique institutions (N = 1162), there are statistically significant differences by Carnegie type (x^2 = 17.7, df = 5, p < .01). Percentages are baccalaureate (11%), doctoral (9%), other special focus (7%), master's (5%), medical/health (4%), and associate's (2%).

95. By CTL staffing quartile (N = 948, x^2 = 32.2, df = 3, p < .001), percentages are 1 individual (3%), 2–3 individuals (4%), 4–6 individuals (11%), and 7+ individuals (15%).

96. In analyses of unique institutions (N = 1162), there are statistically significant differences by Carnegie type (x^2 = 61.5, df = 5, p < .001). Percentages are doctoral (91%), medical/health (81%), master's (76%), baccalaureate (75%), other special focus (72%), and associate's (64%).

97. In analyses of unique institutions, there are statistically significant differences by instructional FTE (N = 1068, x^2 = 84.2, df = 3, p < .001). Percentages are Quartile 1: 16–181 (61%), Quartile 2: 183–319 (76%), Quartile 3: 320–648 (85%), and Quartile 4: 649+ (92%). By CTL staffing quartile (N = 948, x^2 = 51.4, df = 3, p < .001), percentages are 1 individual (68%), 2–3 individuals (83%), 4–6 individuals (89%), and 7+ individuals (92%).

98. By presence of digital learning staff in the CTL (N = 1196, x^2 = 10.9, df = 1, p < .001), percentages are has digital staff (84%), does not have (76%).

99. Jonathan Zimmerman, *The Amateur Hour A History of College Teaching in America* (Baltimore, MD: Johns Hopkins University Press, 2021).

100. Charlene M. Dewey, "The Emergence of Academies of Educational Excellence: A Survey of U.S. Medical Schools," *Academic Medicine* 80, no. 4 (2005): 359.

101. AAMC, "Faculty Academies at US Medical Schools," https://www.aamc.org/data-reports/curriculum-reports/interactive-data/faculty-academies-us-medical-schools.

102. Nancy Searle, Britta M. Thompson, Joan A. Friedland, James Lomax, Jan E. Drutz, Michael Coburn, and Elizabeth A. Nelson, "The Prevalence and Practice of Academies of Medical Educators: A Survey of U.S. Medical Schools," *Academic Medicine* 85, no. 1 (2010): 48–56.

103. Dewey, "The Emergence of Academies," 2005. Additionally, any institution that is listed as a member on "The Academies Collaborative," a professional association for health sciences teaching academies, site membership list as of December 2021 is counted as having a teaching academy.

104. "Teaching Academy," Morehouse School of Medicine, https://www.msm.edu/Education/teachingacademy/index.php.

105. "Teaching Academy," Office of Faculty and Academic Affairs, https://ofaa.gumc.georgetown.edu/teaching-resources/teaching-academy/.

106. In analyses of unique Carnegie types (N = 1162), there are statistically significant differences (x^2 = 122.6, df = 5, p < .001). Percentages are medical/health (52%), doctoral (45%), other special focus (28%), master's (19%), baccalaureate (16%), and associate's (14%).

107. In analyses of unique institutions (N = 1099), there are statistically significant differences by MSI status (x^2 = 9.9, df = 1, p < .01). Percentages are MSI (18%), PWI (29%).

108. In analyses of unique institutions (N = 1068), there are statistically significant differences by instructional FTE (x^2 = 121.0, df = 3, p < .001). Percentages are Quartile 1 (16–181): 10%; Quartile 2 (183–319): 20%; Quartile 3 (320–648): 26%; and Quartile 4 (649+): 50%. By CTL staffing quartile (N = 948, x^2 = 52.7, df = 3, p < .001), percentages are 1 individual (15%), 2–3 individuals (29%), 4–6 individuals (33%), and 7+ individuals (47%).

109. Hutchins and Shulman, "The Scholarship of Teaching," 11–15.

110. Peter Felten and Nancy Chick, "Is SoTL a Signature Pedagogy of Educational Development?" *To Improve the Academy* 37, no. 1 (2018): 7, 12, http://dx.doi.org/10.3998/tia.17063888.0037.114.

111. Hillary Steiner, Laura Cruz, and Clare Cruz, "Signature Moves: An Environmental Scan of the Intersection between Educational Development and SoTL" (unpublished manuscript, consulted 2022).

112. Gibbs, "Reflections on the Changing Nature," 4–14; Kezar, *Scaling and Sustaining Change*.

113. In analyses of unique institutions (N = 1162), there are statistically significant differences by Carnegie type (x^2 = 53.0, df = 5, p < .001). Percentages are doctoral (25%), medical/health (22%), master's (13%), baccalaureate (11%), associate's (5%), and other special focus (0%).

114. In analyses of unique institutions (N = 1068), there are statistically significant differences by instructional FTE (x^2 = 47.3, df = 3, p < .001). Percentages are Quartile 1 (16–181): 6%; Quartile 2 (183–319): 12%; Quartile 3 (320–648): 14%; and Quartile 4 (649+): 26%. By CTL staffing quartile (N = 948, x^2 = 21.2, df = 3, p < .001), percentages are 1 individual (10%), 2–3 individuals (17%), 4–6 individuals (13%), and 7+ individuals (26%). In analyses of unique institutions (N = 1099), there are also statistically significant differences by MSI status (x^2 = 3.9, df = 1, p < .05). Percentages are MSI (10%), PWI (16%).

115. Mary C. Wright, Cynthia J. Finelli, and Deborah Meizlish, "Facilitating the Scholarship of Teaching and Learning at a Research University," *Change: The Magazine of Higher Learning* 43, no. 2 (2011): 50–56.

116. For the rubric, see Michael Dennin, Zachary D. Schultz, Andrew Feig, Noah Finkelstein, Andrea F. Greenhoot, Michael Hildreth, Adam K. Leibovich, James D. Martin, Mark B. Moldwin, Diane K. O'Dowd, Lynmarie A. Posey, Tobin L. Smith, and Emily R. Miller, "Aligning Practice to Policies: Changing the Culture to Recognize and Reward Teaching at Research Universities," *CBE Life Sciences Education* 16, no. 4 (2018).

117. There are statistically significant differences by CTL size (N = 948, x^2 = 10.3, df = 3, p < .05). Percentages are 1 individual (0%), 2–3 individuals (0%), 4–6 individuals (3%), and 7+ individuals (2%). In analyses of unique institutions (N = 1068), there are statistically significant differences by instructional FTE (x^2 = 8.7, df = 3, p < .05). Percentages are Quartile 1 (16–181): 0%; Quartile 2 (183–319): 1%; Quartile 3 (320–648): 0%; and Quartile 4 (649+): 2%.

118. Noha Elassy, "The Concepts of Quality, Quality Assurance and Quality Enhancement," *Quality Assurance in Education* 23, no. 3 (2014): 250–61.

119. In analyses of unique institutions (N = 1162), there are statistically significant differences by Carnegie type (x^2 = 15.2, df = 5, p < .05). Percentages are doctoral (11%),

master's (11%), associate's (9%), other special focus (7%), medical/health (3%), and baccalaureate (3%).

120. In analyses of unique institutions (N = 1100), there are statistically significant differences by control (x^2 = 24.4, df = 2, p < .001). Percentages are private for-profit (13%), public (12%), private not-for-profit (4%). There are statistically significant differences by CTL size (N = 948, x^2 = 28.5, df = 3, p < .001). Percentages are 1 individual (4%), 2–3 individuals (7%), 4–6 individuals (13%), and 7+ individuals (17%).

121. Constance E. Cook, Mary C. Wright, and Chris O'Neal, "Action Research for Instructional Improvement: Using Data to Enhance Student Learning at Your own Institution," *To Improve the Academy* 25 (2007): 123–38; Emerson and Mosteller, "Development Programs for College Faculty."

122. Coppin State University, "Center for Excellence in Teaching and Learning," https://www.coppin.edu/faculty-and-staff/faculty-organizations-and-committees /center-excellence-teaching-and-learning.

123. In analyses of unique institutions (N = 1162), there are statistically significant differences by Carnegie type (x^2 = 57.5, df = 5, p < .001). Percentages are doctoral (11%), baccalaureate (3%), master's (2%), associate's (1%), other special focus (0%), and medical/ health (0%). There are statistically significant differences by CTL size (N = 948, x^2 = 41.0, df = 3, p < .001). Percentages are 1 individual (0%), 2–3 individuals (3%), 4–6 individuals (6%), and 7+ individuals (13%). In analyses of unique institutions (N = 1068), there are also statistically significant differences by instructional FTE (x^2 = 50.9, df = 3, p < .001). Percentages are Quartile 1 (16–181): 0%; Quartile 2 (183–319): 2%; Quartile 3 (320–648): 3%; and Quartile 4 (649+): 12%.

124. By CTL age quartile, percentages are 0–9 years old (1%), 10–19 years (8%), 20–29 years (17%), 30+ years (20%) (N = 183, x^2 = 11.4, df = 3, p < .05).

125. In analyses of unique institutions (N = 1162), there are statistically significant differences by Carnegie type (x^2 = 91.3, df = 5, p < .001). Percentages are doctoral (58%), medical/health (42%), master's (39%), baccalaureate (24%), associate's (24%), and other special focus (21%).

126. In analyses of unique institutions (N = 1100), there are statistically significant differences by control (x^2 = 10.4, df = 2, p < .01). Percentages are public (43%), private not-for-profit (33%), and private for-profit (25%).

127. There are statistically significant differences by CTL size (N = 948, x^2 = 104.5, df = 3, p < .001). Percentages are 1 individual (25%), 2–3 individuals (36%), 4–6 individuals (48%), and 7+ individuals (71%). In analyses of unique institutions (N = 1068), there are also statistically significant differences by instructional FTE (x^2 = 99.1, df = 3, p < .001). Percentages are Quartile 1 (16–181): 24%; Quartile 2 (183–319): 31%; Quartile 3 (320–648): 39%; and Quartile 4 (649+): 64%.

128. Percentages are has digital staff (54%); does not have digital staff (33%) (N = 1196, x^2 = 44.3, df = 1, p < .001).

129. Anna L. Carew, Geraldine Lefoe, Maureen Bell, and Lenore Armour, "Elastic Practice in Academic Developers," *International Journal for Academic Development* 13, no. 1 (2008): 51–66.

130. Laura Cruz, "The Idea of Educational Development: An Historical Perspective," *To Improve the Academy* 37, no. 1 (2018).

131. Lee, "Program Types and Prototypes," 21–33.

132. Mintz, "Why We Need Centers for Educational Innovation."

Chapter 4. How Are We Organized?

1. Kathryn A. Sutherland, "Holistic Academic Development: Is It Time to Think More Broadly about the Academic Development Project?" *International Journal for Academic Development* 23, no. 4 (2018): 1.

2. Andrea Beach, Mary Deane Sorcinelli, Ann E. Austin, and Jaclyn Rivard, *Faculty Development in the Age of Evidence: Current Practices, Future Imperatives* (Sterling, VA: Stylus Publishing, 2016), 35.

3. Bruce Kelley, Laura Cruz, and Nancy Fire, "Moving Toward the Center: The Integration of Educational Development in an Era of Historic Change in Higher Education," *To Improve the Academy* 36, no. 1 (2017): 1–8, http://dx.doi.org/10.1002/tia2 .20052.

4. John A. Centra, *Faculty Development Practices in U.S. Colleges and Universities* (Princeton, NJ: Educational Testing Service, 1976), 32.

5. Beach et al., *Faculty Development*, 163.

6. Kelley, Cruz, and Fire, "Moving Toward the Center."

7. This analysis is based on unique Carnegie types (N = 1162, x^2 = 78.1, df = 5, p < .001). Percentages are doctoral universities (73%), followed by associate's (66%), master's (65%), other special focus (59%), baccalaureate (41%), and medical / health-associated (38%) institutions.

8. This analysis is based on unique institutions (N = 1100, x^2 = 38.6, df = 2, p < .001). Percentages are public (69%), private not-for-profit (51%), and private for-profit (50%).

9. There are statistically significant differences by CTL staffing levels (N = 948, x^2 = 104.2, df = 3, p < .001). Percentages are 1 individual (45%), 2–3 individuals (64%), 4–6 individuals (76%), and 7+ individuals (89%). In analyses of unique institutions, there are statistically significant differences by instructional FTE (x^2 = 28.6, df = 3, p < .001). Percentages are Quartile 1 (16–181): 55%; Quartile 2 (183–319): 55%; Quartile 3 (320–648): 68%; and Quartile 4 (649+): 73%.

10. Sieve: 67%, non-Sieve: 59% (N = 1106, x^2 = 7.09, df = 1, p < .01); Hub: 60%, non-Hub: 68% (x^2 = 5.6, df = 1, p < .05); Incubator: 58%, non-Incubator: 65% (x^2 = 5.0, df = 1, p < .05); Temple: 65%, non-Temple: 62% (x^2 = 1.1, df = 1, ns).

11. Jerry G. Gaff, "Current Issues in Faculty Development," *Liberal Education* 63, no. 4 (1977): 511–19.

12. William H. Bergquist and Steven R. Phillips, *A Handbook For Faculty Development* (Washington, DC: Council for the Advancement of Small Colleges, 1975), 182.

13. POD Network, "What Is Educational Development?" Last modified June 2016, https://podnetwork.org/about/what-is-educational-development/.

14. Beach et al., *Faculty Development*, 60, 72.

15. Beach et al., *Faculty Development*, 72.

16. Kenneth E. Eble and William J. McKeachie. *Improving Undergraduate Education through Faculty Development* (San Francisco: Jossey Bass, 1985), 5.

17. In 2022, Mills College merged with Northeastern University. The Mills Center for Faculty Excellence no longer has a web presence.

18. This analysis is based on unique institutions (N = 1162, x^2 = 46.2, df = 5, p < .001). Percentages are medical/health (64%), doctoral (60%), master's (51%), other special focus (45%), baccalaureate (38%), and associate's (37%) institutions.

19. There are statistically significant differences by CTL staffing levels (N = 948, x^2 = 11.3, df = 3, p < .05). Percentages are 1 individual (43%), 2–3 individuals (56%), 4–6 individuals (56%), and 7+ individuals (50%). In analyses of unique institutions, there are statistically significant differences by instructional FTE (N = 1068, x^2 = 44.9, df = 3, p < .001). Percentages are Quartile 1 (16–181): 33%; Quartile 2 (183–319): 48%; Quartile 3 (320–648): 53%; and Quartile 4 (649+): 62%.

20. Correlations are Temple (r = 0.05), Incubator (r = 0.04), Hub (r = 0.02), and Sieve (r = 0.00).

21. Peggy L. Maki, *Assessing for Learning: Building a Sustainable Commitment across the Institution* (Herndon, VA: Stylus Publishing, 2004), 2.

22. Beach et al., *Faculty Development*, 2016; Tracy Bartholomew, "Analysis of Educational Development Position Advertisements," *POD Network News* (Fall 2016).

23. Peter T. Ewell, "Assessment and Accountability in America Today: Background and Context," in *New Directions for Institutional Research*, vol. S1, edited by Victor M. H. Borden and Gary R. Pike (New York: Wiley, 2008), 9.

24. Mary C. Wright, Molly Goldwasser, Wayne Jacobson, and Christopher Dakes, "Assessment from an Educational Development Perspective," *To Improve the Academy* 36, no. 1 (2017): 39–49, http://dx.doi.org/10.3998/tia.17063888.0036.101.

25. The Carnegie analysis is based on unique institutions (N = 1162, x^2 = 59.6, df = 5, p < .001). Percentages are doctoral universities (38%), medical / health-related centers (20%), master's institutions (20%), other special focus contexts (19%), associate's colleges (17%), and baccalaureates (12%). For personnel size (N = 948, x^2 = 88.9, df = 3, p < .001), percentages are 1 individual (15%), 2–3 individuals (18%), 4–6 individuals (29%), and 7+ individuals (51%). In analyses of unique institutions, there are statistically significant differences by instructional FTE (x^2 = 64.5, df = 3, p < .001). Percentages are Quartile 1 (16–181): 14%; Quartile 2 (183–319): 16%; Quartile 3 (320–648): 23%; and Quartile 4 (649+): 41%.

26. This analysis is based on unique institutions (N = 1100, x^2 = 8.2, df = 2, p < .05). Percentages are public (26%), private for-profit (25%), and private not-for-profit (19%).

27. N = 1106. x^2 = 46.1, df = 1, p < .001.

28. Eble and McKeachie, *Improving Undergraduate Education*; Lance C. Buhl and Laura A. Wilson, eds., "Section V: Student Development: Intellectual Growth and Writing," *To Improve the Academy* 68 (1984); Jennifer Ahern-Dodson and Monique Dufour "Supporting Faculty as Writers and Teachers: An Integrative Approach to Educational Development," *To Improve the Academy* 40, no. 1 (2021); See also Joan Mullin, Peter Carino, Jane Nelson, and Kathy Evertz's 2006 publication from the perspective of writing center professionals: "Administrative (Chaos) Theory: The Politics and Practices of Writing Center Location," in *The Writing Center Director's Resource Book*, edited by Christina Murphy, Byron Stay, and Kim Abels (New York: Taylor and Francis, 2006), 225–35.

29. Beach et al., *Faculty Development*, 35–36, 163–64.

30. Michelle Eodice, Anne Ellen Geller, and Neal Lerner, *The Meaningful Writing Project: Learning, Teaching, and Writing in Higher Education* (Provo: Utah State University Press, 2017).

31. Originating at Brown University in 1982, writing fellows are "selected from diverse disciplines and then trained (and paid) to serve as first readers for papers written in selected courses throughout the curriculum . . . [and] communicate with the writers they are tutoring." Tori Haring-Smith, "Changing Students' Attitudes: Writing Fellows Programs," in *Writing across the Curriculum: A Guide to Developing Programs*, edited by Susan H. McLeod and Margot Soven (Newbury Park, CA: Sage, 2000), 124.

32. This analysis is based on unique Carnegie types (N = 1162, x^2 = 46.5, df = 5, p < .001). Percentages are doctoral (32%), master's (25%), baccalaureate (23%), medical/health (14%), other special focus (10%), and associate's (10%). In analyses of unique institutions, there are statistically significant differences by instructional FTE (N = 1068, x^2 = 35.7, df = 3, p < .001). Percentages are Quartile 1 (16–181): 12%; Quartile 2 (183–319): 22%; Quartile 3 (320–648): 24%; and Quartile 4 (649+): 34%.

33. Percentages are 1 individual (17%), 2–3 individuals (27%), 4–6 individuals (25%), and 7+ individuals (32%) (N = 948, x^2 = 13.5, df = 3, p < .01).

34. Percentages are women's (50%), coeducational (23%). (N = 1102, x^2 = 5.0, df = 1, p < .05).

35. N = 1105, x^2 = 10.1, df = 1, p < .01.

36. George Kuh, *High-Impact Educational Practices: What They Are, Who Has Access to Them, and Why They Matter* (Washington, DC: American Association of Colleges and Universities, 2008), 13–22; Joan Marie Blakey, Shirley Theriot, Mary Cazzell, and Melanie Sattler, "Is Service-Learning Worth It? A Mixed-Methods Study of Faculty's Service-Learning Experiences," *International Journal of Research on Service-Learning and Community Engagement* 3, no. 1 (2015); L. Dee Fink. "Forward," in *Reconceptualizing Faculty Development in Service-Learning/Community Engagement: Exploring Intersections, Frameworks, and Models of Practice*, edited by Becca Berkey, Emily A. Eddins, Patrick M. Green, and Cara Meixner (Sterling, VA: Stylus Publishing, 2018); Sarah Surak and Alexander Pope, "Engaging the Educators: Facilitating Civic Engagement through Faculty Development," *Journal of Higher Education Outreach and Engagement* 20, no. 3 (2016): 140–62; Mary Deane Sorcinelli, Ann E. Austin, Pamela L. Eddy, and Andrea L. Beach, *Creating the Future of Faculty Development: Learning From the Past, Understanding the Present* (Bolton, MA: Anker, 2006), 1–5; Beach et al., *Faculty Development*, 36.

37. Becca Berkey, Emily A. Eddins, Patrick M. Green, and Cara Meixner, eds., *Reconceptualizing Faculty Development in Service-Learning/Community Engagement: Exploring Intersections, Frameworks, and Models of Practice* (Sterling, VA: Stylus Publishing, 2018).

38. Marshall Welch and Star Plaxton-Moore, "Faculty Development for Advancing Community Engagement in Higher Education: Current Trends and Future Directions," *Journal of Higher Education Outreach and Engagement* 21, no. 2 (2017): 131–65.

39. This is defined by those with the following key terms in their titles: *service learning, community engagement,* or *community-engaged learning.*

40. This analysis is based on unique institutions (N = 1100, x^2 = 10.9, df = 2, p < .01). Percentages are public (13%), private not-for-profit (7%), and for-profit (0%).

41. This analysis is based on unique institutions (N = 1180, x^2 = 21.5, df = 1, p < .001). Percentages are Carnegie engaged (19%), non–Carnegie engaged (9%).

42. This analysis is based on unique institutions (N = 1162, x^2 = 35.7, df = 5, p < .001. Percentages are doctoral (18%), master's (12%), associate's (8%), baccalaureate (6%), other special focus (3%), and medical/health (1%) contexts.

43. Percentages are 1 individual (7%), 2–3 individuals (12%), 4–6 individuals (12%), and 7+ individuals (20%) (N = 948, x^2 = 15.6, df = 3, p < .01). In analyses of unique institutions, there are statistically significant differences by instructional FTE (N = 1068, x^2 = 34.2, df = 3, p < .001). Percentages are Quartile 1 (16–181): 4%; Quartile 2 (183–319): 9%; Quartile 3 (320–648): 11%; and Quartile 4 (649+): 20%.

44. Caile Spear, Kara Brascia, Mike Stefanic, and Anna Bailey, "Boise State University," in Berkey et al., *Reconceptualizing Faculty Development,* 108–17.

45. Percentages are Temple 14%, non-Temple 10%; Sieve 12%, non-Sieve 10%; Incubator and non-Incubator: 11%; Hub 10%, non-Hub 13%.

46. See Marshall Welch and Star Plaxton-Moore, "Ready or Not? An International Study of Preparation of Educational Developers," *To Improve the Academy* 29 (2018): 260–73; and Emily O. Gravett and Andreas Broscheid, "Models and Genres of Faculty Development," in Berkey et al., *Reconceptualizing Faculty Development,* 85–106.

47. Kelley, Cruz, and Fire, "Moving Toward the Center," 1–8.

48. Kelley, Cruz, and Fire, "Moving Toward the Center," para. 18.

49. Jennifer H. Herman, "Staffing of Teaching and Learning Centers in the United States: Indicators of Institutional Support for Faculty Development," *Journal of Faculty Development* 27, no. 2 (2013): 33–37.

50. Herman, "Staffing of Teaching and Learning Centers," 34.

51. US Department of Education, National Center for Education Statistics, Integrated Postsecondary Education Data System (IPEDS), 2020, nces.ed.gov/ipeds.

52. Indiana University Center for Postsecondary Research, 2018, Carnegie Classifications 2018 public data file, http://carnegieclassifications.iu.edu/downloads/CCIHE2018-PublicDataFile.xlsx.

53. This analysis is based on unique Carnegie types and excludes CTLs with a committee structure (N = 927, F = 26.4, df = 5, 922), p < .001). Bonferroni post-hoc test shows significant differences for doctoral institutions and all other institutional types (p < .001) except other special focus.

54. Means are 30+ years (15.1), 20–29 years (5.6), 10–19 (4.4), 0–9 years (6.6) (N = 159, F = 5.5, df = 3, 156, p < .001). Bonferroni post-hoc test shows significant differences for 30+ years and all other CTL ages (p < .01).

55. Herman, "Staffing of Teaching and Learning Centers," 33–37.

56. Debra D. Dawson, Judy Britnell, and Alicia Hitchcock, "Developing Competency Models of Faculty Developers: Using World Café to Foster Dialogue," in *To*

Improve the Academy, edited by L. A. Nilson and J. E. Miller (San Francisco: Jossey-Bass, 2010), 3–24; Marie A. Wunsch, "From Faculty Developer to Faculty Development Director: Shifting Perspectives and Strategies," *To Improve the Academy* 12, no. 1 (1993).

57. David A. Green and Deandra Little, "On the Other Side of the Wall: The Miscategorization of Educational Developers in the United States?" *To Improve the Academy* 36, no. 2 (2017), 2.

58. Deandra Little and David A. Green, "Betwixt and Between: Academic Developers in the Margins," *International Journal for Academic Development* 17, no. 3 (2012): 203–15.

59. Sorcinelli et al., *Creating the Future of Faculty Development*, 1–5; Green and Little, "On the Other Side," 2017.

60. This analysis is based on unique Carnegie types (n = 927, x^2 = 21.9, df = 5, p < .001). Percentages are baccalaureate (63%), master's (55%), doctoral (55%), other special focus (42%), medical/health (41%), and associate's (40%).

61. Vicki L. Baker, Laura Gail Lunsford, and Meghan J. Pifer, "Institutional Structures, Support, and Evaluation," in *Developing Faculty in Liberal Arts Colleges: Aligning Individual Needs and Organizational Goals*, edited by Vicki Baker, Laura Gail Lunsford, and Meghan Pifer (New Brunswick, NJ: Rutgers University Press, 2017).

62. Specifically, "centers of one" (i.e., just the CTL leader) (50%) and those with 2–3 individuals (60%) are more likely to have a CTL leader with faculty status, compared to CTLs with 4–6 (44%) or 7+ individuals (44%) (N = 925, x^2 = 18.7, df = 3, p < .001).

63. This analysis is based on unique Carnegie types (N = 479, x^2 = 72.4, df = 30, p < .001). Specific percentages for full professors are medical/health (63%), baccalaureate (42%), other special focus (40%), master's (39%), doctoral (38%), and associate's (17%). Percentages for associate professors are baccalaureate (37%), master's (33%), doctoral (31%), associate's (23%), other special focus (20%), and medical/health (13%). Percentages for "faculty (rank not specified)" are associate's (34%), doctoral (14%), baccalaureate (11%), medical/health (10%), other special focus (10%), and master's (9%).

64. This analysis is based on unique institutions (N = 454, x^2 = 19.0, df = 6, p < .01).

65. This analysis is based on unique institutions (N = 912, x^2 = 351.4, df = 85, p < .001). Percentages for "director" are baccalaureate (70%), master's (69%), other special focus (61%), doctoral (59%), associate's (38%), and medical/health (33%). Percentages for "dean" are medical/health (43%), baccalaureate (17%), associate's (14%), other special focus (9%), master's (4%), and doctoral (4%).

66. Beach et al., *Faculty Development*, table 1.5.

67. Percentages for PhD are baccalaureate (82%), doctoral (81%), master's (80%), other special focus (64%), associate's (48%), medical/health (40%). Percentages for MD/DO are medical/health (40%), other special focus (7%), doctoral (< 1%), associate's (0%), baccalaureate (0%), master's (0%). This analysis is based on unique Carnegie types (N = 644, x^2 = 298.2, df = 30, p < .001).

68. Green and Little, "On the Other Side," 2017; Beach et al., *Faculty Development*, 2016.

69. There is much less information on center websites about non-director credentials. However, I was able to record 840 degrees for personnel at 248 centers. Here,

doctoral degrees and master's degrees are noted with equal frequency (37% each), followed by bachelor's (16%), EdD (5%), MD (1%), and other (4%).

70. Beach et al., *Faculty Development*, 26.

71. Green and Little, "On the Other Side," 2017.

72. Bartholomew, *Analysis of Educational Development*, 2016.

73. Karen Bellnier, "Average Size of Faculty Centers?" POD Network discussion list post, POD Network, 2020, https://groups.google.com/a/podnetwork.org/g/discussion/c/3M_GeQ7eLag/m/rtvooQr4AQAJ; E. Y. Kim, "Seeking CTL/CTE Comparison Data," POD Network discussion list post, June 24, 2021, https://groups.google.com/a/podnetwork.org/g/discussion/c/tbgIkkD7_uQ/m/AiUwhx1-AAAJ; Daniel Stanford, "Should a Doctorate Be Required for Leaders in Our Field?" POD Network discussion list post, fall 2016, https://groups.google.com/a/podnetwork.org/g/discussion/c/k3bV8NXIfo8/m/JutFjWD7BgAJ.

74. Connie Schroeder, Phyllis Blumberg, and Nancy Van Note Chism, eds., *Coming in from the Margins: Faculty Development's Emerging Organizational Development Role in Institutional Change* (Sterling, VA: Stylus Publishing, 2010); Torgny Roxå and Katarina Mårtensson, "Agency and Structure in Academic Development Practices: Are We Liberating Academic Teachers or Are We Part of a Machinery Suppressing Them?" *International Journal for Academic Development* 22, no. 2 (2017): 95–105; Little and Green, "Betwixt and Between," 203–15.

75. Susan Gano-Phillips, "Optimizing Center Staffing and Advisory Boards to Promote Involvement in Institutional Change," in Schroeder, Blumberg, and Chism, *Coming in from the Margins*, 219–20.

76. Gano-Phillips, "Optimizing Center Staffing," 219–220.

77. Richard McDermott, "Learning across Teams: The Role of Communities of Practice in Team Organizations," *Knowledge Management Review* (May/June 1999), 4.

78. Colby College Center for Teaching and Learning, https://www.colby.edu/ctl/advisory-board/.

79. Beach et al., *Faculty Development*, table 3.1.

80. Molloy College Faculty Professional Center, https://www.molloy.edu/academics/faculty-and-staff-resources/-faculty-professional-center/fpc-committee.

81. Susan Colby, Laura Cruz, Danielle Cordaro, and Clare Cruz, "Fellow Travelers: Taking Stock of Faculty Fellows Programs in the Age of Organizational Development," *To Improve the Academy* 41, no. 2 (2022).

82. Deborah Meizlish and Mary C. Wright, "Preparing Advocates for Faculty Development: Expanding the Meaning of 'Growing Our Own,'" *To Improve the Academy* 27 (2009): 385–400; Kristin J. Rudenga and Joseph Lampert, "Mentoring Graduate Student Staff in a Center for Teaching and Learning: Goals and Aligned Practices," *To Improve the Academy* 37, no. 2 (2018), http://dx.doi.org/10.3998/tia.17063888.0037.207.

83. Beach et al., *Faculty Development*, 51.

84. Virginia S. Lee, "Program Types and Prototypes," in *A Guide to Faculty Development*, edited by Kay J. Gillespie and Douglas L. Robertson (San Francisco: Jossey-Bass, 2010), 32.

85. McDermott, "Learning across Teams," 4.

86. Kelley, Cruz, and Fire, "Moving Toward the Center," 1–8.

87. Sally Kuhlenschmidt, "Distribution and Penetration of Teaching-Learning Development Units in Higher Education: Implications for Strategic Planning and Research," *To Improve the Academy* 29, no. 1 (2011): 274–87.

Chapter 5. How Do We Make Visible Our Work?

1. Jonathan Zimmerman, *The Amateur Hour: A History of College Teaching in America* (Baltimore, MD: Johns Hopkins University Press, 2021), ix.

2. Kenneth E. Eble and William J. McKeachie, *Improving Undergraduate Education through Faculty Development* (San Francisco: Jossey Bass, 1985), 24.

3. Peter Felten, Alan Kalish, Allison Pingree, and Kathryn Plank, "Toward a Scholarship of Teaching and Learning," *To Improve the Academy* 25 (2007), http://dx.doi.org/10.3998/tia.17063888.0025.010.

4. Aaron Pallas, Anna Neumann, and Corbin M. Campbell, *Policies and Practices to Support Undergraduate Teaching Improvement* (Cambridge, MA: American Academy of Arts and Sciences, 2017), 18–19.

5. William Condon, Ellen R. Iverson, Cathryn A. Manduca, Carol Rutz, and Gudrun Willet, *Faculty Development and Student Learning: Assessing the Connections* (Bloomington: Indiana University Press, 2016).

6. Mark R. Connolly, Julia N. Savoy, You-Geon Lee, and Lucas B. Hill, *Building a Better Future STEM Faculty: How Doctoral Teaching Programs Can Improve Undergraduate Education* (Madison: Wisconsin Center for Education Research, University of Wisconsin–Madison, 2016); see also Samantha Adams Becker, Malcolm Brown, Michele Cummins, and Veronica Diaz, *NMC Horizon Report: 2017 Higher Education Edition* (Austin, TX: New Media Consortium, 2017).

7. Kyle T. Fassett, Stephen C. Hiller, Allison BrckaLorenz, and Thomas F. Nelson Laird, "Teaching Development Opportunities and Faculty Practice at Four-Year Institutions," *College Teaching*, 2021, https://doi.org/10.1080/87567555.2021.1999894; Joe Strickland and Allison BrckaLorenz, *Teaching Professional Development* (FSSE Psychometric Portfolio) (Bloomington: Indiana University, 2019), https://hdl.handle.net/2022/24485.

8. Jessie Brown and Martin Kurzweil, *Instructional Quality, Student Outcomes, and Institutional Finances* (Washington, DC: American Council on Education, 2017); Yvonne Steinert, Karen Mann, Brownell Anderson, Bonnie Maureen Barnett, Angel Centeno, Laura Naismith, David Prideaux, John Spencer, Ellen Tullo, Thomas Viggiano, Helena Ward, and Diana Dolmans, "A Systematic Review of Faculty Development Initiatives Designed to Improve Teaching Effectiveness: A 10-Year Update: BEME Guide" (No. 40) *Medical Teacher* 38, no. 8 (2016): 1–18, http://dx.doi.org/10.1080/0142159X.2016.1181851.

9. Judith Levinson-Rose and Robert J. Menges, "Improving College Teaching: A Critical Review of Research," *Review of Educational Research* 51, no. 3 (1981): 418.

10. Ann Stes, Mariska Min-Leliveld, David Gijbels, and Peter Van Pategem, "The Impact of Instructional Development in Higher Education: The State-of-the-Art of the Research," *Educational Research Review* 5 (2010): 25.

11. John Kucsera and Marilla Svinicki, "Rigorous Evaluations of Faculty Development Programs," *Journal of Faculty Development* 24, no. 2 (2010): 7.

12. Susan R. Hines, "How Mature Teaching and Learning Centers Evaluate Their
Services," *To Improve the Academy* 30 (2011): 277–89, http://dx.doi.org/10.3998/tia
.17063888.0030.024; Mary Deane Sorcinelli, "The Evaluation of Faculty Development
Programs in the United States: A Fifty-Year Retrospective (1970s–2020)," *Excellence and
Innovation in Learning and Teaching* 2 (2020): 5–17.

13. Denise Chalmers and Di Gardiner, "An Evaluation Framework for Identifying the
Effectiveness and Impact of Academic Teacher Development Programmes," *Studies in
Educational Evaluation*, 46 (2015): 81–91; Susan R. Hines, "Evaluating Centers for Teaching
and Learning: A Field-Tested Model," *To Improve the Academy* 36, no. 2 (2017): 89–100,
http://dx.doi.org/10.3998/tia.17063888.0036.202; Carol A. Hurney, Edward J. Brantmeier,
Meghan R. Good, Douglas Harrison, and Cara Meixner, "The Faculty Learning Outcomes
Assessment Framework," *Journal of Faculty Development* 30, no. 2 (2016): 69–77; Caroline
Kreber and Paula Brook, "Impact Evaluation of Educational Development Programmes,"
International Journal for Academic Development 6, no. 2 (2001): 96–108; Mary C. Wright,
"Measuring a Teaching Center's Effectiveness," in *Advancing the Culture of Teaching on
Campus: How a Teaching Center Can Make a Difference*, edited by Constance Cook and
Matt Kaplan (Sterling, VA: Stylus Publishing, 2011), 38–49.

14. Nancy Van Note Chism and Borbála Szabó, "Teaching Awards: The Problem of
Assessing Their Impact," *To Improve the Academy* 16 (1997): 181–200; Hines, "Evaluating
Centers for Teaching and Learning," 89–100; Kucsera and Svinicki, "Rigorous Evalua-
tions of Faculty Development Programs," 5–18.

15. Janice Miller-Young and Cheryl N. Poth, "'Complexifying' Our Approach to
Evaluating Educational Development Outcomes: Bridging Theoretical Innovations with
Frontline Practice," *International Journal for Academic Development* (February 2021): 3,
https://doi.org/10.1080/1360144X.2021.1887876.

16. Ranald Macdonald, "Developing a Scholarship of Academic Development: Setting
the Context," in *The Scholarship of Academic Development* (New York: McGraw Hill,
2003), 4.

17. John A. Centra, *Faculty Development Practices in U.S. Colleges and Universities*
(Princeton, NJ: Educational Testing Service, 1976), 13.

18. Miri Levin-Rozalis, "Evaluation and Research: Differences and Similarities,"
Canadian Journal of Program Evaluation 18, no. 2 (2003): 1–31.

19. POD Network, *Defining What Matters: Guidelines for Comprehensive Center for
Teaching and Learning (CTL) Evaluation* (POD Network, 2018), 3, https://podnetwork
.org/content/uploads/POD_DWM_R3-singlepage-v2.pdf.

20. Bianca Montrosse-Moorhead and James C. Griffith, "Toward the Development
of Reporting Standards for Evaluations," *American Journal of Evaluation* 38, no. 4
(2017): 596; Michael Q. Patton, *Utilization-Focused Evaluation* 4th ed. (Thousand Oaks,
CA: Sage, 2008).

21. Paul P. Ashwin and Keith Trigwell, "Investigating Staff and Educational
Development," in *Enhancing Staff and Educational Development*, edited by David
Baume and Peter Kahn (New York: Routledge), 117–31.

22. Megan Sanders and Amy Hermundstad Nave, "How Do We Show Our Impact? Patterns in Annual Reports," poster presented at the annual POD Network Conference (Seattle, WA), November 2022.

23. Donald L. Kirkpatrick, "Evaluation of Training," in *Training and Development Handbook: A Guide to Human Resource Development*, edited by R. L. Craig (New York: McGraw Hill, 1976); Hines, "Evaluating Centers for Teaching and Learning," 2017; Kreber and Brook, "Impact Evaluation," 96–108.

24. Because Brown University's intellectual property policy states that the university owns intellectual property of staff utilizing university resources, I would like to state that Justin's work was personally financed.

25. Nancy Van Note Chism and Borbála Szabó, "Who Uses Faculty Development Services?" *To Improve the Academy* 15, no. 1 (1996): 115–16.

26. Chism and Szabó, "Who Uses Faculty Development Services?," 120.

27. M. J. Bishop and Anne Keehn, *Leading Academic Change: An Early Market Scan of Leading-Edge Postsecondary Academic Innovation Centers* (Adelphi, MD: William Kirwan Center for Academic Innovation, 2015), https://www.educause.edu/sites/default/files/library/presentations/E15/PS11/LeadingAcademicChangeProjectReport.pdf.

28. Strickland and BrckaLorenz, *Teaching Professional Development*, table 5.

29. Allison BrckaLorenz, email message to author, January 3, 2022.

30. Allison BrckaLorenz, email message to author, January 3, 2022; and Allison BrckaLorenz, Rong Wang, and Thomas F. Nelson Laird, "Graduate Student Instructors, the Courses They Teach, and the Support They Value," *New Directions for Teaching and Learning* 163 (2020): 25–34.

31. Rosabeth Moss Kanter, *Men and Women of the Corporation* (New York: Basic Books, 1977); Everett M. Rogers, *Diffusion of Innovations* (New York: Free Press, 1962).

32. American Council of Education and POD Network (collaborative authorship by Eli Collins Brown, Catherine Haras, Carol Hurney, Jonathan Iuzzini, Emily Magruder, Mary Deane Sorcinelli, Steven C. Taylor, and Mary C. Wright, *A Center for Teaching and Learning Matrix*, POD Network and American Council of Education (ACE), 2019, https://podnetwork.org/resources/center-for-teaching-and-learning-matrix/.

33. If the center provided its own similar computation, that metric was used instead. In one case, where the center's number of unique faculty participants surpassed the IPEDS count, the resulting percentage (greater than 100%) was discarded from this analysis.

34. Faculty Innovation Center, *Annual Report* (Austin: University of Texas at Austin, 2017), 3, https://facultyinnovate.utexas.edu/sites/default/files/FIC-Annual-Report-FINAL.pdf.

35. Faculty Innovation Center, *Annual Report*, https://facultyinnovate.utexas.edu/sites/default/files/FIC-Annual-Report-FINAL.pdf.

36. Chalmers and Gardiner, "An Evaluation Framework"; Emily M. Walter, Andrea L. Beach, Charles Henderson, Cody Williams, and Ivan Ceballos-Madrigal, "Understanding Conditions for Teaching Innovation in Postsecondary Education: Development and Validation of the Survey of Climate for Instructional Improvement (SCII)," *International Journal of Technology in Education* 4, no. 2 (2021): 166–99, https://doi.org/10.46328/ijte.46.

37. Felten et al., "Toward a Scholarship of Teaching"; Brenda Leibowitz, "Reflections on Academic Development: What Is in a Name?," *International Journal for Academic Development* 19, no. 4 (2014): 357–60.

38. Chism and Szabó, "Who Uses Faculty Development Services?," 120.

39. Eble and McKeachie, *Improving Undergraduate Education.*

40. Asheville UNC Center for Teaching and Learning, *Center for Teaching and Learning (CTL) Annual Report* (Asheville: University of North Carolina at Asheville, 2020), https://ctl.unca.edu/meet-us/mission-and-history/.

41. POD Network, *Defining What Matters*, 7.

42. Levinson-Rose and Menges, "Improving College Teaching," 409.

43. American Council of Education, *A Center for Teaching and Learning Matrix*; Ann Ferren and Kay Mussell, "Strengthening Faculty Development Programs through Evaluation," *To Improve the Academy* 6 (1987): 133–43; Wright, "Measuring a Teaching Center's Effectiveness."

44. Murray Saunders, "Insights into Programmatic Evaluative Practice in HE: A Commentary," in *Reconceptualising Evaluation in Higher Education: The Practice Turn*, edited by Murray Saunder, Paul Trowler, and Veronica Bamber (Berkshire, UK: Open University Press, 2011), 119.

45. David Matthews, "Fear of Looking Stupid," *Inside Higher Ed*, July 6, 2017, https://www.insidehighered.com/news/2017/07/06/anthropologist-studies-why-professors-dont-adopt-innovative-teaching-methods; Carl C. Wieman, *Improving How Universities Teach Science: Lessons From the Science Education Initiative* (Cambridge, MA: Harvard University Press, 2017).

46. Jon F. Wergin, "Beyond Carrots and Sticks," *Liberal Education* 87, no. 1 (2001): 50–54.

47. Point Loma Center for Teaching and Learning, *2018–19 Annual Report* (San Diego, CA: Point Loma Nazarene University, 2019), 7, https://assessment.pointloma.edu/wp-content/uploads/sites/9/2020/02/Center-for-Teaching-and-Learning-2018-2019-Annual-Report.pdf.

48. Amherst Center for Teaching and Learning, *2017–18 Annual Report* (Amherst, MA: Amherst College, 2018), 8, https://www.amherst.edu/system/files/media/2017%2520-%25202018%2520Annual%2520Report%252C%2520Center%2520for%2520Teaching%2520and%2520Learning%252C%2520Final.pdf.

49. Georgia College Center for Teaching and Learning, *Annual Report: 2019–20* (Milledgeville: Georgia College, 2020), 17–20, https://www.gcsu.edu/sites/default/files/documents/2021-04/CTL%20Annual%20Report%202019-2020.pdf.

50. Amherst Center for Teaching and Learning, *2017–18 Annual Report*, 3.

51. POD Network, *Defining What Matters*, 7.

52. Kreber and Brook, "Impact Evaluation."

53. Becker et al., *NMC Horizon Report*, 2007; Stes et al., "The Impact of Instructional Development."

54. Reinert Center for Transformative Teaching and Learning, *2016–17 Annual Report* (Saint Louis, MO: Saint Louis University, 2017), 19, https://www.slu.edu/cttl/docs/activity-reports/annual-reports/annual-report-2016-2017.pdf; see also Condon et al.,

Faculty Development, 117, for the argument that self-efficacy and motivation to change are "efficient and compelling measures of impact."

55. Columbia Center for Teaching and Learning, *Annual Report: 2019–2020* (New York: Columbia University, 2020), 57, https://cpb-us-w2.wpmucdn.com/edblogs .columbia.edu/dist/8/1109/files/2016/07/ctl-annual-report-2020.pdf.

56. Asheville UNC Center for Teaching and Learning, *Center for Teaching and Learning*, 8.

57. Faculty Collaborative for Teaching Innovation, *Annual Report 2018–19* (Santa Clara, CA: Santa Clara University, 2019), 7, https://www.scu.edu/media/offices/provost /assessment/Collaborative-Report-2018-19.pdf.

58. Center for the Advancement of Teaching, *Annual Report 2018–19* (Miami: Florida International University, 2019), 8, https://cat.fiu.edu/about-us/annual-report /index.html.

59. *Faculty Development, AY 2016–2017* (Charleston: Eastern Illinois University, 2017), 8, https://www.eiu.edu/fdic/2016-2017%20Admin%20Assess%20Unit%20 Profile%20Report%20-%20Final.pdf.

60. Center for Faculty Excellence, *2017–18* (Omaha: University of Nebraska Omaha, 2018), 15, https://www.flipsnack.com/unocfe/2017-2018-uno-center-for-faculty -excellence-ebook.html.

61. Office of Faculty Advancement, Leadership and Inclusion, *Annual Report: 2019–20* (Atlanta, GA: Emory University School of Medicine, 2020), 4, https://med .emory.edu/about/faculty/faculty-development/_documents/faali-annual-report-2020 -final.pdf.

62. Sinclair Center for Teaching and Learning, *Annual Report of Faculty Development Provided by the Center for Teaching and Learning, 2018–19* (Dayton, OH: Sinclair Community College, 2019), 41–42, https://ctl.sinclair.edu/leadership/annual-report-2018 -2019/.

63. Sorcinelli, "The Evaluation of Faculty Development Programs."

64. Kathryn M. Plank and Alan Kalish, "Program Assessment for Faculty Development," in *A Guide to Faculty Development* 2nd ed., edited by K. J. Gillespie and D. L. Robertson (San Francisco: Jossey Bass, 2010), 136.

65. Lindsay Wheeler and Dorothe Bach, "Understanding the Impact of Educational Development Interventions on Classroom Instruction and Student Success," *International Journal for Academic Development* 26, no. 1 (2020): 24–40; Condon et al., *Faculty Development*.

66. Sheridan Center for Teaching and Learning, *Annual Report 2019* (Providence, RI: Brown University, 2019), https://www.brown.edu/sheridan/sites/sheridan/files/docs /Annual%20Report%202019.pdf.

67. Searle Center for Learning and Teaching, *Annual Report: 2017–18* (Evanston, IL: Northwestern University, 2018), 24, 25, 42, https://www.northwestern.edu/searle/about /annual-report-2017-2018.pdf.

68. University of Louisville Delphi Center for Teaching and Learning, *2019–20 Annual Report* (Louisville, KY: University of Louisville, 2020) 8, 21, https://louisville .edu/delphi/-/files/annual_report/Delphi_Annual_Report_2019_2020.pdf.

69. Mary C. Wright, Cassandra Volpe Horii, Peter Felten, Mary Deane Sorcinelli, and Matt Kaplan, "Faculty Development Improves Teaching and Learning," *POD Speaks* 2 (2018): 1–5.

70. Chism and Szabó, "Who Uses Faculty Development Services?," 61.

71. Sinclair Center, *Annual Report*, 39.

72. Kirkpatrick, "Evaluation of Training."

73. Cheryl Amundsen and Laura D'Amico, "Using Theory of Change to Evaluate Socially-Situated, Inquiry-Based Academic Professional Development," *Studies in Educational Evaluation* 61 (2019): 196–208; Deborah Meizlish, Mary C. Wright, Jay Howard and Matthew Kaplan, "Measuring the Impact of a New Faculty Program Using Institutional Data," *International Journal for Academic Development* 23, no. 2 (2017): 72–85.

74. Centre College Center for Teaching and Learning, *Annual Report: June 1, 2019-May 31, 2020* (Danville, KY: Centre College, 2020), 17, https://ctl.centre.edu/about /publications-archives/.

75. Office for the Advancement of Teaching and Learning, *Annual Report, 2018–2019* (South Kingston: University of Rhode Island, 2019), 59, https://web.uri.edu/atl/files/ATL -Annual-Report-Final2-.pdf.

76. University of Tennessee–Chattanooga Grayson H. Walker Center for Teaching and Learning, *Annual Report (July 1, 2018–June 30, 2019)* (Chattanooga: University of Tennessee–Chattanooga, 2019), 4, https://www.utc.edu/sites/default/files/2020-08/2019 -annual-report.pdf.

77. Howard P. Greenwald and Ann P. Zukowski, "Assessing Collaboration: Alternative Measures and Issues for Collaboration," *American Journal of Education* 39, no. 3 (2018): 1–14.

78. POD Network, *Defining What Matters*.

79. "Partnerships." University of California, Los Angeles Center for the Advancement of Teaching, https://teaching.ucla.edu/about/partnerships/.

80. Seattle University Center for Faculty Development, *Annual Report 2019/20* (Seattle, WA: Seattle University, 2020), 2, https://www.seattleu.edu/media/center-for -faculty-development/files/aboutus/2019-20-Annual-Report—Center-for-Faculty -Development—for-website.pdf.

81. Kreber and Brook, "Impact Evaluation."

82. Chalmers and Gardiner, "An Evaluation Framework."

83. POD Network, *Defining What Matters*, 6–9.

84. Kreber and Brook, "Impact Evaluation"; see also Miller-Young and Poth, "'Complexifying' Our Approach."

85. Kirkpatrick, "Evaluation of Training"; Ciaran Sugrue, Tomas Englund, Tone D. Solbrekke, and Trine Fossland, "Trends in the Practices of Educational Developers: Trajectories of Higher Education," *Studies in Higher Education* 43, no. 12 (2017): 2336–53.

86. Hurney et al., "The Faculty Learning Outcomes," 70.

87. Chism and Szabó, "Who Uses Faculty Development Services?," 61.

88. Leslie M. Harper, Michelle Maden, and Rumora Dickson, "Across Five levels: The Evidence of Impact Model," *Evaluation* 26, no. 3 (2019): 7.

89. Saunders, "Insights into Programmatic Evaluative Practice," 3.

90. Cynthia Weston, Jennie Ferris, and Adam Finkelstein, "Leading Change: An Organizational Development Role for Educational Developers," *International Journal of Teaching and Learning in Higher Education* 29, no. 2 (2017): 270–80; see also Harper, Maden, and Dickson, "Across Five Levels."

91. Sorcinelli, "The Evaluation of Faculty Development Programs."

92. Chism and Szabó, "Who Uses Faculty Development Services?" 610.

93. Peter T. Ewell, "Assessment and Accountability in America Today: Background and Context," in *New Directions for Institutional Research* vol. S1, edited by Victor M. H. Borden and Gary R. Pike (New York: Wiley, 2008), 7–18; Sugrue et al., "Trends in the Practices of Educational Developers."

94. Amundsen and D'Amico, "Using Theory of Change"; Miller-Young and Poth, "'Complexifying' Our Approach."

Conclusion. Re-Centering Teaching and Learning in US Higher Education

1. Sally Kuhlenschmidt, "Distribution and Penetration of Teaching-Learning Development Units in Higher Education: Implications for Strategic Planning and Research," *To Improve the Academy* 29, no. 1 (2011): 274–87. For a description of faculty development needs at tribal colleges and universities, see Ahmed Al-Asfour and Suzanne Young, "Faculty Professional Development Needs and Career Advancement at Tribal Colleges and Universities." *Journal of Faculty Development*, 31, no. (2017): 1–8.

2. Mitchell L. Stevens, Elizabeth A. Armstrong, and Richard Arum, "Sieve, Incubator, Temple, Hub: Empirical and Theoretical Advances in the Sociology of Higher Education," *Annual Review of Sociology* 34 (2008): 127.

3. Connie Schroeder, "Aligning and Revising Center Mission Statements," in *Coming in from the Margins: Faculty Development's Emerging Organizational Development Role in Institutional Change*, edited by Connie Schroeder, Phyllis Blumberg, and Nancy Van Note Chism (Sterling, VA: Stylus Publishing, 2010), 235–59.

4. Bruce Kelley, Laura Cruz, and Nancy Fire, "Moving Toward the Center: The Integration of Educational Development in an Era of Historic Change in Higher Education," *To Improve the Academy* 36, no. 1 (2017): 1–8, http://dx.doi.org/10.1002/tia2 .20052.

5. Jonathan Zimmerman, *The Amateur Hour: A History of College Teaching in America* (Baltimore, MD: Johns Hopkins University Press, 2021).

6. Donald L. Kirkpatrick, "Evaluation of Training," in *Training and Development Handbook: A Guide to Human Resource Development*, edited by R. L. Craig (New York: McGraw Hill, 1976); Susan R. Hines, "How Mature Teaching and Learning Centers Evaluate Their Services," *To Improve the Academy* 30 (2011): 277–89; Caroline Kreber and Paula Brook, "Impact Evaluation of Educational Development Programmes," *International Journal for Academic Development* 6, no. 2 (2001): 96–108.

7. Graham Gibbs, "Reflections on the Changing Nature of Educational Development," *International Journal for Academic Development* 18, no. 1 (2013): 8.

8. Adrianna Kezar, *Scaling and Sustaining Change and Innovation: Lessons Learned from the Teagle Foundation's 'Faculty Work and Student Learning' Initiative* (New York:

Teagle Foundation, 2015), https://www.teaglefoundation.org/Teagle/media/Global MediaLibrary/documents/resources/Scaling-and-Sustaining-Innovation-and-Change .pdf?ext=.pdf.

9. Mary C. Wright, Debra Lohe, Molly Hatcher, Anna Flaming, and Jennifer Frederick, "New Evaluation Guidelines to Examine Impact in Times of Change," workshop presented at the POD Network Annual Conference, Portland, OR, November 2018.

10. For other helpful resources on CTL strategic planning, see Simon P. Albon, Isabeau Iqbal, and Marion L. Pearson, "Strategic Planning in an Educational Development Centre: Motivation, Management, and Messiness," *Collected Essays on Learning and Teaching* vol. 9 (Vancouver: University of British Columbia, 2016) as well as Laura Cruz, Michelle Parker, Brian Smentkowski, and Marina Smitherman, *Taking Flight: Making Your Center for Teaching and Learning Soar* (Sterling, VA: Stylus Publishing, 2020).

11. Tara Gray and Susan Shadle, "Launching or Revitalizing a Teaching Center: Principles and Portraits of Practice," *Journal of Faculty Development* 23, no. 2 (2009): 5–12.

12. Means for aims are 1 personnel (2.6), 2–3 personnel (2.7), 4–6 personnel (2.7), 7+ personnel (2.7). These differences are not statistically significant at the $p < .05$ level. Means for strategies are 1 personnel (1.6), 2–3 personnel (1.8), 4–6 personnel (1.8), 7+ personnel (1.6) ($N = 875$, $F = 2.7$, $df = 3$, 872, $p < .05$). These differences are not statistically significant at the $p < .05$ level. Means for tactics are 1 personnel (1.9), 2–3 personnel (2.3), 4–6 personnel (2.6), 7+ personnel (3.0) ($N = 948$, $F = 49.5$, $df = 3$, 944, $p < .001$). Bonferroni post-hoc test shows significant differences between center of one and all other CTL sizes ($p < .001$), as well as 7+ personnel and all other sizes ($p < .001$).

13. Schroeder et al., *Coming in from the Margins*, 2010.

14. Nancy Van Note Chism and Borbála Szabó, "Who Uses Faculty Development Services?" *To Improve the Academy* 15, no. 1 (1996): 115–28; Joe Strickland and Allison BrckaLorenz, *Teaching Professional Development* (FSSE Psychometric Portfolio) (Bloomington, IN: Faculty Survey of Student Engagement, 2019).

15. William Condon, Ellen R. Iverson, Cathryn A. Manduca, Carol Rutz, and Gudrun Willet, *Faculty Development and Student Learning: Assessing the Connections* (Bloomington: Indiana University Press, 2016); Michael S. Palmer, Adriana Streifer, and Stacy Williams-Duncan, "Systematic Assessment of a High-Impact Course Design Institute," *To Improve the Academy* 35, no. 2 (2016): 339–61; Mary C. Wright, Cassandra Volpe Horii, Peter Felten, Mary Deane Sorcinelli, and Matt Kaplan, "Faculty Development Improves Teaching and Learning," *POD Speaks* 2 (2018): 1–5.

16. Samantha Adams Becker, Malcolm Brown, Michele Cummins, and Veronica Diaz, *NMC Horizon Report: 2017 Higher Education Edition* (Austin, TX: New Media Consortium, 2017); Mark R. Connolly, Julia N. Savoy, You-Geon Lee, and Lucas B. Hill, *Building a Better Future STEM Faculty: How Doctoral Teaching Programs Can Improve Undergraduate Education* (Madison: Wisconsin Center for Education Research, University of Wisconsin–Madison, 2016.)

17. KerryAnn O'Meara, Mark Rivera, Alexandra Kuvaeva, and Kristen Corrigan, "Faculty Learning Matters: Organizational Conditions and Contexts That Shape Faculty Learning," *Innovative Higher Education* 42 (2017): 355–76.

18. Wright, *Always at Odds? Creating Alignment between Faculty and Administrative Values* (Albany: SUNY Press, 2008).

19. Jessie Brown and Martin Kurzweil, *Instructional Quality, Student Outcomes, and Institutional Finance* (Washington, DC: American Council on Education, 2017); Yvonne Steinert, Karen Mann, Brownell Anderson, Bonnie Maureen Barnett, Angel Centeno, Laura Naismith, David Prideaux, John Spencer, Ellen Tullo, Thomas Viggiano, Helena Ward, and Diana Dolmans, "A Systematic Review of Faculty Development Initiatives Designed to Improve Teaching Effectiveness: A 10-Year Update: BEME Guide" (No. 40). *Medical Teacher* 38, no. 8 (2016): 1–18.

20. Adrianna Kezar, "What Is the Best Way to Achieve Broader Reach of Improved Practices in Higher Education?" *Innovative Higher Education* 36 (2011): 235–47; Adrianna Kezar, *Scaling and Sustaining Change and Innovation*; Everett M. Rogers, *Diffusion of Innovations* (New York, Free Press, 1962); Nancy Van Note Chism, Matthew Holley, and Cameron J. Harris, "Researching the Impact of Educational Development: Basis for Informed Practice," *To Improve the Academy* 31 (2012): 129–45.

21. For example, Cole et al. find that "more public praise and support from leaders offer an entry point to fostering a culture that values innovation." Eddie R. Cole, Amber D. Dumford, and Thomas F. Nelson Laird, "Senior Leaders and Teaching Environments: Faculty Perceptions of Administrators' Support of Innovation," *Innovative Higher Education* 43 (2018): 57–70; see also Mary C. Wright, Debra Lohe, Tershia Pinder-Grover, and Leslie Ortquist-Ahrens, "The Four Rs: Guiding CTLs with Responsiveness, Relationships, Resources, and Research," *To Improve the Academy* 37, no. 2 (2018): 271–86.

22. Aubra Bulin, Derisa Grant, Marissa Salazar, and Marina Smitherman, eds., "Educational Development in the Time of Crisis," special issue, *To Improve the Academy* 39, no. 3 (Spring 2021); John Paul Tassoni, ed., "CTLs in the Time of COVID: A Message from the Editor-in-Chief," special issue, *Journal on Centers for Teaching and Learning* 12 (2021), https://openjournal.lib.miamioh.edu/index.php/jctl/article/view/215.

23. Josh Kim and Edward Maloney, *Learning Innovation and the Future of Higher Education* (Baltimore, MD: Johns Hopkins University Press, 2020), 46.

academic development, 8, 27
academic integrity, 91
academic units, 26, 28. *See also* departments
accessibility, 91
accreditation, 41–43, 129, 132–33, 150
ACE-POD Matrix, 22, 167
action teams, 60, 100
active learning, 91, 93, 95, 151; classrooms, 95
advising and mentoring, 32, 91, 123, 196. *See also* mentoring
advisory boards. *See* CTL advisory boards
advocacy, 66, 70, 122, 127
affinity groups, 99–100
Aims Community College (Faculty Teaching and Learning Center), 32
Alamo Colleges District, 226n29
Albany Law School (Center for Excellence in Law School Teaching), 29, 229n33
Albertus Magnus College (Center for Teaching and Learning Excellence), 33, 230n49
alignment: aims and strategies, 79–80; annual reports, 199; assignments, 95; as CTL priority, 138, 208–9; dialogue and collaboration communities and change aims, 101–2, 105; institutional aims, 47, 202; strategies and tactics, 203, 208–9
American Association of Colleges and Universities (AAC&U), 40
American Council on Education (ACE). See *ACE-POD Matrix*
American Public University System (Center for Teaching and Learning), 44
American River College (Center for Teaching and Learning), 42, 88
American University (Center for Teaching, Research and Learning), 89, 123

Amherst College (Center for Teaching and Learning), 114, 185
Angelo State University (Faculty Learning Commons), 35
Anna Maria College (Center for Teaching Excellence), 43, 72
annual reports. *See* CTL annual reports
anti-racist teaching, 94, 98
Appalachian State University (Center for Excellence in Teaching and Learning for Student Success), 92, 99, 148
Arizona University (Teaching and Learning Program), 99
Armstrong, Elizabeth, 4, 51
Art Center College of Design (Office of Faculty Development), 111, 116
Arum, Richard, 4, 51
assessment: accreditation, 129, 139, 191; aims, 137, 188; assessment-infused CTLs, 149–50, 172; award focus, 124, 150; CTL name, 149; culture of, 191; definition of, 72, 149; educational development approach to, 149; fellows, 129, 171; grants, 116–17, 150; programs, 91, 95, 101, 133, 150; Sieve approach, 53, 71–72, 78, 84, 129, 135, 137–38, 202; staff, 150; of student learning, 53, 95, 149; tactics, 149–50
associate's institutions: annual reports, 179; change strategy, 79–80, 119, 202; constituencies, 25–28; CTL aims, 32, 46; integrative emphases, 143, 154, 157, 159; leaders, 162; permeation of CTLs, 14, 20, 200; personnel size, 157–59; reach, 181; tactics, 111–12, 120, 135–36. *See also* community colleges
A. T. Still University of Health Sciences (Teaching and Learning Center), 117

employment, 171; Kuhlenschmidt methodology, 10, 12; mentoring programs, 114–15; outcomes, 176, 211; prevalence of programs, 85; support for writing and scholarship, 151. *See also* graduate student instructors

graduate student instructors (GSI): award, 123; mentoring, 115; orientations, 112–13, 187; CTL reach, 180–81, 196; teaching academies, 126

graduate teaching assistant (GTA). *See* graduate student instructors (GSI)

Grand Canyon University (Center for Innovation in Research and Teaching), 74, 107–8, 134

grand rounds, education, 91

Grand Valley State University (Robert and Mary Pew Faculty Teaching and Learning Center), 97

grants, 61, 64–65, 115–16, 120, 196

Gravett, Emily, 75–76

Great Lakes Colleges Association, 13

Green, David, 160, 164–66

Grinnell College (Center for Teaching, Learning, and Assessment), 117, 149

GSI. *See* graduate student instructors

Guevara, Carlos, 48

Hall, Leslie, 182–83

Haras, Catherine, 167

Harvard University, 38, 125, 146

HBCUs, 15–16. *See also* MSIs

Henderson, Charles, 76–78

Herman, Jennifer, 157–59, 174

Higher Education Research and Development Society of Australasia (HERDSA), 75

Hispanic-Serving Institutions (HSIs), 15–16, 99. *See also* MSIs

Historically Black Colleges and Universities. *See* HBCUs

HITS (Hub-Incubator-Temple-Sieve): alignment of strategy/tactics, 208; change, 203; change tactics, 84, 135–36; CTL evaluation, 177; framework, 52–54, 78–81, 202

holistic educational development, 141

holistic professional learning (HPL)–infused CTLs, 144–48, 172; annual reports, 198; tactics, 146–48. *See also* career development; leadership development; research

honors programs, 212

hooks, bell, 97

Howard University (Center for Excellence in Teaching, Learning, and Assessment), 89

HPL. *See* holistic professional learning–infused CTLs

Hub: alignment between strategy and tactics, 208; articulated in statements of purpose, 57–58; cautions, 59–60; defined, 52, 202; growth, 58, 214; impact, 58–60, 87, 100, 104–5; organizational mandates, 155; strategic CTL orientation, 55–57, 79; strengths, 58–59; tactics, 84–105, 136–37

humanities, 165–66

Hurney, Carol, 167

Illinois State University (Center for Teaching, Learning, and Technology), 87, 144

impact of CTL work: on academic job search success, 211; on collegial networks, 176, 211–12; on faculty retention, satisfaction, and productivity, 211; Hub approaches, 58–60, 87, 100, 104–5; Incubator approaches, 64–65; on institutions, 191, 212; on student learning, 176, 189, 211–12; on teaching behaviors, 176, 186; Temple approaches, 69–70

inclusion, 37, 40–41, 55, 99, 149, 185, 192, 220. *See also* diversity, equity, and inclusion

Incubator: alignment between strategy and tactics, 208–9; articulated in statements of purpose, 63; cautions, 64–65; defined, 52, 202; impact, 64–65, 107–9, 112–16; strategic CTL orientation, 60–63, 79; strengths, 63–65; tactics, 84, 106–20, 136–37; writing-infused CTLs, 152

Indiana University Bloomington (Center for Innovative Teaching and Learning), 124

Indiana University Kokomo (Center for Teaching, Learning, and Assessment), 149

Indiana University–Purdue University Indianapolis (Center for Teaching and Learning), 61, 192
Indiana University Southeast (Institute for Learning and Teaching Excellence), 42, 66
information literacy, 91
innovation: affordances of focus, 22; CTL aim, 31, 36–37, 46–47, 56–57; innovation-focused CTLs, 37; tactics, 101–2, 105, 116–17, 123, 125. *See also* change
Inside Higher Education, 82
institutional impact, 191–94, 212
institutional mission: CTL aim, 31, 41–42, 46, 201; diverse missions and presence of CTLs, 15–16, 215; tactics, 101, 124, 137, 205; theories of change, 80, 205
Institutional Review Board (IRB), umbrella arrangements, 131
institutional size. *See* size, institutional
institutional strategic plans, 116, 191
institution-wide events, 84, 86–87, 96–97, 103, 147, 204
instructional development, 9, 27, 145, 186
instructional FTE, 26, 32, 43–44, 54, 74, 157, 159, 216
instructional technology. *See* technology
instructor outcomes, 186–89
integrative emphases, 139–55
intergenerational CTLs, 65
Iowa State University (Center for Excellence in Learning and Teaching), 89, 114
IPEDS (Integrated Postsecondary Education Data System), 1, 14, 157–58, 181
Iuzzini, Jonathan, 167

James Madison University (Center for Faculty Innovation), 94, 102, 124
John A. Logan College (Teaching and Learning Center) 28, 43
journal clubs, 97–98
justice, 39–40, 42, 99, 124. *See also* diversity, equity, and inclusion

Kalamazoo College (Teaching Commons), 66
Kansas City (Kansas) Community College (Center for Teaching Excellence), 131
Kansas State University (Teaching and Learning Center), 40

Kelley, Bruce, 141, 143, 155, 173–74
Kentucky Wesleyan College (Center for Engaged Teaching), 192
Kennesaw State University (Center for Excellence in Teaching and Learning), 133
King's College (Center for Excellence in Teaching and Learning), 37
Kirkwood Community College (Center for Excellence in Learning and Teaching), 109, 113
Kreber, Carolin, 178, 186, 193–94
Kuhlenschmidt, Sally, 10–12, 18–19, 158, 174

LaGuardia Community College, 115
Land, Ray, 42, 53
La Salle University (De La Salle Institute for Advanced Teaching and Learning), 40, 92, 233n92
Lansing Community College (Center for Teaching Excellence), 35, 127, 231n63
large classes, teaching, 91
leadership, of centers. *See* CTL leadership
leadership development. *See* holistic professional learning–infused CTLs
learning. *See* student learning; faculty learning
learning communities: alignment with CTL aims, 137, 205; Hub tactic, 98–99, 138; impacts of, 59–60
learning management system (LMS), 93, 143, 215
learning space design/support, 32, 132, 143
Lee College (Empirical Educator Center), 43, 234n105
Lee, Virginia, 82, 138, 172
Leeward Community College (Innovation Center for Teaching and Learning), 114
Lenoir-Rhyne University (Center for Teaching and Learning), 34
Levinson-Rose, Judith, 176, 184
Lewis University (University Faculty Development Committee), 33
liberal arts colleges, 56, 112, 161, 170. *See also* baccalaureate institutions
libraries/librarians, 140, 142, 147, 164, 170
Little, Deandra, 160, 164–66
Lukacik, Fran, 140

North Carolina State University (Office for Faculty Excellence), 171

North Dakota State University (Office of Teaching and Learning), 124

Northeast Alabama Community College, 65

Northwestern University (Searle Center for Advancing Learning and Teaching), 190

not-for-profits. *See* private not-for-profit institutions

Oakland University (Center for Excellence in Teaching and Learning), 171

observations, 108–9, 120; peer observation training, 108

OER. *See* Open Educational Resources

Ohio State University (Michael V. Drake Institute for Teaching and Learning), 67

online teaching and learning. *See* digital teaching and learning; technology.

open classroom initiatives, 109–10

Open Educational Resources (OER), 91, 104–5, 108, 116, 192

Oregon Health and Science University (Teaching and Learning Center), 70, 241n86

Oregon State University (Center for Teaching and Learning), 112

organizational change. *See* change

organizational development: consultations, 108; CTL mandate, 142; CTL purpose statements, 75; CTL role in, 7; defined, 145; measurement of impact, 177, 182, 191; potential pivot of the field, 34, 47–48, 191; workshops, 90, 92.

organizational integrations, 141–55, 172

orientations: alignment with CTL aims, 137, 205; constituencies, 112–13; duration, 112; to educational development practice, 53; impact, 64, 111; Incubator approach, 61, 110–13, 120; new chair, 148; new faculty, 52, 61–64, 110–12; new GSI, 112–13, 250n79; new staff, 113

Ortquist-Ahrens, Leslie, 36, 62, 101, 140

other special focus contexts: annual reports, 179; change strategies, 79–80; constituencies, 25–27; CTL aims, 46; CTL leaders, 162; integrative emphases, 148; permeation of CTLs, 14; personnel size, 157, 159; tactics, 103, 107, 113, 120, 128, 135–36, 204

outcomes. *See* faculty learning; impact of CTL work; student learning

Ozarks Technical Community College (OTC Faculty Development), 22

Palmer, Michael, 85

pandemic. *See* COVID-19 pandemic

participation: metrics, 179–83; rationale for measuring, 183–84

Pasadena City College (Office of Professional and Organizational Development), 148

personnel. *See* CTL personnel

Phillips, Steven, 145

POD Network: Centers and Programs Directory, 11, 215; conference, 51, 53, 209; defined, 1; discussion list, 11, 167; number of members, 7; realms of practice, 145; SIGs, 166; surveys of members, 5–6, 178–79; *To Improve the Academy*, 151; use of member lists by researchers, 10. See also *ACE-POD Matrix*

Point Loma Nazarene University (Center for Teaching and Learning), 185, 192

policy, 74, 92, 131

podcasts, 97–98, 102

postdoctoral scholars (postdocs), 26, 29, 89–90, 96, 113, 227, 229

Pratt Institute (Center for Teaching and Learning), 40

Predominantly White Institutions (PWIs), 20, 127, 131, 162

pre-orientation programs, 190

Princeton University (McGraw Center for Teaching and Learning), 65, 95

private for-profit institutions: integrative emphases, 154; permeation of CTLs, 15, 19, 200; personnel size, 158–59; tactics, 97

private not-for-profit institutions: annual reports, 179; change strategies, 62; CTL leaders, 163; integrative emphases, 154; permeation of CTLs, 15, 19, 200; personnel size, 159; tactics, 97

professional development, 10, 34–35, 122, 176, 229n38

professional learning community, 98

SCoT (Students Consulting on Teaching), 84, 110
Scottsdale Community College (Center for Teaching and Learning), 32
Seattle University (Center for Faculty Development), 98, 193
selectivity (institutional) and CTL permeation, 17–19
senior leaders: CTL assessment, 177; CTL head titles, 163; public praise of a CTL's work, 269n21; support for CTL, 212–13; transitions, 23, 202
service, 31, 101
service learning. *See* community engagement; service learning / community engagement (S-LCE)–infused CTLs
service learning / community engagement (S-LCE)–infused CTLs, 153–55
Sewanee: The University of the South (Center for Teaching), 109
SGID. *See* Small-Group Instructional Diagnoses
Shaw University (Center for Teaching and Learning), 124
Shenandoah University (Center for Teaching, Learning, and Technology), 99
Shinaberger, Jennifer, 142, 150, 184
Shippensburg University of Pennsylvania (Center for Excellence in Teaching and Learning), 114
Sieve: alignment, 208; annual reports, 196; articulated in statements of purpose, 74–76; assessment-infused CTLs, 150; cautions, 76–78; defined, 70–74, 202, 236n12; growth, 75, 214; impact, 76–78; strategic CTL orientation, 70–74, 79; strengths, 78; tactics, 84, 128–37; technology-infused CTLs, 144
signature CTL change strategies, 202
signature programs, 6
signature strategies, 80–81
Simmons University (Center for Faculty Excellence), 152
Sinclair Community College (Center for Teaching and Learning), 126, 188, 190
size, CTLs: aims, 210–11; board size, 170; CTL leader, 162–65; personnel size, 156–60, 168, 173; strategies, 210–11; tactics, 97, 107, 120, 128, 133, 136, 210–11

size, institutional: constituencies, 26; CTL aims, 36, 39, 44; CTL leader, 162–63; CTL permeation, 18–20; CTL personnel, 157; integrative emphases, 144; strategies, 54, 57; tactics, 107, 120, 128
Skidmore College (Center for Leadership in Teaching and Learning), 99
Small Group Instructional Diagnoses (SGIDs), 109
social networks, 58–59, 212
social sciences, 166
Society for Teaching and Learning in Higher Education (STLHE), 75
sociological imagination, 2
Sonoma State University (Center for Teaching and Educational Technology), 132
Sorcinelli, Mary Deane, 6, 32, 34, 53, 85–86, 106, 112, 145, 151, 161, 164, 166–67, 189
SoTL. *See* Scholarship of Teaching and Learning
South Dakota State University (Center for the Advancement of Teaching and Learning), 131
Southern Adventist University (Center for Teaching Excellence and Biblical Foundations of Teaching and Learning), 134
Southern Connecticut State University (Office of Faculty Development), 134
Southwestern University (Center for Teaching, Learning, and Scholarship), 98
space, 66, 70
special focus institutions: annual reports, 179; change strategies, 79–80, 204; constituencies, 25–27; CTL aims, 46; CTL leaders, 162; permeation of CTLs, 14; personnel size, 157, 159; tactics, 103, 107, 113, 120, 128, 135–36
staff: annual reports, 179, 189–90; assessment-focused, 129, 132, 150, 172; awards, 123–24; CTL constituency, 26–28, 30, 45, 142, 201; CTL personnel, 156–60, 168, 173–74; credentials of CTL staff, 259–60n69; digital, 37, 63, 74, 107, 120, 135, 143, 149, 172, 206, 215; direct academic support, 118; HPL-focused, 172; integrative areas, 172, 206; need for,